WHAT'S MY NAME, FOOL?

Sports and Resistance in the United States

DAVE ZIRIN

Praise for Dave Zirin and
What's My Name, Fool?

Dave Zirin is an angry young man, and he's not bashful about telling you why—no quarter asked, no holds barred. In his new book, *What's My Name, Fool?*, he calls out the many inequities he sees on the level playing fields. It's good to read such an impassioned critic taking sport to task in a manner we haven't heard in some time.

Frank Deford, *Sports Illustrated*, National Public Radio's *Morning Edition*, and HBO's *Real Sports*

The sports industry has long needed an alternative voice, someone to rage away at issues of money, race, and celebrity. Dave Zirin is that voice.

Lester Munson, *Sports Illustrated*

I am a baseball fan, and I love this book. It is so refreshing to have a sportswriter who writes with such verve and intelligence, who also has a social conscience, and who refuses to keep those parts of his life separate. This is a rare contribution to social history, something I have been looking for, a sports history that understands how the issues of race and class are inextricable from the world of sports.

Howard Zinn, third baseman, switch hitter, historian

Out from the greed, myths, freeloading, cover-ups, censorships, and gouging of big time commercial sports comes the clear voice, honest pen, and vigilant eyes of David Zirin. Put this book down only to pray, eat, and sleep.

Ralph Nader

Dave Zirin is that rarest of commodities in sportswriting: an original voice. His writing reveals the ever present but ignored bridge between sports and struggle. *What's My Name, Fool?* will be loved by both athletes who hate politics and activists who hate sports. As for progressives who are closet sports fans, finally here is a book for you.

Mary Ratcliff, editor, *San Francisco Bay View*

Dave Zirin approaches sport and its integral role in society with a keen political eye. He is perceptive, forceful, and analytically on target. This guy throws strikes.

Michael James, Athletes United for Peace

In *What's My Name, Fool?* Dave Zirin proves that he is the only sportswriter working who can stand tall where athletes and ideas meet and deliver a knockout.

Eddie Mustafa Muhammad, Light Heavyweight champion and founder, J.A.B. boxing union

Dave Zirin is one of the brightest, most audacious voices I can remember on the sportswriting scene, and my memory goes back to the 1920s.

Lester Rodney, *Daily Worker* sports editor 1936–58

Dave Zirin has an amazing talent for covering the sports and politics beat. Ranging like a great shortstop, he scoops up everything! He profiles the courageous and inspiring athletes who are standing up for peace and civil liberties in this repressive age. A must read!

Matthew Rothschild, editor, *The Progressive*

Dave Zirin's inspiring account of sports nonconformists, from race rebels to antiwar athletes, is a halftime speech for radicals. This book is a left uppercut to the solar plexus of the sports-industrial complex.

Andrew Hsiao, former sports editor, *Village Voice*

Dave Zirin is that rare thing—a writer who combines a passion for sport, deep knowledge of its history, and a fearlessly radical critique of the role the rich and powerful play in it.

Mike Marqusee, author, *Redemption Song: Muhammad Ali and the Spirit of the Sixties*

At BlackSportsNetwork.com, we had been looking for writers who could deliver sharp and insightful stories that speak first and foremost to African American sports fans. Dave has continually delivered thought provoking ideas that offer a unique difference from the mainstream sports landscape. A rare talent indeed!

David Cole, CEO and publisher, Black Sports Network

Dave Zirin's *What's My Name, Fool?* is an absolute treasure. Agree or disagree (and I often disagree) you always walk away thinking about what you read—and how many sports columnists can you say that about?

Bill McCaffrey, *Inside Sports*, Maryland Public Television

Dave Zirin is America's best sportswriter.

Lee Ballinger, *Rock and Rap Confidential*

Dave Zirin has unique wit, vast sports knowledge, and delightful candor. It is refreshing to see someone who can cut through the fluff and get to the heart of any sports issue. You want sports with an edge? You picked the right book.

Ed DeMayo, CEO, Basketball.com

Zirin doesn't get bogged down in heavy theorizing. He writes with compassion, humor, and a saber-like sharpness that deftly shreds owners and mainstream sportswriters alike.

Jeffrey St. Clair, co-editor, *CounterPunch*

Dave Zirin is one of the few sportswriters who is both original and real. Zirin goes beyond the front page and the overdone and instead delivers to his readers interesting stories with a unique perspective.

Mario Scalise, *Chicago Sports Review*

Dave Zirin shows us not only that sports can be a window through which we can examine the complex workings of race and class in this twisted, commercialized culture, but that it can also be a site of resistance. If I was a religious believer, I'd say that Dave Zirin is the second coming of Lester Rodney, but I'm not, and, besides, they're both Jewish. But I have no doubt that Rodney's spirit fills Zirin's soul. Lucky us!

Peter Rachleff, author, *Hard-Pressed in the Heartland*

Zirin with a pen in his hands is as graceful and potent as Tiger with a golf club or Bonds with a bat. He hits hard, and he hits with meaning and purpose. In the train wreck that is contemporary sports commentary, Dave Zirin is the ambulance that arrives to clean up the mess.

A. Lamont Germany, Producer & Host, *SportsRap*, WEAA 88.9FM Baltimore, MD

Sports in the U.S. today is big business, and no one exposes the powerful interests who use it for profit and propaganda better than Dave Zirin. He identifies with and gives voice to those athletes and players who have become symbols of resistance.

Phil Gasper, contributor to *International Socialist Review* and *CounterPunch*

Dave Zirin loves the essence of sports, but he hates the corporate stench. He explains both with a clear, concise, caring, and wise style that is well worth reading.

Michael Albert, ZNet

In the tradition of Lester Rodney and Ralph Wiley, Dave Zirin bridges the gap between social issues and pop culture with a smooth blend of radical passion and street smart prose. He's the thinking man's sports fan and the sports fan's thinking man.

Mickey Z., author, *The Seven Deadly Spins: Exposing the Lies Behind War Propaganda*

With unusual flair and acuity Zirin trains his eye on the political dimensions of sport, beautifully illustrating its potential to transform culture. When it comes to the intersection of sports and politics, Dave Zirin is the wittiest and most engaging essayist writing today. This book belongs on the shelves of all sportslovers who believe that athletes are people, too.

Bryan Sacks, publisher, *Breakaway Monthly*

Dave Zirin is the rare writer who treats athletes as citizens, not as spectacles. Worldly but not cynical, political but not preachy, never sentimental and frequently hilarious, Zirin's columns show a side of sports that the owners and the marketing execs do not want you to see.

Chris Toensing, editor, *Middle East Report*

When it comes to the politics of sports, I'd read this book first. With passion, insight, and incredible humor, he cheers athletes struggling to make sports democratic and fair, and makes clear which owners and institutions need to be benched.

Clay Steinman, professor, Media and Cultural Studies, Macalester College

What's My Name, Fool?
Sports and Resistance in the United States

Dave Zirin

Chicago, Illinois

To Michele:
Through upturns and downturns, you are my heart.

First published 2005 by Haymarket Books
P.O. Box 180165, Chicago, IL 60618
773-583-7884
www.haymarketbooks.org

Cover design by Eric Ruder
Cover photo of Muhammad Ali © Getty Images
Book design by Paul D'Amato

Library of Congress Cataloging-in-Publication Data

Zirin, Dave.
  What's my name, fool? : sports and resistance in the United States /
Dave Zirin.
    p. cm.
  ISBN-13: 978-1-931859-20-2 (pbk. 13 digit)
  ISBN-10: 1-931859-20-5 (pbk. 10 digit)
  1. Sports—Social aspects—United States. 2. Sports—Social aspects. I.
Title: Sports and resistance in the United States. II. Title.
  GV706.5.Z57 2005
  306.4'83'0973—dc22
                              2005010553
Printed in Canada

Contents

Acknowledgements

What's My Name, Fool? could not have been completed without the creative, emotional, and financial support of the following people. First and foremost, thanks to the good people at Haymarket Books: Anthony Arnove, Julie Fain, and Ahmed Shawki, for believing that a book on sports was worth their time and energy.

Eternal gratitude to Elizabeth Terzakis—editor extraordinaire—who had the task of ironing out every disturbed, nonsensical metaphor and disciplining me to limit the erotic references to Dick Cheney. Any sentence herein with a modicum of grace is the result of her efforts. Anything crude, offensive, or nauseating is present over her objections (or behind her back).

Thanks to Dao Tran, Eric Ruder, David Whitehouse, Paul D'Amato, and Virginia Harabin for their invaluable help in the production of this book.

Thanks to my mentor and friend, Dave Meggyesy, for his support and guidance.

Thanks to Mike Marqusee for writing *Redemption Song: Muhammad Ali and the Spirit of the Sixties.*

Thanks are due as well to Annie Zirin, Jason Yanowitz, and Michele Bollinger for enduring some of the early drafts.

Thanks to my parents, Jane Zirin and Jim Zirin, for their ceaseless support.

Special mention to everyone who has ever kept sports fun: Arya Shirazi, Damian Smith, Lute Breuer, Ed "Pop" Bollinger, John Coursey, the "Care Bears," Dave Ashton and Nico Berry, "The Don" Rob Scavone, and Keeanga Taylor.

Finally, endless thanks to Nick Chin, my former co-editor and comrade at the *Prince George's Post*.

And last but never least, to Sasha Jane Truth Zirin, my miracle baby. Thank you for putting a smile on my face that may require surgery to remove. Anyone who doesn't like this book has made my baby cry. Just consider that, when you start reading. ◆

Foreword by David Meggyesy

Dave Zirin is one of our most talented and progressive young sports writers. Zirin understands better than any other sports writer I know the connection between the world of sport and the larger political and social matrix of our culture as we roll into the twenty-first century. His writing reminds me of Bob Lipsyte, former sports columnist of the *New York Times*.

Zirin is an avowed progressive, a lover of sport, and a talented and committed journalist. He traces his historical sports writing roots to Lester Rodney, former sports editor of the Communist Party's *Daily Worker*. Few people know Lester Rodney's columns in the *Daily Worker* generated necessary public awareness about the racist nature of Major League Baseball in its exclusion of African-American baseball players. There is little doubt that Rodney's campaign paved the way for Jackie Robinson's entry into the Major League. Parenthetically, the Boston Red Sox eighty-seven-year curse had less to do with Babe Ruth and more to do with a racist franchise that refused to employ African-American baseball players until 1959—Willie Mays for example. During Rodney's time—and to some degree this continues today—baseball journalists were nothing more than public relations flacks for their respective teams and

David Meggyesy is a former NFL linebacker and the author of *Out of Their League*.

Major League Baseball itself. Zirin, like Rodney in the 1940s, breaks the mold and consciously connects the dots between sport and the larger issues of class, race, gender, money, and politics from a progressive perspective.

Sport and society walk hand in hand through our lives and the historical time in which we live. In the late 1960s, the Athletic Revolution (so named by the late Jack Scott), Harry Edward's Olympic Project for Human Rights, and the late Leonard Schecter's writings in the now-defunct *Look* magazine began to critically examine the role of sport in society and the values embedded and expressed in sport. Along parallel lines, the athletes—myself in football, Tommie Smith and John Carlos in Olympic track and field, Muhammad Ali in boxing, and Billie Jean King in women's tennis—not only made the critique, but brought it home to our respective sports.

For myself, it was becoming involved with the Civil Rights and Anti-Vietnam War movements, petitioning my Cardinals teammates to protest the war, being benched for my "political activities," quitting the Cardinals, and writing *Out of Their League*. When Tommie Smith and John Carlos raised their black-gloved fists on the victory stand at the 1968 Mexico City Olympics and Muhammad Ali refused to be drafted to fight in the Vietnam War, they were protesting racism and African-American poverty. Billie Jean King became a giant protesting the exclusion and second-class citizenship of female athletes and founded the Women's Sports Foundation.

In the 1960s, when I was becoming, as we used to say back then, "radicalized" and "unchaining my brain," I was playing football for the St. Louis Cardinals and attending Washington University's sociology graduate school during the off-season. The connection between my insular world of professional football and the larger political world was becoming evident. It was not a pretty picture. When the NFL would not honor the assassination of President John Kennedy by canceling the following weekend's games, NFL owners' greed trumped moral considerations of respect and tragedy. In the middle and late 1960s, the NFL's support of the Vietnam War, with its jingoistic pro-military Super Bowl halftime shows, disregarded half the country's opposition to the war. The NFL was in the "selling the war" business.

I was also becoming aware of the issues of racism and professional athletes' "economic slavery" on the St. Louis Cardinals. On the Cardinals and other NFL teams, African-American football players were "stacked" in certain positions—running back, cornerback—and denied access to others—quarterback and linebacker. NFL teams had virtually perpetual rights to players' services. Free agency, the right to seek other employment upon contract expiration, did not exist. They had you for life, we used to say.

Much of this history is covered in *What's My Name, Fool?* and serves as a backdrop to Zirin's commentary on current issues that, believe it or not, cover similar ground. The world has not progressed that much. There are contemporary athletes who are protesting racism and poverty, the Iraq War, United States imperialism, inequities of wealth, and the corruption of our political process by money and the media.

The new ground Dave Zirin covers also includes the increasing impact of *SportsWorld* as mass entertainment delivering messages of mass consumerism and celebrity. How mass spectator sport emerged as a carrier of the "dominant values" that underpin our capitalist consumer culture is a story in itself. Values such as competition, respect for rules and authority, fairness, winner take all, aggression, teamwork, hard work, playing by the rules, winning, and merit are central to the sport myth and are also central to the myth of material success in our society. Whether or not these values offer a positive and humane vision pointing to a better life for all of us in our future is an open question.

The reality is that these values, gathered together as the "success myth," tend to pertain more to players and workers than franchise owners and other elites. In this elite world of business and politics, class, race, connections, cronyism, favoritism, ruthlessness, propaganda, and amassing wealth are critical elements in the success equation. Zirin weighs heavily and well into this underbelly of mass sport and, by extension, corporate and political elites.

The larger point I'm making here is that what goes on in the world of sport mirrors what is going on in the larger society. The beauty of looking at the human condition within sport, embedded in our particular culture and society, is to also look at the larger culture in a more focused and concentrated way. This is so because sport is understood to be a meritocracy, the best man or woman plays and wins the contest. Lester Rodney's campaign to allow African Americans the opportunity to play Major League Baseball caught reality's cutting edge because of the fact that many Negro League baseball players were superior to the best players in Major League Baseball. And the white Major Leaguers said so. It was glaringly clear that the exclusion of African-American players was about race and not ability. The league's racism clashed with the value sport and society placed on merit and fairness, and this contradiction gave Rodney's campaign its compelling power.

What's My Name, Fool? also features interviews with numerous past and contemporary athlete activists who Zirin keys off of to make a larger point or to bring individual issues into current focus with his own writings. The book is contemporary, yet also reaches back to the recent past and gives a historical perspective. For those of us who hold to the vision of creating a more humane and just world, this book "brings it all back home" via the world of sport. Sport is a wonderful and unique human enterprise known to every culture on the planet. How we do sport, how we play our games, is a window to see and a format through which to express that vision of a better world. It takes someone like Dave Zirin to make those connections and critiques, and to make it clear that sport can be a powerful carrier of the best within us, which is respect for each other's humanity and life itself, human relationship and connection, and the joy of play with our fellow humans. ◆

Sports—An Offer We Can't Refuse

In *The Godfather, Part II,* dying mob boss Hymen Roth wheezes the obscene truth to young Don Michael Corleone. "Michael," he whispers, "we're bigger than U.S. Steel." This scene updated for today would have Yankees kingpin George Steinbrenner booming at pubescent Dallas Mavericks owner Mark Cuban, "Screw U.S. Steel. We're bigger than the damn mafia."

Just like Hymen Roth, "Big Stein" would be telling no lies. Professional sports are now the tenth largest industry in the United States, generating $220 billion in revenue every year. And just like Mr. Roth's rackets, it's a business that can stink to high heaven.

Rotten Roots

If, in 1900, a forward thinking person had predicted that sports would some day stand as one of the great pillars of American industry, that person would have been proclaimed mad and then subjected to some combination of leeching and lobotomy. Before the 1880s, everything from the World Series to a daily sports page was just a gleam in Uncle Sam's eye. The Victorian idea that sports undermined character and promoted a slothful work ethic dominated most people's perceptions of organized play. (The Victorians clearly considered child labor and building a better chastity belt more noble pursuits.) Their attitude, however, is easy to understand when you consider class. Competitive sports were a working-class pastime that reflected the brutality of early industrial life. Popular sports of the day included bare-knuckled boxing, "stick-battling," cock fighting, and animal baiting, which involved setting starved dogs against a bull or bear.

But at the end of the nineteenth century, an upstart generation of wealthy industrialists forged a new idea about these innocuous games. Industrialist J. P. Morgan and former President Teddy Roosevelt argued that organized athletics could be the means for instilling the character and values deemed necessary to make America a global power in the century to come. Sports could breed a sense of hard work, self-discipline, and the win-at-all-cost ethic of competition. Roosevelt once said, presumably while swinging a big stick,

> Virile, masterful qualities alone can maintain and defend this very civilization. There is no better way [to develop this] than by encouraging the sports which develop such qualities as courage, resolution, and endurance. No people has ever yet done great and lasting work if its physical type was infirm and weak.

Teddy and his ilk backed their words with bucks. Business scions funded organizations like the YMCA to teach sports and specifically to exclude "undesirable" ethnic groups, women, and Blacks.

As the popularity of sports rose among working people, factory owners began to see the benefit of starting plant teams as a form of labor management. This synthesis bore team factory names that remain today like the Green Bay Packers and the Milwaukee Brewers. The Chicago Bears, who used to be rooted in Decatur, Illinois, were known as the Decatur Staleys, named after the A. E. Staley Company. Their first coach, George "Papa Bear" Halas, was a Staley manager. Organized athletics became less a place to toughen up Teddy Roosevelt's gentlemen of leisure than a narrow window of opportunity for immigrants, white urban youth, and people right off the farm to claw their way out of poverty. Players who captured the country's imagination included a Baltimore orphan named "Babe" Ruth, Native American Olympic star Jim Thorpe, and the first renowned female athlete, a daughter of immigrants named Mildred "Babe" Didrikson. As another first-generation American, Joe DiMaggio, once said, "A ball player's got to be kept hungry to become a big-leaguer. That's why no boy from a rich family ever made the big leagues."

As the United States urbanized, it was evident that people would pay to see sports played at their highest level. The 1920s and 1950s, two decades with very similar economic landscapes, saw this take root. Both were periods of expansion and urbanization. Both eras saw revolutions in technology—radio in the 1920s and then TV in the 1950s—that could deliver sports into people's homes. But, most critically, both were times after brutal world wars that saw a population in the United States looking for relief, escape, and leisure.

Sports and Lee Greenwood

In addition to becoming a profitable form of mass entertainment, pro sports were used by the political and financial elite as a way to package their values and ideas. This is why sports in this country reflect a distinctly U.S. project, rooted in aspirations for greatness as well as conquest and oppression. That's why the United States is so singular in its sports presentation. We are unique in playing the national anthem before every game (and, since 9/11, playing "God Bless America" during baseball's seventh inning stretch—even for all-American teams like the Toronto Blue Jays). We are unique in employing scantily clad women to tell us when to "cheer." We are unique in calling the winners of our domestic leagues "world champions." We are unique in the very sports we imbibe most heartily—especially football. (And don't tout NFL Europe as counter-evidence. There are more U.S. study-abroad students at those games than at your typical Amsterdam hash bar.) In many cities, the average Sunday NFL game contains more patriotic overkill than a USO show in Kuwait. First there's a military drum line to midfield. Then a standing sing-along to "I'm Proud to Be an American (Where at Least I Know I'm Free)" by Lee Greenwood. And then comes the "Star-Spangled Banner." You are certainly "free" to not stand, as long as you know that the person behind you will feel "free" to pour beer on your head. Save me, Lee Greenwood!

Why Sports Matters

Many throughout the U.S. are repelled by pro sports today for a laundry list of reasons. People who otherwise enjoy competitive play performed at its highest levels don't want to be party to the cutthroat competition at its core. Many are also put off by the insane salaries of the games' top players, others by the backroom dealings that produce publicly funded stadiums at taxpayer expense. Then there is the abuse of steroids and other performance enhancing drugs, which some feel have taken long-hallowed baseball records and reduced them to rubbish. When you pile on the way racism and sexism can be used to sell sports, it can all seem about as appealing as a Sunday in the park with George Steinbrenner.

The way that the games have been shaped by profit and patriotism has quite understandably led many people to conclude that sports are little more than a brutal reflection of the savage inequalities that stream through our world. As esteemed left-wing critic Noam Chomsky noted in *Manufacturing Consent*,

> Sports keeps people from worrying about things that matter to their lives that they might have some idea of doing something about. And in fact it's striking to see the intelligence that's used by ordinary people in sports [as opposed to political and social issues]. I mean, you listen to radio stations where people call in—

they have the most exotic information and understanding about all kinds of arcane issues. And the press undoubtedly does a lot with this.… Sports is a major factor in controlling people. Workers have minds; they have to be involved in something and it's important to make sure they're involved in things that have absolutely no significance. So professional sports is perfect. It instills total passivity.

Chomsky quite correctly highlights how people use sports as a balm to protect themselves from the harsh realities of the world. He is also right that the intelligence and analysis many of us invest in sports far outstrips our dissecting of the broader world. It is truly amazing how we can be moved to fits of fury by a missed call or a blown play, but remain too under-confident to raise our voices in anger when we are laid off, lose our healthcare, or suffer the slings and arrows of everyday life in the United States. The weakness in Chomsky's argument, however, is that it disregards how the very passion we invest in sports can transform it from a kind of mindless escape into a site of resistance. It can become an arena where the ideas of our society are not only presented but also challenged. Just as sports can reflect the dominant ideas of our society, they can also reflect struggle. The story of the women's movement is incomplete without mention of Billie Jean King's match against Bobby Riggs. The struggle for gay rights has to include a chapter on Martina Navratilova. When we think about the Black freedom struggle, we picture Jackie Robinson and Muhammad Ali in addition to Martin Luther King Jr. and Malcolm X. And, of course, when remembering the movement for Black Power, we can't help but visualize one of the most stirring sights of our sports century: Tommie Smith and John Carlos's black-gloved medal-stand salute at the 1968 Olympics.

Chomsky's view also reflects a lack of understanding of why sports are, at their core, so appealing. Amid the politics and pain that engulf and sometimes threaten to smother big-time sports, there is also artistry that can take your breath away. To see Michael Vick zigzag his way through an entire defense, or Mia Hamm crush a soccer ball past a goalie's outstretched hands, or LeBron James use the eyes in the back of his head to spot a teammate cutting to the basket can be a glorious sight at the end of a tough day. It is a bolt of beauty in an otherwise very gray world. As a good friend said to me long ago, "Magic Johnson will always be my Miles Davis."

Lester "Red" Rodney, the editor of the *Daily Worker* sports section from 1934 to 1958 and a groundbreaking fighter in the battle to smash baseball's color line, puts it perfectly:

> Of course there is exploitation but there is fun and beauty too. I mean, what's more beautiful than a 6-4-3 double play perfectly executed where the shortstop fields a ground ball and flips it toward second base in one motion, the second baseman takes the throw in stride, pivots, avoids the base runner, and fires it to first on time. That's not a put-on. That's not fake. That's beyond all the social analysis of the game. The idea of people coming together and amazing the rest of us.

Sports as a whole do not represent black and white, good or bad, red state or blue state issues. Sports are neither to be defended nor vilified. Instead we need to look at sports for what they are, so we can take apart the disgusting, the beautiful, the ridiculous, and even the radical.

This book aims to recall moments of resistance past and rescue the underreported shows of struggle and humanity by athletes of the present, so we can appreciate the beauty of sports independent of the muck and fight for a future where skill, art, glory, and the joy of play belong to all of us. ◆

CHAPTER ONE

It All Starts With Lester Rodney

It all starts with Lester "Red" Rodney. Rodney was the first jounalist to express the idea that sports could be an arena for not only reaction but also beauty and resistance. Through the U.S. Communist Party newspaper, the *Daily Worker,* and over the objections of many in the Party itself, he launched a political sports page that was light-years ahead of its time.

Rodney's sports section was alive with the intertwining of sports and struggle. Through his writings, he helped initiate the first campaign to integrate baseball in the 1930s, and was the first writer to scout a young second baseman named Jackie Robinson. Rodney also covered the famed 1938 boxing match between "The Brown Bomber" Joe Louis and Adolf Hitler favorite Max Schmeling. Yet, despite these and other remarkable accomplishments, Rodney's background as a political radical has kept him buried below the horizon of the sports landscape.

Still going strong at the age of ninety-four, Rodney remembers his early love of sports and the experiences of the Great Depression that hurtled him toward radical politics. "I went to high school in Bensonhurst and ran track back when they had the dominant track team in New York City, never losing a meet in four years," he recalls with a somewhat sad smile. "I got a partial track scholarship to Syracuse but the Depression had just hit, and knocked my whole family out. We lost our home, everything. I graduated high school in '29, right into the mouth of the crash and I had to forget Syracuse and go to work."

It was while taking night classes at NYU in the early 1930s that Rodney first met the activists in the campus Communist Party. Like thousands of others in that era, he found the magnetic attraction of radical ideas to be irresistible. "People who weren't around during the 1930s can't fully grasp what it was like politically," he remembers, with growing animation. "In New York if you were on a college campus and you weren't some kind of radical, Communist, socialist, or Trotskyist, you were considered brain-dead, and you probably were! That's what all the conversation was about during the Depression. But what caught my eye was that [the *Daily Worker*] also had a weekly column on sports."

The radical in Rodney loved most of the newspaper, but the sports fan in him took a look at that column and "absolutely cringed." Today, Rodney calls it "patronizing," and he is perhaps being too kind. Looking at archives of the *Daily Worker*, it seems that the only purpose of its early sports section was to tell workers how stupid they were to like sports. Articles included lines such as, "The purpose of baseball is nothing more than to distract workers from their miserable conditions" and "peddling dope and talking [about] boxing are one and the same."

But the support for this perspective—the Party's "old guard"—were being worn away. As Rodney remembers, "The party was beginning to change its demographic makeup. The ones who were pouring into the party were young people, born here in the States, and there were many trade unionists that played ball and were interested in sports. Ten years earlier, the party was probably 75 percent foreign born and they brought the prejudice of European immigrants about sports,

Former *Daily Worker* sports editor Lester Rodney still showcases his athletic chops as a top-ranked tennis player in the over-80 division. (Marc Geller)

seeing it as 'grown people, wasting their time on children's games.' They couldn't understand its appeal. When I met my wife's father for the first time, he said, 'What do you do?' I said, 'I write sports.' He laughed uneasily and asked 'But what do you really do?'"

Rodney sent the editors of the *Daily Worker* a letter "mildly suggesting" that, while they were correct in writing about what's wrong with sports, they also needed to ask why sports are so meaningful to U.S. workers in the first place.

"I didn't make some big argument that a collective effort of a team, the coming together, and finding satisfaction in getting the job well done, is some kind of revolutionary act," he recalls with a jaunty grin. "But I did say that the paper ought to relax and cover sports as well as respect people who are interested in sports." To Rodney's amazement, the editor of the *Daily Worker*, Clarence Hathaway, called him in and hired him to spearhead his vision of what the sports page should be—this despite the fact that he wasn't even a member of the party at the time.

Strong disagreements over having a sports section with a broader appeal still existed on the paper's editorial board, however. "There was one person who said, 'This is ridiculous. We have a socialist paper that barely has enough money to put out eight pages, and here we're going to devote one-eighth of that paper to games?' But the editor, Hathaway, he was from Minnesota, he said, 'Let's check with the readers.' And they actually had a poll. They asked readers to vote on whether the *Daily Worker* should have a daily sports section that covers big league baseball and college sports and so on in addition to trade union activities and people overwhelmingly voted that they wanted it."

It was at this point that Rodney set about his real work: not just editing a broad sports page that reported scores and stats to radical readers, but covering sports in a way they had never been covered before—with an eye on their social impact. For him, this project crystallized when he covered the historic Louis/Schmeling fight. "I didn't have a full realization of what the meaning of sports could be. Looking back, when you look at the meaning of Joe Louis, and what he meant when he knocked out Max Schmeling in that second fight and—it's just incredible. Abner Barry was a Black columnist of the day, and he was assigned to Harlem during the second fight. He told how, during the fight, the streets were eerily deserted, like a scene from after the dropping of the atom bomb in a movie. But the minute the fight was over the streets were teeming with people, and young kids were laughing and giving the mock Hitler salute. And this was happening in every city in the country, including southern cities. In Knoxville [Tennessee] Blacks poured out into the streets and fought with the police who tried to keep them from marching. So you say there's no social meaning to Joe Louis? There was a young Black man being led to death row and he cried out 'Save me, Joe Louis!' It sounds corny and hokey, but it's true. You can almost say in a sense that Joe Louis may have been just as important as Jackie Robinson, just on a different level, one of the differences being that Joe Louis was uneducated and not articulate, and at that time he was asked and he agreed to not make waves. That's hard for people to understand today. Here's a person in the thirties, and this is years before the Civil Rights movement."

Rodney was an acute observer of the intersection of race and sports, but he did more than just record from the sidelines. He used the *Daily Worker*'s sports page to launch the first sustained campaign to end the color line in Major League Baseball, which enforced Jim Crow on the playing field. "It was only a matter of time after I started when I said, 'Look at this huge void here! No one is talking about this!' When Negro League teams came in, we highlighted who the good Negro players were and gave something of their background and history. That took investigative reporting. The other papers just said, 'The Kansas City Monarchs will play the Baltimore Giants at such and such a time tomorrow' with no mention that any of them could have played big league baseball or even Minor League baseball and were banned from both. It's amazing. You go back and you read the great newspapers in the thirties, you'll find no editorials saying, 'What's going on here? This is

America, land of the free, and people with the wrong pigmentation of skin can't play baseball?' Nothing like that. No challenges to the league, to the commissioner, to league presidents, no interviewing the managers, no talking about Satchel Paige and Josh Gibson, who were obviously of superstar caliber. After a while, some of the white comrades who had never paid attention to sports before began saying, 'Is this an all-white sport?' People didn't think about it. It was the culture of the times and it was accepted. We also developed a relationship with the Black press and printed each other's articles about the Negro League players and the color line, which in those highly segregated times opened up new audiences for both of us.... It was this tremendous vacuum waiting. Anybody who became sports editor of the *Daily Worker* would have gone into this. It was too obvious."

Rodney stepped into this vacuum, took the fight to integrate baseball off the sports page, and turned it into an activist campaign. It became a key part of the group's antiracist work in the 1930s. "I spoke to the leaders of the YCL [Young Communist League]. They were enthusiastic about the sports page. We talked about circulating the paper. It just evolved as we talked about the color line and some kids in the YCL suggested, 'Why don't we go to the ballparks—to Yankee Stadium, Ebbets Field, the Polo Grounds—with petitions?' They for the most part never encountered any hostility from fans. People would say, 'Gee, I never thought of that.' And then they'd say, 'Yeah, I think if they're good enough then they should have a chance.' We wound up with at least a million and a half signatures that we delivered straight to the desk of [baseball commissioner] Judge Landis."

The *Daily Worker* had an influence far in excess of its circulation, partly because of a concentrated trade-union readership. "When May Day came along," Rodney remembers, smiling, "the Transport Workers Union, or Furriers, or District 65, would march with signs that said 'End Jim Crow in Baseball!'" From then on, Rodney seized every opportunity to raise the question of integration on the sports page.

"In 1937, we were in the dressing room at Yankee Stadium and somebody asked a young Joe DiMaggio, 'Joe, who's the best pitcher you've faced?' And without hesitation, young Joe said, 'Satchel Paige.' He didn't say, 'Satchel Paige, who ought to be in the big leagues,' he just said, 'Satchel Paige.' [DiMaggio had played Paige in an exhibition game on the West Coast.] So that was a huge headline in the next day's *Daily Worker* sports page, in the biggest type I had: 'Paige best pitcher ever faced—DiMaggio.' No other paper reported that. If the other reporters would hand that in, their editor would say, 'Come on, you're not stirring this thing up.' But I want to be clear that we didn't see it as a virtue that we were the only people reporting on this. We wanted to broaden this thing and end the damned ban." The campaign evolved step by step, and Rodney would put the question of integration to white ballplayers whenever he had the chance. "It was meaningful when players like Johnny Vander Meer or Bucky Walters said, 'I don't see why they shouldn't play.' That shot down the myth the owners would repeat that white players would never stand for it."

As Rodney fought to end the color ban, he never stopped covering and highlighting the Negro League teams, giving them press at a time when they were at the margins of the sporting world. One of the players closest to Rodney personally was Negro League legend Satchel Paige. Rodney still gets upset when he thinks about Paige's talents, thwarted on the Negro League circuit. "It is an American tragedy. He was arguably the best pitcher this country has produced, or one of the top three, and in his prime he was playing in the Negro Leagues. Some people still say, 'Well, maybe he wanted to stay with his own.' I shot that down with an interview I did with him in which he challenged Major League Baseball to give him a tryout. He was twenty-nine at the time, and I told him, 'Satch, Dazzy Vance is in the Hall of Fame and he didn't reach his peak until he was thirty-four.' He said, 'Okay, well I'll surely be in there by then.' Thirteen more years went by and he was a forty-two-year-old rookie. America's gotten off the hook pretty lightly on this. Josh Gibson was the greatest catcher who ever put on a uniform. If you want to say Johnny Bench was the greatest catcher you ever saw, Gibson was at least as good as Bench defensively. And at bat he was nothing less than a right-handed hitting Babe Ruth. That's how good he was. He became embittered and began drinking. It came too late for him. That kind of tragedy was for him more than Satchel because Satchel at least got a chance to make a cameo appearance and show the world how good he would have been."

Rodney remembers the Negro Leagues fondly, but the good times don't cover the truth of what it meant to play there. "Although these players were embittered, they had fun, they enjoyed it, and like any oppressed people they had their own spirit. That doesn't mean that they wanted to be playing in Podunk, and that they didn't want to be center stage of the national pastime and making that kind of money. I am highlighting Satchel Paige and Josh Gibson, but there were any number of players. [African-American sportswriter] Wendell Smith estimated that the Homestead Grays, the Black team in Pittsburgh [and later Washington, D.C.] around 1939, had six players in particular of potential all-star, big league quality."

The 1930s turned into the 1940s, and World War II played an important role in the push to integrate Major League Baseball. As Rodney, a veteran, remembers, "Here were Black guys dying for their country and they wouldn't be eligible to play in the national pastime." One such veteran was Jackie Robinson, who broke the color ban in 1947 playing with the Brooklyn Dodgers. "The grief that Jackie took the first two years, when he pledged not to fight back or even to glare back, young people today can't really grasp. Think of Tiger Woods. Let's just suppose he's walking along the fairway and the people in the stands are screaming racial epithets at him and vile things to the white players about him. He knows that some of the white players on the tour have banded together with a petition to bar him, and when he gets to the putting green somebody throws out a big black cat in front of him, which happened to Jackie in Philadelphia. You've got to imagine all that, plus the physical thing. Jackie was hit by more pitches by far than anybody else in the league his rookie year. Enos Slaughter veered and came down on his heel when he was at first base. Lenny Marillo, I remember, slid into him and jumped on him. They had immunity; they knew he wouldn't fight back. So Jackie was suppressing his very being, his personality."

By Robinson's third year, Rodney saw the real Robinson—tough and outspoken—emerge. "White ballplayers with those qualities, like Eddie Stanky and Leo Durocher, they're called scrappers, the tough winners. As soon as Jackie emerged as an aggressive ballplayer, the *Sporting News*, the baseball bible at that time, called him 'shrill and irritating.' The double standard immediately made itself felt. Some people are thrust into roles in history that they didn't seek or maybe even comprehend. Jackie was different. He was a fiercely intelligent man. He knew exactly what he was doing. Which is why this proud man didn't somewhere along the line say, 'This is too much, the hell with it, I'm out of here.' He knew his role and he accepted it. And the Black players who followed him knew what he meant too. Joe Morgan, the announcer and hall of fame second baseman, was on the field for an old-timers' occasion at Yankee Stadium. Jackie was at that time gray and his eyesight was going. Joe had never met Jackie so he ran after him as he was being led off the field, and he came back and his wife asked him, 'What did you tell him?' and Joe said, 'I just said thank you.'"

Despite Robinson's own somewhat conservative and complicated politics, he was friendly with Rodney, the "Press Box Red." "I interviewed him often. [Dodgers general manager] Branch Rickey was a sophisticated anticommunist, and he obviously passed down the word that Jackie should not get too close to the communist press. So what does 'too close' mean? If I walked up to him at the batting cage before a game and said 'Jackie, last night you hit that double off Warren Spahn,' he'd talk to me just like anyone. I got a tip once that he and [African-American Hall of Fame Dodgers catcher] Roy Campanella were up at the Harlem Y, spending time with the kids there. So I went up there and had a wonderful interview with both of them. Sports writers sometimes say that Campanella and Robinson didn't get along because Campanella wasn't militant enough. That is such nonsense. Campanella knocked around the Negro Leagues, had to eat in the back of the restaurants, and had to get on the bus without taking a shower and play in another game. He certainly knew what Jim Crow was."

Just as the emerging Civil Rights movement affected the confidence of Black athletes on the field, their play—and their courage—helped inspire the struggle for Civil Rights, especially in the South. Rodney remembers a dramatic exhibition game in Atlanta in which all the dynamics of the Black freedom struggle were on display, years before they reached fruition. "This exhibition game wound up with the Black fans being allowed in because they had overflowed the segregated stands, they had poured in from outlying districts to see the first integrated game in Georgia history. The Klan had said, 'This must not happen.' That night there was this tremendous sight of Robinson, [Dodgers African-American pitcher] Don Newcombe, and Campanella coming out and the Black fans behind the ropes and in the stands standing and roaring their greeting. A large sector of whites were just sitting and booing. Then other white people, hesitantly at first, stood up and consciously differentiated themselves from the booers and clapped. This was an amazing spectacle. This was the Deep South, many years before the words 'civil rights' were widely known. So it had its impact. People used to say 'Never in Shreveport,' 'Never in Mobile,' 'Never in New Orleans,' but it did, and the Atlanta scene happened everywhere Black and white took the field that year. Roy Campanella once said to me something like, 'Without the Brooklyn Dodgers you don't have Brown v. Board of Education.' I laughed. I thought he was joking, but he was stubborn. He said, 'All I know is, we were the first ones on the trains, we were the first ones down South not to go around the back of the restaurant, first ones in the hotels.' He said, 'We were like the teachers of the whole integration thing.'"

For white players on the Dodgers, many from small towns in the South, dealing with Jackie Robinson's presence challenged their own conceptions of race, especially when it meant protecting Robinson, and themselves, from racist fans or opponents. "[White Dodgers player] Pete Reiser, when he was seeing what was happening to Robinson said, 'Well, democracy means that everyone is equal, so that means we should treat everybody equal.' Pee Wee Reese, the captain, he took it a layer deeper and said, 'Well that's true, but Jackie is catching special hell because he's the only Black player. Maybe we ought to do something to make it more equal.' And that is an amazing thing to say thirty-seven years before the words affirmative action were ever uttered. Reese was from Louisville, Kentucky and he was conflicted at first when he heard that they were having a Black player, but he was a decent person, and the abstraction wears away after a while."

Reese made history at a game in Cincinnati when, as fans called for Robinson's head, the Dodgers captain casually slung his arm around Jackie's shoulder. Rodney was there to see it. "I was thrilled, but I wasn't totally shocked because I had already seen Reese evolving. It was just a wonderful thing to do. And Cincinnati fans were shouting such vile things and nobody was stopping them. But by the middle of Jackie's second year in 1948, it stopped. You began to get the feeling that the racists knew they were in the minority, and they may still be racist to the core but at least their mouths were shut! And you never heard that again."

But it was Dodgers star outfielder Carl Furillo who experienced the most dramatic change. "You have no idea what that meant to me, having heard him say 'I ain't gonna play with no niggers,' initially. Then in 1955, when they finally beat the Yankees in the World Series and had a big celebration party in Brooklyn's old Bossert Hotel, when Jackie and [his wife] Rachel came in, Furillo jumped out of his chair like he got an electric prod. He was the first one hugging Jackie, their cheeks pressed together, saying, 'We did it! We did it!' You tell that to a kid today, they say, 'What's the big deal?' Today we see players in the NBA hugging, but then it was meaningful. That's what sports can do. Historically, when the 'powers that be' clamped the Jim Crow ban on baseball, which was by far the national pastime by the turn of the century, and fought like hell to keep it there for another fifty years, the breaking down of these walls was one of the things they were worried about. It sounds to some people a bit stretchy, but they knew that baseball was that meaningful. That's why, on an official level, the racism continued. Before the 1950 season, Ford Frick, who was the president of the American League, issued a warning about sliding roughly into bases and he only mentioned one name in particular: Jackie Robinson. That's what he went through: a double standard."

To this day, Rodney gets emotional when thinking about Jackie Robinson and his impact. "I gave a speech in 1997 at a forum about the fiftieth anniversary of his debut. At this forum, I said, 'There are very few people of whom you can say with certainty that they made this a somewhat better country. Without doubt you can say that about Jackie Robinson.' Then I said, and this brought me an ovation and was featured in the *New York Times* the next day, 'His legacy was not, "Hooray, we did it," but "Buddy, there's still unfinished work out there."'" He was a continuing militant, and that's why the Dodgers never considered this brilliant baseball man for the position of coach or manager. It's because he was outspoken and unafraid. That's the kind of person he was. In fact, the first time he was asked to play at an old-timers' game at Yankee Stadium, he said 'I must sorrowfully refuse until I see more progress being made off the playing field on the coaching lines and in the managerial departments.' He made people uncomfortable. In fact, it was that very quality which made him something special. He always made you feel that 'Buddy, there's still unfinished work out there.'"

This is the way Lester "Red" Rodney makes any sports journalist of conscience feel today. A look at the current sporting landscape reveals no shortage of topics that Rodney would have seized upon—not only to elaborate on the beauty of sports, but also to expose any instances of injustice that dare stray onto the field. There is still unfinished business, but thanks to Rodney, we have a road map for the journey. ♦

CHAPTER TWO

Jackie Robinson and the Politics of Stealing Home

It was 1955. The Brooklyn Dodgers were close to winning their first World Series, playing none other than hated crosstown rivals, the New York Yankees. Dodgers infielder Jackie Robinson danced off third base with the daring of a tightrope walker. Stealing home is one of the most difficult feats in sports, and Robinson was its acknowledged master.

During the pitcher's windup, Robinson exploded toward home plate. Yankee catcher Yogi Berra—the approximate size and shape of a mailbox—took the pitch and, seeing Robinson in the corner of his eye, squared off over the plate with all the apparent flexibility of tempered steel. The play was close, hair-trigger close, and Robinson was most likely out. But then—a miracle occurred. The umpire called him safe. The crowd roared. Yogi went ballistic. Robinson casually dusted himself off and jogged into the dugout with the nonchalance of someone who had done it before and would do it again.

Taken out of context, Robinson's steal is simply a snapshot of a world-class athlete at the height of his powers. But given the historical circumstances, that simple play was an emblem of the possibilities for change. Eight years earlier, in 1947, Jackie Robinson stood alone, facing off against one of the staunchest citadels of U.S. segregation, Major League Baseball. He was getting spiked, slapped, and spat on every time he took the field. Eight years earlier, Robinson could have beaten Berra's tag by a country mile and still been called out. But in 1955, he was safe.

In the intervening years, Robinson received mountains of hate mail from a motley crew of anti-integrationists, Dixiecrats, and stone-cold killers. He weathered every storm, first with the silent, seething fortitude demanded of him by his manager and team owner and later, as his confidence grew and popular attitudes started to shift, with a searing outspokenness that forced people to take sides. Fast-forward to 1968, and Robinson was once again a target of derision—but this time for young Black militants and revolutionaries who saw him as a front man for a nation and a civil rights program that wasn't responding to their anger and urgency. In the eyes of those struggling for Black freedom in the 1960s, Robinson's image was cast by an acid-tongued Malcolm X. Praising the young Cassius Clay, Malcolm consigned Robinson to a dubious place in American history: "[Clay] is the finest Negro athlete I have ever known and he will mean more to his people than Jackie Robinson. Robinson is an establishment hero. Clay will be our hero."

Robinson's lifelong, vocal commitment to the Republican Party and his voluntary condemnation of Paul Robeson before the House Un-American Activities Committee (HUAC) in 1949 caused him to be shunned by the new radicals of the 1960s. From their perspective, he was on one side of a divide with Cassius Clay—soon to be Muhammad Ali—on the other. In the heat of struggle, as cities burned, this perception of Robinson residing on the wrong side of the barricades was seared into the minds of a generation. But if we accept this formulaic framework today, we miss out on a Jackie Robinson who used his sporting prowess as a springboard to advance the struggle for equality, perhaps more than any athlete in history. There is far too much to learn from Jackie Robinson

Brooklyn Dodgers third baseman Jackie Robinson (42) steals home and slides under catcher Yogi Berra's mitt in the 1955 World Series. (AP)

to casually disregard his towering contribution to the cause of building a better world.

Robinson was a Hall of Fame player who defined daring and speed. He played for ten years, with a .311 lifetime batting average. He was a competitor known for dancing on the bases and driving pitchers to fits of distraction, stealing home a record eighteen times. My Brooklyn-born and -raised father would soothe me to sleep with stories of his base running, saying, "When I close my eyes, I can still see him on the base paths." By all conventional measures, Robinson was an exceptional ballplayer. But because he opened the door to a generation of talent like Willie Mays, Henry Aaron, and Ernie Banks, and smashed the color line at great personal cost, his legacy far outpaces his stat sheet. As baseball scribe Roger Kahn once wrote, "To see Robinson's career in numbers is to see Lincoln through Federal budgets and to miss the Emancipation Proclamation. Double plays, stolen bases, indeed the bat, ball, and glove, were only artifacts with which Jackie Robinson made...you and me a shade more free."

Roots

Jack Roosevelt Robinson was born in rural Georgia in 1919, one of five children. His family moved to Pasadena, California, with dreams of escaping the heart of Jim Crow, but soon found that the Golden State was not immune to the disease of discrimination. His sister, Willa Mae, described growing up in California as "a sort of slavery, with whites slowly, very slowly, getting used to us." Robinson's father soon ran off in search of other opportunities. As Robinson remembered in his 1972 autobiography, "My father's will and spirit were slowly broken down by the economic slavery imposed upon him, the exorbitant costs of food and rent and other necessities.... I could only think of him with bitterness. He too may have been a victim of oppression, but he had no right to desert my mother and five children."

With their father gone, the Robinson family's hardscrabble existence—now supported only by their mother's wages as a domestic servant—was marked by an exacerbated poverty. "Sometimes there were only two meals a day," Robinson wrote in his autobiography, "and some days we wouldn't have eaten at all if it hadn't been for the leftovers my mother brought home from her job."

Although Pasadena offered little or no chance for an African American to attain a high-paying job or hold political office, it did offer athletic opportunities. Jackie's older brother, Mack, was the first breakout star of the family, winning a silver medal at the 1936 Berlin Summer Olympics. Upon his return home, however, Mack found that the only job open to him was sweeping the Pasadena streets. Showing a defiant streak like the one that would characterize his younger brother, Mack made a point of sweeping in his leather Olympic jacket, which prompted local whites to call the police and charge him with being "provocative."

While his brother was winning medals and "provoking" racists, Jackie went to Pasadena Junior College and then accepted a sports scholarship from the University of California at Los Angeles (UCLA) where he excelled at football and baseball. He was a loner who didn't drink or smoke and was very religious. He was also very sensitive to every slight, racial or otherwise. Teammate Woody Strode commented, "Jackie was a very intelligent, good-looking man who had steely hard eyes that would flash angry in a heartbeat. People would ask me, why is Jackie always so sullen?" Jackie would be compelled, more than once, to risk everything he would become in order to stand up to racist police officers harassing his friends or sports opponents making racial slurs.

Robinson continued to stand up when he joined the army during World War II. At a military base, he was brought up on court martial charges for refusing to give up his seat on a bus. Another time, he heard a white superior officer call a Black private a "stupid nigger son of a bitch." Jackie calmly stepped in and said, "You shouldn't speak to a soldier in those terms." He was then told, "Oh fuck you too nigger!" At this point, according to one witness, "Jackie almost killed the guy." Only the intervention of heavyweight boxing champion Joe Louis, an admirer of Jackie's UCLA athletic achievements, prevented another court martial trial. It's safe to say that, without his athletic background, Jackie Robinson would have spent the Civil Rights movement in prison, or worse.

After the army, Jackie aimed to settle down with his wife Rachel and become a gym teacher. But before making much headway toward this dream, he joined the Negro Leagues as a twenty-six-year-old rookie. In 1946, Robinson caught the eye of Brooklyn Dodgers general manager and part owner Branch Rickey. The previous winter, Major League owners had voted fifteen to one against integrating baseball, with Rickey the lone dissenter. Rickey thought Robinson could be the one to break through the unofficial color line that garroted the league.

The choice of Robinson was a shock to almost everyone in baseball, Robinson included: "I was thrilled, scared, and excited. Most of all I was speechless." Some thought the first Black player championed should be an aging Negro League legend like Satchel Paige or Josh Gibson. Others thought Robinson was a good, but not great, player and that he would fail. But Branch Rickey was looking for more than just a great ballplayer. He was looking for a "type." He believed that breaking the color line wouldn't be just about skill. Breaking the color line would require the ability to endure harassment, threats, and daily pressure to perform without acting out or striking back. In the articulate college graduate and army veteran, Rickey felt he had his man: someone ready and willing to take on—without cracking—a mighty and official resistance to change.

Turn the Other Cheek

In their first meeting, Rickey said to Robinson, "I know you have the skills. But do you have the guts?" Meaning, in effect, Do you have the guts to take torrents of abuse and not respond?" A decade before the rise of Dr. Martin Luther King Jr. and his movement of nonviolent resistance, Rickey was asking Robinson, a player with no tolerance for racism and a notoriously short temper, to turn the other cheek. Robinson agreed to the challenge, not really knowing what he would have to face.

From the beginning, abuse came in handfuls, and not just from opponents. His first Minor League manager was Mississippi-born Clay Hopper. When told Robinson would join the Dodgers' farm team, the Montreal Royals, Hopper immediately complained to Rickey. With lips quivering, he asked, "Mr. Rickey, do you REALLY think a nigger's a human being?" During Minor League games, Robinson got a preview of what he would confront in the majors: calls never going his way, black cats thrown onto the field during at bats, and death threats that shadowed him and his family. As Jackie remembered, "The toll these incidents took was greater than I realized. I was overestimating my stamina and underestimating the beating I was taking. I couldn't sleep or eat."

Blacks from Harlem to Watts responded by following the Montreal Royals every game with zeal, seeing every at bat as a morality play about whether African Americans had the "necessities" to achieve success in baseball. Sam Lacy, legendary sports columnist for the *Baltimore Afro-American*, wrote, "I felt a lump in my throat each time a ball was hit in his direction. I was constantly in fear of his muffing an easy roller under the stress of things and I uttered a silent prayer of thanks as with closed eyes I heard the solid whack of Robinson's bat against the ball."

Eventually, Robinson's relentless competitiveness and stoicism in the face of racism began to win his critics. By the time Jackie was called up to the majors, even Clay Hopper, in what would become a familiar type of transformation, had completely changed his tune, telling Robinson, "You're a great player and a fine gentleman and it's been wonderful having you on the team."

When Jackie started playing for the Dodgers, the racial taunts, slurs, and threats didn't stop. In fact, they got worse. Before he had played a single game, teammates like "Dixie" Walker and others petitioned to get him off the squad. He was on a team without teammates. Other clubs took every opportunity to throw at his head or spike his legs, and no one came to his defense. He was a twenty-seven-year-old rookie who, according to sports writer Jimmy Cannon, "is the loneliest man I've ever seen."

But the situation couldn't last. It began to change on April 22, 1947, when the Philadelphia Phillies, led by manager Ben Chapman, chanted "Nigger"—and worse—at Robinson throughout the game. At first, Robinson ignored them as instructed; his teammates also did nothing. "I felt tortured," Robinson wrote in his autobiography,

> …and I tried to just play ball and ignore the insults but it was really getting to me. For one wild and rage crazed moment I thought, 'To hell with Mr. Rickey's noble experiment. To hell with the image of the patient black freak I was supposed to create.' I could throw down my bat, stride over to that Phillies dugout, grab one of those white sons of bitches, and smash his teeth in with my despised black fist. Then I could walk away from it all.

In the end, it was Jackie's teammates who couldn't take it anymore. Dodger leader Eddie Stanky yelled into the Phillies dugout, "Listen you yellow-bellied cowards! Why don't you pick on someone who can fight back?!" The Dodgers then picked up bats and edged forward until Chapman and his Phillies backed down. Branch Rickey recognized the significance of the moment. "The Phillies," he later observed, "did more to unify the Dodgers than any manager could have."

The crowds that gathered in opposing ballparks also may have shifted the Brooklyn team. No matter what the city, large

African-American crowds would show up to games and root for the Dodgers, making every game feel almost like a home game. Black novelist John A. Williams explained this phenomenon: "Many of us who went to the park to see Jackie did so to protect him, to defend him from harm, if necessary, as well as to cheer him on."

The Jackie Robinson Behind the Image

By the year's end, Jackie had won the first-ever Rookie of the Year Award and led the league in stolen bases. He had become an instant legend in Black America, and his demeanor, that of a "patient black freak," made him a hero for large swaths of an emergent liberal white America as well. In a national poll, he ranked as the "second most admired American," ahead of President Harry S. Truman and General Dwight D. Eisenhower, and behind only Bing Crosby. The image of Robinson as a quiet, subservient, soft-spoken gentleman was, of course, totally false. Robinson's true personality was angry, combative, and confrontational. For him, real progress occurred in 1948, when Rickey gave him more leeway to argue with umpires and even spike a player back if he got hit first. Yet the idea persisted—for many whites especially—that Robinson, the veteran, the man who "succeeded the right way," without rancorous protests, was the model for African Americans. The U.S. government, in the early stages of the Cold War, needed such an image to project internationally that the United States was a color-blind society and not, as claimed by the USSR, a bastion of racism.

It was because of this (misleading) image and in this context that Robinson was called before the House Un-American Activities Committee (HUAC). Singer, actor, and civil rights activist Paul Robeson—who, in addition to being the most famous African American in the world at the time, had ties with the American Communist Party and was militantly opposed to

American racism and imperialism—had told HUAC that Blacks would never pick up arms against the Soviet Union. HUAC saw this comment as an opportunity to undermine Robeson's popularity and political authority by challenging his patriotism. To legitimize their attack, they asked Robinson to testify before the committee. NAACP lawyers wanted to defend Robinson's right not to speak, but he refused their offer. Rickey wanted him to testify, and besides, Robinson, who was, after all, more interested in politics than power hitting, craved the platform. Jackie was an anticommunist, yet he understood the importance of Robeson to the Black community. He thought he could use the HUAC hearing to speak out for racial justice and lightly chide Robeson without hurting him. He was wrong.

Robinson read a prepared statement. "Every single Negro who is worth his salt is going to resent slurs and discrimination because of his race, and he's going to use every bit of intelligence he has to stop it. This has got absolutely nothing to do with what Communists may or may not do. Just because it is a Communist who denounces injustice in the courts, police brutality, and lynching when it happens doesn't change the truth of the charges. Blacks were stirred up long before there was a CP and will be stirred up after unless Jim Crow has disappeared." Such a statement, both in the absence of a civil rights movement and directly in the face of a HUAC committee dominated by Dixiecrat segregationists, is simply remarkable.

However, it is Robinson's next remark regarding Paul Robeson that is etched in the history books as the blow that took down the seemingly indomitable Robeson. "I haven't any comment to make except that the statement [about Blacks refusing to fight the USSR]—if Mr. Robeson actually made it—sounds very silly to me. Negroes have too much invested in America to throw it away for a siren song sung in bass." With those words, he gave HUAC both license and cover to attack and persecute Robeson. And persecute him they did. In a few short years, Robeson—world-famous recording and performing artist, valedictorian, and football star of his class at Rutgers—had been virtually erased from public memory. Robinson later called his contribution to this attack "the greatest regret of my life." It is without question an indelible mark on Robinson's political legacy. But it would do his own political evolution a disservice to see him as merely a "pawn" of HUAC or Branch Rickey. In this period before the Civil Rights movement, the politics of McCarthyism choked the life out of Robeson and the entire Left—from liberal to radical to communist. Robinson was a proud veteran and saw himself as a "role model" demonstrating how Blacks could succeed in Cold War America. He agreed with people like future Supreme Court Justice Thurgood Marshall that Robeson's pro-Soviet politics made him a liability in more mainstream civil rights activists' attempts to curry favor with friendly forces in government and the courts. But Jackie would soon realize that Robeson was correct in his assertion that freedom cannot be given by the oppressor but must be demanded by the oppressed.

By the time the 1949 season began, Robinson had gained more confidence to speak and threw down a warning to umpires: "I am not going to be anyone's sitting duck. I know what's going on out there." He was also winning the undying friendship of white teammates, including shortstop Pee Wee Reese. Before one game in Cincinnati, when a local white supremacist group threatened to assassinate Robinson on the field, Reese laughed to reporters and said, "I think we will all wear 42 [Robinson's number] and have ourselves a shooting gallery."

But not everyone was won over. The *Sporting News* answered Robinson's new voice with a warning of its own: "America will resent and repel with all their force the agitator, the sharper with an angle, the fellow who is less than an American because he chooses to be a rabble rouser." Affection for him in white America—outside of Brooklyn—began to wane. Robinson's new confidence to speak out against racism earned him the scorn of previously friendly sports writers like Jimmy Cannon. "The range of Jackie Robinson's hostility appears to have no frontiers. He is a juggler of sorts, flashily keeping feuds in motion, alienating even Brooklyn partisans with his undisciplined protests." Robinson's "undisciplined protests" consisted of standing up to players attempting to spike his legs, arguing with umpires, and being who he actually was: a fiercely proud, hot-headed athlete who wouldn't take a back seat to anybody. If Robinson had been white, Cannon would have most likely praised his spitfire, win-at-all-costs temperament. But the sight of someone Black going toe-to-toe with umpires and All Stars alike was more than he and other previously sympathetic sportswriters could stomach.

This kind of criticism only made Robinson more eager than ever to speak out against Jim Crow and racism. In these dark years of McCarthyism, before the light of the Montgomery Bus Boycotts, "Only Jackie Robinson," as his biographer Arnold Rampersad wrote, "insisted day in day out on challenging America on questions of race and justice."

1955 was a particularly complicated year. By then, a new generation of African-American players had come into the league and established themselves as stars. Amazingly, only three teams didn't have Black players in their farm systems. Mays, Aaron, Ernie Banks, and Brooklyn catcher Roy Campanella wowed crowds across the country. 1955 was the year of the Montgomery Bus Boycotts and the first backlash against the emerging mood for civil rights. It was the year that fourteen-year-old Emmett Till was beaten to death for being "too familiar" with a white woman. The White Citizen Councils had swelled to 300,000 members. Over one hundred Congressmen signed a document pledging to uphold segregation. Robinson, still a symbol of integration and now never silent, was viciously booed and threatened. The more progressive *Sport Magazine* called him: "The most savagely booed, ruthlessly libeled player in the game, his every appearance greeted by a storm of cat calls and name calling." But Robinson had the last laugh, leading the Dodgers to victory in the 1955 World Series on the strength of that daring steal of home and an umpire's call that owed more to changing attitudes on race than whether Robinson was actually safe.

Jackie Robinson retired from Major League Baseball in 1956 and became a spokesman for the NAACP, quickly earning his place as the their most requested speaker nationwide (number two was Martin Luther King Jr.). Robinson would end speeches by saying, "If I had to choose between baseball's Hall of Fame and first-class citizenship I would say first-class citizenship to all of my people." In 1958, he was the marshal and lead organizer of the Youth March for Integrated Schools, which had an initial goal of getting 1,000 Black and white students to march on the Lincoln Memorial. They got 10,000.

"White Man's Negro"?

In April of 1959, Robinson began writing a column on the sports page of the *New York Post* (then—believe it or not—a liberal paper) on topics that ranged from sports to civil rights. Critics, both Black and white, said that, as an athlete, Robinson didn't have the right to speak out on politics. Dr. King rebuked them, arguing, "He has the right because back in the days when integration wasn't fashionable, he underwent the trauma and the humiliation and the loneliness which comes with being a pilgrim that walks in the lonesome byways toward the high road of Freedom. He was a sit-inner before sit-ins, a freedom rider before freedom rides."

During this time, and until the end of his life, Robinson was a hard-core Republican. This fact is usually brought up to undermine his progressive credentials, or as a queasy attempt by Republicans to claim him as one of their own. But, once again, context is everything. Robinson, from his Georgia birth, had a hardened and quite justifiable view that the Democrats were the party of slavery, segregation, and Jim Crow. When John F. Kennedy gave his famous "New Frontier" speech to the Democratic National Convention, Robinson saw none other than Democratic governor of Arkansas and notorious segregationist Orval Faubus sitting by JFK's side. This confirmed his suspicion that there was nothing "new" in Kennedy's New Frontier. But Robinson would be disappointed time and again by the Republican "commitment" to civil rights. When Dr. King was sentenced to four months on a work gang in Georgia, Jackie asked his "friend" Richard Milhous Nixon to intervene and was ignored. Jackie was shocked.

Though disillusioned with both political parties, Jackie never stopped going to the front lines of civil rights battles and encouraging African Americans to vote. At a stop in Tennessee, on a speaking tour to raise money for the SNCC (Student Nonviolent Coordinating Committee) sit-ins, Robinson said, "We are going to get our share of this country—we are going to fight for it. We must take it step by step and us older folks should support the youngsters in their stand-ins and sit-ins."

As the Black freedom struggle grew and a revolutionary wing developed, Robinson, in spite of his actions, was viewed as a "white man's Negro" due to his abiding faith in electoral politics and his belief in integration. He was an icon of "the old way of doing things" in the eyes of many. His verbal feud with Malcolm X heightened this impression. Robinson wrote in his *Post* column, "Malcolm is very militant on Harlem street corners where militancy is not that dangerous. I don't see him in Birmingham…. He is terribly militant on soapboxes and street corners yet he has not faced the police dogs or gone to jail for freedom." Robinson could not have known that he was touching on the pressure point of Malcolm's pain and frustration with the Nation of Islam. The Nation position—voiced by Malcolm X when he said, "What kind of man would send his kids to be attacked by dogs and hoses? Why would we want to integrate with people who don't want us?"—was, at the end of the day, an abstention from struggle, as Malcolm X well knew. Yet, although they were political opponents, Robinson and Malcolm X had something in common: their ideas shifted in the struggles of the 1960s.

When HUAC opened investigations on the Nation of Islam, Jackie wrote a column asking, "What about an investigation of the White Citizen Councils?" Frustrated by the snail's pace of Kennedy's program on civil rights, he wrote "The revolution that is taking place in this country cannot be squelched by police dogs or high power hoses." During the Birmingham campaign, he flew to join King and wrote, "If King was harmed, the restraint of many people all over this nation might burst its bonds and bring about a brutal bloody holocaust the like of which this country has not seen." Robinson was a lead organizer for the great 1963 March on Washington. And on September 16, 1963, after four young Black girls were killed by a bomb at the 16th Street Baptist Church in Birmingham, Alabama, he wrote: "God bless Dr. Martin Luther King.... But if my child had been killed, I'm afraid he would have lost me as a potential disciple of his credo of non-violence."

In 1964, the Black freedom struggle began to move North, and economic segregation proved much more intractable than Jim Crow. Starting in Harlem, the era of the northern ghetto riots began. Gone was the ideal of patient suffering. Gone too was the underlying ideal of an integrated America in which justice would prevail for all. When Malcolm X was killed, Robinson wrote an obituary that, unlike most, didn't bury Malcolm but praised him. He quoted Malcolm saying to him, "Jackie, in the days to come your son and my son will not be willing to settle for things we are willing to settle for." Robinson's ideas further changed as the Vietnam War came crashing into his life. His son, Jackie Jr., saw combat in Southeast Asia and returned deeply scarred: carrying a gun, scared of shadows, and addicted to drugs.

Jackie, the fervent anticommunist, began to change his views of the war. "As I look around today and observe how lost and frustrated and bitter our young people are, I find myself wishing that there was some way to reach out to them and let them know that we want to help. I confess I don't know the way." This sentiment deepened in Robinson when King came out against the war, dividing the Civil Rights movement. At first, Robinson vehemently disagreed. But King called him and they spoke for several hours, after which Robinson pledged never to criticize him again.

By the end of 1968, he supported the much-criticized movement among Black athletes to boycott the Olympics, writing, "I do support the individuals who decided to make the sacrifice by giving up the chance to win an Olympic medal. I respect their courage. We need to understand the reason and frustration behind these protests…it was different in my day; perhaps we lacked courage." And in 1969, this "veteran," "Republican," and "anticommunist" wrote, "I wouldn't fly the flag on the fourth of July or any other day. When I see a car with a flag pasted on it, I figure the guy behind the wheel isn't my friend."

Robinson died way too early. He passed away in 1972 from complications caused by diabetes. He was fifty-two years old. As Red Smith wrote upon his death, "The word for Jackie Robinson is 'unconquerable.'… He would not be defeated. Not by the other team and not by life." Robinson's number 42 has been retired by all of baseball. We should retire all static views of Robinson as well. ◆

CHAPTER THREE

Rumble, Young Man, Rumble: Muhammad Ali and the 1960s

Film footage of Muhammad Ali is used to sell everything from soft drinks to cars. We are spoon-fed an easily digestible image of the young Ali, an improbably charismatic boxer, dancing in the ring and crowing, "I am the greatest!" The Ali of the present is also easy to take in, a very public figure despite his near total inability to move or speak, his voice silenced both by years of boxing and by Parkinson's disease. The establishment embraces this Ali as a walking saint. In 1996, Ali was sent to light the Olympic Torch in Atlanta. In 2002, he "agreed to star in a Hollywood-produced advertising campaign, designed to explain America and the war in Afghanistan to the Muslim world." In 2004, he appeared in a cuddly Super Bowl ad, telling a young, blond child that the future was his. Later that year, he threw out the first pitch at baseball's All-Star game.

The present Ali has been absorbed by the establishment as a legend—a harmless, helpful icon. There is barely a trace left of the ragged truth: Never has an athlete been more reviled by the mainstream press, more persecuted by the U.S. government, or more defiantly beloved throughout the world than Muhammad Ali. Yet this Ali, the catalyst that forced professional sports—and the country as a whole—to examine the issues of racism and war, no longer exists.

The reason for this is not difficult to fathom. The golden

rule of big-time sports is that "jocks" are not supposed to be political, unless it involves saluting the flag, supporting the troops, selling a war, or, in the case of Boston Red Sox pitcher Curt Schilling, supporting President Bush. All of that is acceptable. But a radical in running shoes is not. When Toni Smith, the basketball captain at little Division III's Manhattanville College, turned her back on the flag in 2003, the attack was rabid. In March of the same year, when Wake Forest basketball All-American Josh Howard said about the U.S. war on Iraq, "It's all over oil...that's how I feel," not only was Howard derided publicly, but NBA draft reports stated, "Antiwar remarks reflect rumored erratic behavior."

The hidden history of Muhammad Ali and the revolt of the Black athlete in the 1960s is therefore a living history. By reclaiming it from the powers that be, we not only gain a better understanding of the struggles of the 1960s, we also see how struggle can shape every aspect of life in the United States—even sports.

Boxing

No sport has chewed athletes up and spit them out—especially Black athletes—quite like boxing. For the very few who "make it," it is never the sport of choice. Boxing has always been for the poor, for people born at the absolute margins of society. The first boxers in the United States were slaves. Southern plantation owners amused themselves by putting together the strongest slaves and having them fight it out while wearing iron collars. After the abolition of slavery, boxing was unique among sports because it was desegregated as early as the turn of the last century. This was not because the people who ran boxing were in any way progressive. They make the people who run boxing today resemble gentlemen of great character. Those early promoters simply wanted to make a buck off the rampant racism in American society by pitting

Black vs. white for public spectacle. Unwittingly, these early fight financiers opened up a space in which the white supremacist ideas of the day could be challenged. This was the era of deeply racist pseudo-science. The attitude of social Darwinist quacks was that Blacks were not only mentally inferior but also physically inferior to whites. Blacks were cast as too lazy and too undisciplined to ever be taken seriously as athletes.

When Jack Johnson became the first Black heavyweight-boxing champion in 1908, his victory created a serious crisis for these ideas. The media whipped up a frenzy around the need for a "Great White Hope" to restore order to the world. Former champion Jim Jeffries came out of retirement to restore that order, saying, "I am going into this fight for the sole purpose of proving that a white man is better than a Negro."

At the fight, which took place in 1910, the ringside band played, "All Coons Look Alike to Me," and promoters led the nearly all-white crowd in the chant "Kill the nigger." But Johnson was faster, stronger, and smarter than Jeffries, knocking him out with ease. After Johnson's victory, there were race riots around the country—in Illinois, Missouri, New York, Ohio, Pennsylvania, Colorado, Texas, and Washington, D.C. Most of the riots consisted of white lynch mobs attempting to enter Black neighborhoods and Blacks fighting back. This reaction to a boxing match was the most widespread simultaneous racial uprising in the U.S. until the riots that followed the 1968 assassination of civil rights leader Dr. Martin Luther King Jr. Right-wing religious groups immediately organized a movement to ban boxing, and Congress actually passed a law that prohibited the showing of boxing films. Black leaders, such as Booker T. Washington, pushed Johnson to condemn the African-American uprising. But Johnson remained defiant. He not only spoke out on all issues of the day, he also broke racist social taboos by marrying white women, and as a result faced harassment and persecution for most of his life. Johnson was forced into exile in 1913 on the trumped-up charge of transporting a white woman across state lines for prostitution.

The "Johnson backlash" meant that it would be twenty years before the rise of another Black heavyweight champ—"The Brown Bomber," Joe Louis. Louis was quiet where Johnson had been outspoken. An all-white management team handled Louis very carefully, and had a set of rules he had to follow, including, "never be photographed with a white woman, never go to a club by yourself, and never speak unless spoken to." But the Brown Bomber's timid public face became fierce in the ring. Louis scored sixty-nine victories in seventy-two professional fights—fifty-five of them knockouts.

Despite the docile image demanded by his handlers, Joe Louis—and his dominance in the ring—represented dignity and resistance to Blacks and to the radicalizing working class of the 1930s. This played out most famously during Louis's two fights against German boxer Max Schmeling in 1936 and 1938. German Nazi leader Adolf Hitler promoted Schmeling as the epitome of "Aryan greatness," and in their first bout, Schmeling knocked out Louis. Hitler and Nazi propagandist Joseph Goebbels had a field day, and the southern press in the United States laughed it up. One columnist for the *New Orleans Picayune* wrote, "I guess this proves who really is the master race."

The Louis-Schmeling rematch in 1938 was even more politically loaded—a physical referendum on Hitler, the Jim Crow South, and antiracism. The U.S. Communist Party organized radio listenings of the fight from Harlem to Birmingham that became mass meetings—complete with armed guards at the door. Hitler closed down movie houses so all of Germany would be compelled to listen to the fight. The cinema doors probably should have been kept open; Louis devastated Schmeling in one round, with lightning combinations that stunned the big German. In a notorious move, Hitler cut all of Germany's radio power when it was clear that the knockout was coming.

The Brown Bomber held the heavyweight title for twelve years, the longest reign in history. He beat all comers, the overwhelming majority of them white, successfully defending his title a record twenty-five times. He was, according to poet Maya Angelou, "The one invincible Negro, the one who stood up to the white man and beat him down with his fists. He in a sense carried so many of our hopes, and maybe even our dreams of vengeance." Thirty years after the fight against Schmeling, Martin Luther King Jr. reinforced its significance by reminding readers of *Why We Can't Wait* that

> More than 25 years ago, one of the southern states adopted a new method of capital punishment. Poison gas supplanted the gallows. In its earliest stages a microphone was placed inside the sealed death chamber so that scientific observers might hear the words of the dying prisoner to judge how the victim reacted in this novel situation. The first victim was a young Negro. As the pellet dropped into the container, and the gas curled upward, through the microphone came these words. "Save me Joe Louis. Save me Joe Louis. Save me Joe Louis."

In a society so violently racist, boxing became an outlet for people's anger—an arena where the thwarted ability, unrecognized talent, and relentless fighting spirit that shaped the Black experience in the U.S. could be acted out in all its intensity and proportionate rage.

"King of the World"

Muhammad Ali's identity was forged in the 1950s and 1960s, as the Black freedom struggle heated up and boiled over. He was born Cassius Clay in Louisville, Kentucky, in 1942. His father, a frustrated artist, made his living as a house painter. His mother, like Jackie Robinson's mother, was a domestic worker. The Louisville of 1942 was a segregated horse-breeding community, where being Black meant being seen as a servant. But the young Clay could box. And he could talk. He had a mouth like no fighter, athlete, or public Black figure anyone had ever heard. Joe Louis used to say, "My manager does my talking for me. I do my talking in the ring." Clay did his own talking, inside and outside the ring. The press called him the Louisville Lip, Cash the Brash, Mighty Mouth, and Gaseous Cassius. He used to say he talked so much because his hero was Gorgeous George, a flamboyant, verbose, white pro wrestler of the late 1950s. But once, in an unguarded moment, he said, "Where do you think I'd be next week if I didn't know how to shout and holler? I'd probably be down in my hometown washing windows and saying yassuh and nossuh and knowing my place."

And Ali, of course, could back up the talk. His boxing skills won him the gold medal in the 1960 Greek Olympics at age eighteen. When he returned from the Olympiad—and this is the first step in his political arc—the young Clay held a press conference at the airport, his gold medal swinging from his neck, and riffed:

> To make America the greatest is my goal
> So I beat the Russian and I beat the Pole
> And for the USA won the medal of Gold.
> The Greeks said, You're better than the Cassius of Old.

Clay loved his gold medal. Fellow Olympian Wilma Rudolph remembered, "He slept with it, he went to the cafeteria with it. He never took it off." The week after returning home from the Olympics, Clay went with his medal swinging around his neck to eat a cheeseburger in a Louisville restaurant—and was denied service. He threw his beloved medal into the Ohio River. This started the eighteen-year-old on a po-

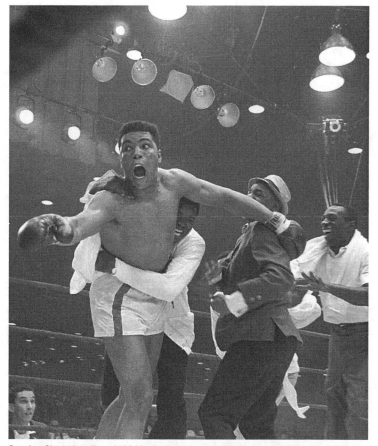

Cassius Clay's handlers hold him back as he reacts after he is announced the new heavyweight champion of the world on a seventh round technical knockout against Sonny Liston at Convention Hall in Miami Beach, Florida, on Feb. 25, 1964. (AP)

litical journey that would define his era.

The young Clay actively looked for political answers and began finding them when he heard Malcolm X speak at a meeting of the Nation of Islam (NOI). He heard Malcolm X say, "You might see these Negroes who believe in nonviolence and mistake us for one of them and put your hands on us thinking that we are going to turn the other cheek—and we'll put you to death just like that." The young fighter and Malcolm X became political allies and fast friends. Malcolm stayed with Clay as he trained for his fight against "The Big Ugly Bear," champion Sonny Liston. With Malcolm around, rumors that Clay was going to join the NOI flew through the sports pages, and the press hounded him, wanting to know whether he planned to become a member. At one point he said, "I might if you keep asking me."

When everyone else was forecasting an easy knockout for Liston, Malcolm X predicted otherwise:

> Clay will win. He is the finest Negro athlete I have ever known and he will mean more to his people than Jackie Robinson. Robinson is an establishment hero. Clay will be our hero…. Not many people know the quality of mind he has in there. One forgets that although the clown never imitates a wise man, a wise man can imitate the clown.

Although the verdict was out on whether he was a wise man or a clown, no one except Malcolm X gave him a chance against Liston, a hulking ex-con who had worked for the Mob as a picket-line leg-breaker. But Ali—quicker, stronger, and bolder than they knew—shocked the world and beat Liston. He then said famously, "I'm king of the world!"

When Ali said he was the greatest, it wasn't far from the truth. His trainer Angelo Dundee once said with a smile, "He destroyed [the style of] a generation of fighters by boxing with his hands down. Everyone else who did that got creamed but Ali was so quick he could get away with it." Ali also set a new standard for ring speed. He used to say, "I'm so fast, I can turn off the bedroom lights and get in bed before it gets dark." As writer Gary Kamiya put it,

> No one had ever seen anyone that big move that fast; no one had ever seen anyone that graceful hurt other people so badly. Fighting Ali was like being forced to glide across the floor with Gene Kelly in

a murderous duet; a single deviation from the beat, a hundredth of a second's pause coming out of a liquid twirl, and a baseball bat would explode against your head.

In his professional career, this "Louisville Lip" won fifty-six of sixty-one fights, with thirty-seven knockouts.

Nation of Islam

The day after he beat Liston, Clay announced publicly that he was a member of the NOI. Words cannot do justice to the firestorm this caused. Whatever disagreements one may have with the Nation of Islam, the fact that the heavyweight champion of the world joined the organization of Malcolm X was enormously significant. The Olympic gold medalist had linked arms with a group that called white people "devils" and stood unapologetically for self-defense and racial separation. Not surprisingly, the power brokers of the conservative, mobbed-up, corrupt fight world lost their minds. Famed scribe Jimmy Cannon wrote, "The fight racket since its rotten beginnings has been the red light district of sports. But this is the first time it has been turned into an instrument of hate." Apparently, he had forgotten the entire career of Jack Johnson.

Ali was attacked not only by Cannon and his ilk, but also by the "respectable" wing of the Civil Rights movement. NAACP executive secretary Roy Wilkins went so far as to say, "Cassius Clay may as well be an honorary member of the white citizen councils." Ali's response at this point was very defensive. He repeatedly said that his was a purely religious, not political, conversion. His defensiveness reflected the conservative perspective of the NOI, and the views he expressed were those of the Nation: "I'm not going to get killed trying to force myself on people who don't want me. Integration is wrong. White people don't want it, the Muslims don't want it. So what's wrong with the Muslims? I've never been in jail. I've never been in court. I don't join integration marches and I never hold a sign."

But much like Malcolm X, who at the time was engineering a political break from the Nation, Clay—to the anger of Elijah Muhammad—found it impossible to explain his religious worldview without speaking to the mass Black freedom struggle exploding outside the boxing ring. When it came to maintaining the religious nature of his conversion, he was his own worst enemy—claiming that his transformation had nothing to do with politics in one breath and then in the next saying,

> I ain't no Christian. I can't be when I see all the colored people fighting for forced integration get blown up. They get hit by the stones and chewed by dogs and then these crackers blow up a Negro Church…. People are always telling me what a good example I would be if I just wasn't Muslim. I've heard over and over why couldn't I just be more like Joe Louis and Sugar Ray. Well they are gone and the Black man's condition is just the same ain't it? We're still catching hell.

If the establishment press was outraged, the new generation of activists was electrified. As civil rights leader Julian Bond reminisced,

> I remember when Ali joined the Nation. The act of joining was not something many of us particularly liked. But the notion that he would do it, that he'd jump out there, join this group that was so despised by mainstream America and be proud of it, sent a little thrill through you…. He was able to tell white folks for us to go to hell; that I'm going to do it my way.

For a brief time, the former Clay was known as Cassius X, until Elijah Muhammad gave him the name Muhammad Ali—a tremendous honor bestowed in an attempt to ensure that Ali would side with Elijah Muhammad in his split with Malcolm X. Ali proceeded to commit what he would later describe as his greatest mistake: turning his back on Malcolm X. But the internal politics of the Nation were not what the powers that be and their media noticed. To them, the Islamic name change— something that no world class athlete had ever done before—

was a sharp slap in the face. Almost overnight, calling the champ Ali or Clay indicated where one stood on civil rights, Black Power, and, eventually, the war in Vietnam. For years after the change, the *New York Times'* editorial policy was to refer to Ali as Clay.

This all took place against the backdrop of a Black freedom struggle that rolled from the South to the North. During the summer of 1964, there were 1,000 arrests of civil rights activists, thirty buildings bombed, and thirty-six churches burned by the Ku Klux Klan and their sympathizers. Also in 1964, the first urban uprisings and riots took place in the northern ghettos. The politics of Black Power began to emerge, and Muhammad Ali became the critical symbol of this transformation. As news anchor Bryant Gumbel said, "One of the reasons the civil rights movement went forward was that Black people were able to overcome their fear. And I honestly believe that for many Black Americans, that came from watching Muhammad Ali. He simply refused to be afraid. And being that way, he gave other people courage."

A concrete sign of Ali's early influence was seen in 1965, when Student Nonviolent Coordinating Committee (SNCC) volunteers in Lowndes County, Alabama launched an independent political party. Their new group was the first to use the symbol of a black panther. Their bumper stickers and T-shirts featured the black silhouette of a panther and a slogan straight from the champ: "WE Are the Greatest."

It's this broader context that allows us to understand how Ali came to symbolize the Black revolution while his adversaries represented the people who opposed it. Floyd Patterson, a Black ex-champion, wrapped himself tightly in the American flag, and challenged Ali, saying, "This fight is a crusade to reclaim the title from the Black Muslims. As a Catholic I am fighting Clay as a patriotic duty. I am going to return the crown to America." On the night of the fight, Ali brutalized Patterson for nine rounds, dragging it out and yelling, "Come on, America! Come on, white America…. What's my name? Is my name Clay? What's my name, fool?" Future Black Panther Party leader Eldridge Cleaver wrote in his 1968 autobiography, *Soul on Ice*, "If the Bay of Pigs can be seen as a straight right hand to the psychological jaw of white America then [Ali/Patterson] was the perfect left hook to the gut."

Vietnam

In early 1966, Ali was classified 1-A—eligible to be drafted—and the army came calling. Ali heard this news surrounded by reporters and blurted out one of the most famous phrases of the decade: "Man, I ain't got no quarrel with them Vietcong." This was an astounding statement. There was little opposition to the war at the time, as the antiwar movement was still in its infancy. *Life* magazine's cover read, "Vietnam: The War Is Worth Winning," the song "Ballad of the Green Berets" was climbing the charts, and standing against this seemingly insurmountable tide was Ali. As long-time peace activist Daniel Berrigan concluded, "It was a major boost to an antiwar movement that was very white. He was not an academic, or a bohemian, or a clergyman. He couldn't be dismissed as cowardly."

The reaction was immediate, hostile, ferocious, and, at times, rather hysterical. Jimmy Cannon wrote,

> He fits in with the famous singers no one can hear and the punks riding motorcycles and Batman and the boys with their long dirty hair and the girls with the unwashed look and the college kids dancing naked at secret proms and the revolt of students who get a check from Dad, and the painters who copy the labels off soup cans and surf bums who refuse to work and the whole pampered cult of the bored young.

Writing for *Sports Illustrated*, Jack Olsen later noted that, "The noise became a din, the drumbeats of a holy war. TV and radio commentators, little old ladies...bookmakers, and parish priests, armchair strategists at the Pentagon and politicians all over the place joined in a crescendo of Get Cassius! Get Cassius! Get Cassius!" Ali was given every opportunity to recant, to apologize, to sign up on some cushy USO gig boxing for the troops and the cameras, to go back to making money. But he refused. This refusal was gargantuan, considering what was bubbling over in U.S. society. There was the Black revolution on the one hand, draft resistance and the antiwar struggle on the other, and the heavyweight champ with one foot planted in each. As poet Sonia Sanchez remarked,

> It's hard now to relay the emotion of that time. This was still a time when hardly any well-known people were resisting the draft. It was a war that was disproportionately killing young Black brothers and here was this beautiful, funny poetical young man standing up and saying no! Imagine it for a moment! The heavyweight champion, a magical man, taking his fight out of the ring and into the arena of politics and standing firm. The message was sent!

An incredible groundswell of support built up for Ali. That is why, despite the harassment and the media attacks and the taps on his phones, he stood firm. At one press conference later that year, he was expected to fully recant. Instead, Ali stood up and said, "Keep asking me, no matter how long, On the war in Vietnam, I sing this song, I ain't got no quarrel with the Vietcong." By now it was 1967 and, in another huge step for the antiwar movement, Martin Luther King Jr. came out against the war. At the press conference where he first proclaimed his opposition, King said, "Like Muhammad Ali puts it, we are all—Black and Brown and poor—victims of the same system of oppression." Ali and King, to the anger of the NOI, struck up a private friendship that we know about now thanks to the good historians at the FBI. Here is one FBI wiretap summary, in which Muhammad Ali is referred to derisively as "C."

MLK spoke to C, they exchanged greetings. C invited MLK to be his guest at the next championship fight. MLK said he would like to attend. C said he is keeping up with MLK and MLK is his brother and he's with him 100 percent but can't take any chances, and that MLK should take care of himself and should "watch out for them whities."

The only time these private friends came together in public was later that year, when Ali joined King in Louisville, where a bitter and violent struggle was being waged for fair housing. Ali spoke to the protesters, saying,

> In your struggle for freedom, justice and equality I am with you. I came to Louisville because I could not remain silent while my own people, many I grew up with, many I went too school with, many my blood relatives, were being beaten, stomped and kicked in the streets simply because they want freedom, and justice and equality in housing.

Later that day, he cemented his position as a bridge between the Black freedom and antiwar struggles when responding to a reporter who kept dogging him about the war. With cameras whirring, Ali connected the dots:

> Why should they ask me to put on a uniform and go 10,000 miles from home and drop bombs and bullets on Brown people in Vietnam while so-called Negro people in Louisville are treated like dogs and denied simple human rights? No I'm not going 10,000 miles from home to help murder and burn another poor nation simply to continue the domination of white slave masters of the darker people the world over. This is the day when such evils must come to an end. I have been warned that to take such a stand would cost me millions of dollars. But I have said it once and I will say it again. The real enemy of my people is here. I will not disgrace my religion, my people or myself by becoming a tool to enslave those who are fighting for their own justice, freedom and equality.... If I thought the war was going to bring freedom and equality to 22 million of my people they wouldn't have to draft me, I'd join tomorrow. I have nothing to lose by standing up for my beliefs. So I'll go to jail, so what? We've been in jail for 400 years.

Said Julian Bond,

> When Ali refused to take that symbolic step forward everyone
> knew about it moments later. You could hear people talking about
> it on street corners. It was on everybody's lips. People who had
> never thought about the war—Black and white—began to think it
> through because of Ali.

Ali's refusal to fight in Vietnam was front-page news all over the world. In Guyana, there was a picket in support of Ali in front of the U.S. embassy. In Karachi, young Pakistanis fasted. A mass demonstration was called in Cairo, Egypt.

On June 19, 1967, an all-white jury in Houston passed judgment on Ali. The typical sentence for refusing to serve was eighteen months. Ali got five years and the confiscation of his passport. He immediately appealed. Ali, undefeated and untouched, was stripped of his title, beginning a three-and-a-half-year exile from the ring. Support came from unlikely sources. Floyd Patterson, who was himself being shaped by the movements around him said,

> What bothers me is Clay is being made to pay too stiff a penalty
> for doing what is right. The prize fighter in America is not sup-
> posed to shoot off his mouth about politics, particularly if his
> views oppose the government's and might influence many among
> the working class that follows boxing.

One group that deeply understood Ali's significance was the U.S. Congress. The day of his conviction they voted 337–29 to extend the draft four more years. They also voted 385–19 to make it a federal crime to desecrate the flag. At this time, 1,000 Vietnamese noncombatants were being killed each week by U.S. forces. One hundred soldiers were dying every day, the war was costing $2 billion a month, and the movement against the war was growing. Ali's defiance was far more than a footnote to the movement. As one observer remembered, "He made dissent visible, audible, attractive, and fearless."

Heavyweight champion Muhammad Ali, left, is shown conferring March 29, 1967, with Dr. Martin Luther King Jr. King later said that the sooner this country does away with the draft, the better off we'll be. Ali attended a court proceeding to prevent his Army induction April 28 in Houston. The court refused, however, to block his call-up. (AP)

By 1968, Ali was out on bail, abandoned by the NOI and hangers-on, and stripped of his title. But he was never less alone because a young generation of Blacks and whites were clamoring to hear what he had to say. And Ali obliged. In 1968, he spoke at 200 campuses, each speech brimming with confidence—as if the U.S. state were no more menacing than Floyd Patterson:

> I'm expected to go overseas to help free people in South Vietnam and at the same time my people here are being brutalized, hell no! I would like to say to those of you who think I have lost so much, I have gained everything. I have peace of heart; I have a clear, free conscience. And I am proud. I wake up happy, I go to bed happy, and if I go to jail, I'll go to jail happy.

In the late sixties, when *Esquire* magazine gave Ali five pages to do with what he would, he crafted a political manifesto. He wrote that Black athletes should "take all this fame the white man gave to us because we fought for his entertainment, and we can turn it around. Instead of beating up each other...we will use our fame for freedom." He went on to make the case for reparations, long before the term ever entered common parlance, suggesting the government take $25 billion earmarked for the Vietnam war and instead build homes in Georgia, Mississippi, and Alabama. "Each black man who needs it is going to be given a home," he wrote. "Now, whites need to say, 'We ain't giving you nothing. We're guilty. We owe it to you.'" By the time of Ali's 1970 interview in the *Black Scholar*, he had become a full-fledged radical. "I was determined to be one nigger that the white man didn't get," he said. "Go on and join something. If it isn't the Muslims, at least join the Black Panthers. Join something bad."

Down Goes Ali

Ali appealed his five-year sentence, and was aided by the tide that had turned against the war. In 1970, a divided Supreme Court struck down his sentence, with one justice saying it would "Give Black people a lift." Ali was victorious. He returned to the ring in 1971 a slower fighter, but as intelligent as any who ever laced up a pair of gloves. The slower Ali discovered something that he'd never had to know in his lightning-quick youth: he had a jaw of iron and could take a punch. Ali advanced up the heavyweight ranks until losing to champion "Smokin" Joe Frazier in 1971. The fifteen-round fight was so brutal it sent both fighters to the hospital. In 1973, Ali lost to and then beat Ken Norton. Then came the "Rumble in the Jungle" against George Foreman in Zaire. In many ways, this historic fight revealed the limits and ambiguity of Black Power—as well as the decline of both Ali's militancy and the movement it inspired.

Dictator Mobutu Sese Seko—a darling of the U.S. government who had tortured and killed Ali's friend Patrice Lumumba and thousands of others while seizing power and looting a quarter of Zaire's wealth—secured the fight arm in arm with Don King, the American paragon of unprincipled promotion. Together they dressed up the fight in the colors of Black Nationalism. Squatter camps along the road leading from the airport were obscured by huge billboards that read: "Zaire: Where Black Power Is a Reality." In the lead-up to the fight, Mobutu rounded up scores of alleged criminals and had a hundred of them executed in order to ensure calm for the foreign press and dignitaries.

But if everything surrounding the "Rumble" was horrid, the fight itself was incredible. The African crowd—who, like Blacks in the United States and the oppressed around the world, saw Ali as their hero—chanted, "Ali, Bombaye!" ("Ali, Kill him!"). Foreman, strong and in his prime, was expected to trounce Ali. Instead, Ali beat Foreman in one of the greatest upsets in sports history. For the first several rounds, Ali let Foreman pummel him with ferocious body shots. The crowd thought Ali would not be long for Zaire, but what they didn't know was that, in the weeks leading up the fight, Ali had practiced this "rope-a-dope" strategy, defending his head and body while keeping his back against the ropes. After Foreman had "punched himself out," Ali suddenly exploded from the ropes, dispatching Foreman in a series of lightning blows in the eighth round. It was one of the most strategically brilliant boxing matches ever fought. It was also Ali's athletic apex.

Ali's fighting career continued as the American ruling class smashed some sections of the Black Power movement and accommodated others. In some respects, Ali represented both sides of the dynamic. He was both smashed and accommodated. The slower Ali wowed crowds with his ability to take a punch, and he took them all until he was physically destroyed. Ali's almost complete incapacitation and consequent isolation coincided with the downturn of the freedom struggle in the mid to late 1970s. He was diagnosed with Parkinson's disease in 1984, but the symptoms began to emerge much earlier. The more isolated he became, the more he turned away from militant politics to spirituality and prayer.

The new, slower Ali was much loved by the same establishment that had once abused him. Louisville named a thoroughfare after him. Presidents invited him to the White House, and, as mentioned, today his transformation is so complete he can be counted on to show up to light the Olympic torch or shill for war. Jim Brown, one athlete who has never stopped organizing, mourned Ali's metamorphosis: "The Ali that America ended up loving was not the Ali I loved the most. The warrior I loved was gone."

But if the present Ali has been absorbed by the mainstream, his past is written and it belongs to us. As war and resistance continue, the faint glow of what Ali actually represented remains a threat. That's why his presence still rankles older reactionaries. After Ali appeared at the 2004 Baseball All-Star Game, Hall of Fame pitcher Bob Feller went on record saying, "I object very strongly to Muhammad Ali being here to throw out the first pitch, and you can print that. This is a man who changed his name and changed his religion so he wouldn't have to serve his country, and, to me, that's disgusting." In addition to being factually inaccurate, this is proof positive that the flame of Ali, no matter how faint, needs to be kept lit. His stirring resistance to racism and war belongs not only to the 1960s, but also to our struggles for social justice, both present and future. ◆

CHAPTER FOUR

The 1968 Olympics Raise the Bar

It was inevitable that this revolt of the black athlete should develop. With struggles being waged by black people in the areas of education, housing employment and many others, it was only a matter of time before Afro-American athletes shed their fantasies and delusions and asserted their manhood and faced the facts of their existence.

—Dr. Harry Edwards

It has been almost forty years since the son of a migrant worker named Tommie Smith and Harlem's John Carlos took the medal stand at the 1968 Olympics and created what is arguably the most enduring image in sports history. But while the image has stood the test of time, the struggle that led to that moment has been cast aside, a casualty of capitalism's commitment to political amnesia.

Smith and Carlos's stunning gesture of resistance was not the result of some spontaneous urge to get face time on the evening news, but a product of the revolt of Black athletes in the 1960s. In the fall of 1967, amateur Black athletes formed OPHR, the Olympic Project for Human Rights, to organize a boycott of the 1968 Olympics in Mexico City. OPHR, its lead organizer, Dr. Harry Edwards, and its primary athletic spokespeople, Smith and 400-meter sprinter Lee Evans, were very influenced by the Black freedom struggle. Their goal was nothing less than to expose how the U.S. used Black athletes to project a lie about race relations both at home and internationally. In their founding statement, they wrote,

> We must no longer allow this country to use a few so-called Negroes to point out to the world how much progress she has made in solving her racial problems when the oppression of Afro-Americans is greater than it ever was. We must no longer allow the sports world to pat itself on the back as a citadel of racial justice when the racial injustices of the sports world are infamously legendary…any black person who allows himself to be used in the above matter is a traitor because he allows racist whites the luxury of resting assured that those black people in the ghettos are there because that is where they want to be. So we ask why should we run in Mexico only to crawl home?

OPHR had three central demands: restore Muhammad Ali's title, remove Avery Brundage as head of the United States Olympic Committee, and disinvite South Africa and Rhodesia from the Olympics. Ali's title had been stripped earlier that year for his resistance to the Vietnam draft. By standing with Ali, OPHR also expressed opposition to the war. Olympic Committee head Avery Brundage was a notorious white supremacist, best remembered today for sealing the deal on Hitler's hosting the 1936 Olympics in Berlin. The demand to disinvite South Africa and Rhodesia conveyed internationalism and solidarity with the Black freedom struggles against apartheid in Africa.

The wind went out of the sails of a broader boycott for many reasons, most centrally because athletes who had trained their whole lives for their Olympic moment quite understandably didn't want to give it up. Some athletes also came forward with accusations of a campaign of harassment and intimidation orchestrated by Brundage; although nothing was ever proven, fear of retribution from the Olympic establishment helped to undermine the boycott. Despite these pressures, many Black Olympians were still determined to make a stand.

The lead-up to the Olympics in Mexico City was electric

Extending gloved hands skyward in protest, U.S. athletes Tommie Smith, center, and John Carlos stare downward during the playing of the Star Spangled Banner after Smith received the gold and Carlos the bronze for the 200-meter run at the Summer Olympic Games in Mexico City on October 16, 1968. Australian silver medalist Peter Norman, wearing an OPHR button, is at left. (AP)

with struggle. Already in 1968, the world had seen the Tet offensive in Vietnam, proving that the U.S. military was vulnerable to defeat; the Prague Spring, during which Czech students challenged tanks from the Stalinist Soviet Union; the assassination of Martin Luther King Jr. and the mass revolts that followed; the growth of the Black Panther Party in the United States; and the largest general strike in world history in France. Then, on October 2, ten days before the Games opened, Mexican security forces massacred hundreds of students who were occupying the National University in Mexico City. Although the harassment and intimidation of the OPHR athletes cannot be compared to this bloody massacre, the intention was the same—to stifle protest.

It was on the second day of the Games that Smith and Carlos took their stand. Smith set a world record, winning the 200 meter gold, and Carlos captured the bronze. Smith then took out the black gloves. When the silver medallist, a runner from Australia named Peter Norman, saw what was happening, he ran into the stands to grab an OPHR patch off a supporter's chest to show his solidarity on the medal stand. As the U.S. flag began rising up the flagpole and the anthem played, Smith and Carlos bowed their heads and raised their fists in a Black power salute, creating what is now a widely recognized image. But most people don't see that their medal stand included more than just the gloves. The two men also wore no shoes, to protest black poverty, and beads, to protest lynching.

Within hours, Smith and Carlos had been stripped of their medals and expelled from the Olympic Village. Avery Brundage justified this by saying, "They violated one of the basic principles of the Olympic games: that politics play no part whatsoever in them." The Los Angeles Times accused Smith and Carlos of a "Nazi-like salute." *Time* magazine's coverage showed the Olympic logo but replaced the motto "Faster,

Higher, Stronger" with "Angrier, Nastier, Uglier." The harshest rebuke, perhaps, came from fellow Olympian, boxer George Foreman, who upon winning the gold medal, waved a miniature American flag and bowed to the Mexico City audience. This was perceived by many as an act of anti-solidarity with Smith and Carlos.

But if Smith and Carlos were attacked from all corners, they also received support from unlikely sources. The Olympic crew team, all white and entirely from Harvard, issued the following statement:

> We—as individuals—have been concerned about the place of the black man in American society in their struggle for equal rights. As members of the U.S. Olympic team, each of us has come to feel a moral commitment to support our black teammates in their efforts to dramatize the injustices and inequities which permeate our society.

OPHR and the actions of Smith and Carlos were a terrific slap in the face to the hypocrisy at the heart of the Olympics. Unfortunately, the Project mirrored a deep flaw also found in other sections of the New Left and Black Power movement: women were largely shut out. Many of OPHR's calls to action had statements about "reclaiming manhood," as if African-American women weren't victims of racism or couldn't be part of a strong voice against it. Despite this exclusion, many women athletes became major voices of solidarity after the fact. The anchor of the women's gold-medal-wining 4x100 relay team, Wyomia Tyus said, "I'd like to say that we dedicate our relay win to John Carlos and Tommie Smith."

It was a watershed moment of resistance. But the image of Carlos and Smith must be seen as more than just a nexus for nostalgia. As we build resistance to war and poverty today, we should look to their actions and organizing as a living history, one we should celebrate. As Tommie Smith said recently of his frozen moment, "It's not something I can lay on my shelf and forget about. My heart and soul are still on that team, and I still believe everything we were trying to fight for in 1968 has not been resolved and will be part of our future." ◆

Lee Evans Keeps on Pushin'

Lee Evans set a World Record in the 400 meters at the 1968 Olympics in Mexico City. He has since coached world-class track teams around the world, from Nigeria to Saudi Arabia, and currently is the track and cross-country coach at South Alabama University. Yet Evans is perhaps best known for being a founding member of the Olympic Project for Human Rights. In this interview, Lee Evans talks about his own and OPHR's efforts to protest racism and oppression both at home and abroad.

Dave Zirin: Please speak about the circumstances in which you grew up.

Lee Evans: Well, both of my parents were from Louisiana and they left by train in 1946 to California. They were part of the migration by African Americans right after the war. My dad was looking for work, having been a sharecropper in Louisiana. I was born in February 1947, in Madera, California. My dad got work on construction sites. He labored building the big dams in California. On some of the big projects, I remember he'd be gone for weeks at a time. I was the middle child. It was seven of us total. I had two older brothers and an older sister and two younger brothers and a younger sister, so I was right in the middle. My mother used to take us out to the fields to help pick whatever was ready to be harvested. I grew up picking cotton and cutting grapes, and we did that from sunup to sundown. That's how I always thought I got my special endurance. Tommie Smith, of course, grew up in similar circumstances, just twenty miles from me. Tommie likes to tell people we met in the grape patch. We did farm labor work, while my dad did cement work. After I grew up we moved to Fresno, California, which is just twenty miles from Madera. Eventually my mother's parents also came to California but not my dad's parents. He had his mother, brothers, and sisters in the South, and we grew up never meeting them. We used to say to my dad, "Let's go visit your family in Louisiana," and he wouldn't go down there. He said, "They got Jim Crow down there. I don't want to go back down there." I had no idea what Jim Crow meant. That's how young I was. I didn't realize what it was until high school. I came across the word "Jim Crow" in a history book and then I found out it was segregation. So my dad didn't go back South until I was a sophomore in college.

What began to radicalize you in the 1960s?

In 1966, I was number one in the world in the 400 meters as a freshman in college. I went to London for a meet, and I met these African people, and they said, "We're going to a meeting tonight, do you want to come with us?" I said sure. So they came and got me at the hotel, and it was a South African resistance meeting. They said a prayer for the brothers who had fallen during the week, and I didn't even know there was a war going on down there. I met Dennis Brutus there and Sam Ramsamy, who is now president of the South African Olympic Committee. So I met these guys, and I really became aware. But I didn't speak out until the fall of 1967, when no one would rent us housing close to the university. At that time, the only Black males on the campus were athletes: basketball, football, or track. Harry Edwards was working on his doctorate and he was around. He got wind about our complaints and called a meeting. This is how it started. We started the Olympic Project for Human Rights. And all this came out of us not finding housing close enough to the university.

What was the Olympic Project for Human Rights?

The Olympic Project for Human Rights was a vehicle for a proposed boycott by African-American athletes of the 1968 Olympic games. We were very unhappy with the way things were run in our sport. We had ten demands. One of them simply was that we could have a Black coach for the team.

Another was about restoring Muhammad Ali's title. Why was that so important?

He was being beaten down by the system the way we felt beaten down all the time, so all of us could identify with him.

What is it about Ali that was so threatening, do you think, to the powers that be?

His independence and the way he ran his mouth. In those days the Black Muslims said that white people were devils and all that stuff, so you know that scared white people to death. Also, Malcolm X recruited Muhammad Ali to Islam, and they were after Malcolm at this time.

The boycott didn't really take hold among the athletes. In retrospect, was that a successful strategy to pursue?

Yes. Harry was media savvy. He said all year that we were going to take a vote at the Olympic trials and all year there was commentary in all the newspapers. Some editors made fools of themselves. They would write, "Look at these narrow, stupid Black guys. They don't know what they're doing." They just said things that exposed themselves to who they really were. The athletes, of course, voted down the boycott. I was hoping it was going to be voted down because I wanted to run in the Olympics. I knew that this would happen, that the proposal was a way for us to get leverage. Tom and I had talked about it, and I said, "Let's say we're going to boycott so we can get some things done," but we all knew that we were going to run in Mexico. Push comes to shove, we were going to be there.

Can you speak about what was accomplished by the OPHR?

The Olympic Project for Human Rights got a lot of things accomplished that continue today. We brought a lot of awareness to a lot of people. First of all, the fact that some Black university students were standing up to the world. Sports columnists hated us. They just wrote horrible stuff about Tommie and myself, and so this made the Black community gather themselves on our side.

1936 gold medalist and track legend Jesse Owens was asked by Avery Brundage to meet with you in Mexico City. What was his take on your desire to use the Olympics as a platform to raise grievances?

Jesse was confused as far as I'm concerned. The USOC [United States Olympics Committee] dogged him, and he knew they dogged him.

What do you mean they "dogged him"?

Treating him badly after his exploits in the [Berlin] Olympic games, when he ran [and won four gold medals]. He came back, didn't have a job, was racing horses for money. We were really annoyed with him because he knew what we were going through, yet he pretended that it didn't exist, and that just blew our minds when he called a meeting with us in Mexico City. I thought he called this meeting because Avery Brundage sent him there. Jesse Owens was sitting on the fifty-yard line with all the important people of the world, the royalties, the Avery Brundages. They have a special section where they sit in the games, right at the fifty-yard line, and Jesse—that's where he was sitting. He thought he was one of them. He had forgot that he was once an athlete struggling like we were. So he came and talked to us like he was Avery Brundage or the King of England or somebody, and really talking stupid to us, and we just shouted him out of the room. And then out of the blue he said, "You know wearing those long black socks [running socks that were an act of identification with the Black freedom struggle] is going to cut off the circulation in your legs." That's what he told us. We said, "This guy is really out of his mind!" This is when we ran him out of there. I still admire him to this day, that's why I say he was confused, coming to talk to us like that, because we knew that he was being victimized. He was a victim, and we felt sorry for him, actually.

What was your initial reaction in your heart when you saw Tommie Smith and John Carlos raise their black-gloved fists on the medal stand?

I said that's a good idea. I was also thinking about what Avery Brundage would do to them. Brundage was asked about the black athletes—about what would he do if we protested at the games. He said, "We would send those boys right home. They should be considered lucky we allow them to be on the team." He never should have said that because we started having meetings again after that, and we said, "We are going to have a protest at the Olympic games." We never could come to a uniform protest. There was always a disagreement: "I can't wear black socks," "I can't wear black on black," "I can't do this, I can't do that." We finally agreed that if you make it to the victory stand, get together with another Black guy you're with and do the same thing. We were going to protest by event, in other words. In the 400 meters, we had decided we were going to wear black berets; that's what we did. Tommie, on the other hand, had gloves in his bag because we thought Avery Brundage presented the gold medals to everybody. So I told Tommie, "I don't want to shake Avery Brundage's hand. Let's get some black gloves and stick them in our pants and before Avery Brundage shakes our hand, we'll put the black glove on and wait until he has a heart attack." So I had two black gloves in my bag also. But as we found out later, Avery Brundage didn't give the gold medal out to everybody, and they kind of shifted around with the different dignitaries. But Tommie, when he was waiting to go outside to run, gave one of the gloves to Carlos. He took the other glove, and they did their thing, and I didn't see anything wrong with it.

What was your reaction when you heard that they were stripped of their medals and sent home? I read reports of you being very, very upset.

Oh yeah, I was because they were my teammates. I was very distraught. I wanted to go home. I said I wasn't going to run. But Tommie and John—they came to me and said I better run and I better win. They came to my room, and that freed my mind up to go run because I was confused, but when they told me that I should run that really freed me up.

You mentioned that you wore a black beret on the stand?

That was our protest. After what Tommie and John did, what anybody else did was like little or nothing.

When the media asked you why you wore a black beret, you said sarcastically that it was because it was raining.

Yeah, but they knew why. We knew that the black beret was a symbol of the Black Panther Party.

What did you think of the Black Panthers at the time?

I thought they were pretty brave guys, but I wouldn't do what they were doing. They were having a shoot-out with the police almost every day. So my job [protesting at the Olympics] was easy. This is one of the things I learned from Malcolm X and Martin Luther King. Everybody can play a part, but everyone has to do something. I used to say to guys I was trying to get to come to meetings, I said, "It's going to be easy for us. We're just going to the Olympic games. I know some guys in Oakland shooting out with the police. So what we're doing is nothing compared to those guys. We're not putting our life on the line."

But, as it turned out, we did put our lives on the line because I had maybe twenty death threats on my life in Mexico City. You have mailboxes in the Olympics. I had the KKK, the NRA, saying "Yeah we're going to shoot you niggers." They even tell you what time they're going to shoot you.

What kind of reaction did you get from other Blacks?

I had a tough time too because the Blacks thought that I didn't do enough, and the whites were just mad. I got it from both sides. The Black people thought I should have done nothing less than dynamite the victory stand. That's the only thing that would have satisfied them because, after Tommie and John, what else could I do?

You've done some unbelievably amazing things since those days in 1968. Can you just say a little about what you've been doing since then, in terms of coaching in Nigeria and Qatar and Saudi Arabia?

I remember as soon as I learned about why I was Black and why I was in this classroom in Fresno, California, as a youngster— that my heritage and my people were ex-slaves, and they came from Africa. As soon as I learned about what Jim Crow meant and I found out that my ancestors were Africans, I wanted to go back to Africa. So that's what I did. I went back to Africa in 1975, and I worked there for about twenty years, and I was fortunate to coach three Olympic medal winners on Nigeria's team.

You also coached in Qatar and Saudi Arabia.

Yes, I was an international coach and, when I turned fifty, I told my wife, "We have to go back to the United States because I don't have any retirement." So I'm in the U.S. trying to get some retirement and after I get some retirement—that means I have to stay here ten years—I'm going to go back to Africa and continue my work over there.

And now you're a coach at South Alabama.

Yeah. I've got seven more years.

Because you have that experience in Africa and in the Middle East, I want to ask you, what do you think about Bush's policies over there, specifically the war on terrorism?

I don't agree with the war in Iraq. You know, I've been to all those places, and Iraq never had any designs on the United States, I can tell you that right now. And I think that all these right-wing Republicans know that. They just want a war so they can do their money-making thing. That's the only reason I can think of. I agree with going after him [Saddam Hussein], but what they're doing in Iraq—and to the Arabs—is stupid. That's why the Arab countries are against it, because they knew that Iraq was no threat to the United States, and Saddam wasn't either. They have no weapons of mass destruction.

Last question: you guys brought the Black freedom struggle into sports. Do you think that needs to happen again?

Yeah, these guys should be aware, but they aren't, unfortunately. It's more about money for them. I think money is polluting their minds. They're not conscious of what's going on, they don't care about other people. That is going to have to change if we are to move forward. ◆

John Carlos Endures

Thirty-seven years ago, John Carlos became one half of perhaps the most famous (or infamous) moment in Olympic history. After winning the bronze medal in the 200-meter dash, he and gold medalist Tommie Smith raised their black glove-clad fists in a display of "Black Power." It was a moment that defined the revolutionary spirit and defiance of a generation. Recently, the thirty-fifth anniversary of that moment passed with nary a word. Here John Carlos speaks about those turbulent times.

Dave Zirin: Many call that period of the 1960s the "Revolt of the Black athlete." Why?

John Carlos: I think *Sports Illustrated* started that phrase, but I don't think of it as the revolt of the Black athlete at all. It was the revolt of the Black men. Athletics was my occupation. I didn't do what I did as an athlete. I raised my voice in protest as a man. I was fortunate enough to grow up in the era of Dr. King, of Paul Robeson, of baseball players like Jackie Robinson and Roy Campanella who would come into my dad's shop on 142nd Street and Lenox in Harlem. I could see how they were treated as Black athletes. I would ask myself, why is this happening?

Racism meant that none of us could truly have our day in the sun. Without education, housing, and employment, we would lose what I call "family-hood." If you can't give your wife or son or daughter what they need to live, after a while you try to escape who you are. That's why people turn to drugs and why our communities have been destroyed. That's why there was a revolt.

When you woke up that morning in 1968, did you know you were going to make your historic gesture on the medal stand or was it spontaneous?

It was in my head the whole year. We first tried to have a boycott, but not everyone was down with that plan. A lot of the athletes thought that winning medals would supersede or protect them from racism. But even if you won the medal, it ain't going to save your momma. It ain't going to save your sister or children. It might give you fifteen minutes of fame, but what about the rest of your life? I'm not saying they didn't have the right to follow their dreams, but to me the medal was nothing but the carrot on the stick.

At the last track meet before the Olympics, we left it that every man would do his own thing. You had to choose which side of the fence you were on. You had to say, "I'm for racism or I'm against racism."

We stated we were going to do something. But Tommie and I didn't know what we were going to do until we got into the tunnel [on the way to the 200 meter finals in Mexico City]. We had gloves, black shirts, and beads. And we decided in that tunnel that, if we were going to go out on that stand, we were going to go out barefooted and—

Why barefooted?

We wanted the world to know that in Mississippi, Alabama, Tennessee, South Central Los Angeles, Chicago, that people were still walking back and forth in poverty without even the necessary clothes to live. We have kids that don't have shoes even today. It's not like the powers that be can't provide these things. They can send a spaceship to the moon, or send a probe to Mars, yet they can't give shoes? They can't give health care? I'm just not naïve enough to accept that.

Why was it important to you both to wear beads on the medal stand?

The beads were for those individuals that were lynched, or killed, that no one said a prayer for, that were hung tarred. It was for those thrown off the side of the boats in the Middle Passage. All that was in my mind. We didn't come up there with any bombs. We were trying to wake the country up and wake the world up, too.

How did your life change when you took that step onto the podium?

My life changed prior to the podium. I used to break into freight trains by Yankee Stadium when I was young…. Then I changed when I realized I was a force in track and field. I realized I didn't have to break into freight trains. I wanted to wake up the people who work and run the trains, so they can seize what they deserve. It's like these supermarkets in southern California that are on strike. They always have extra milk, and they throw it in the river or dump it in the garbage even though there are people without milk. They say we can't give it to you, so we would rather throw it away. Something is very wrong. Realizing that changed me long before 1968.

Was there anything that specifically prepared you for that moment on the medal stand?

I was with Dr. King ten days before he died. He told me he was sent a bullet in the mail with his name on it. I remember looking in his eyes to see if there was any fear, and there was none. He didn't have any fear. He had love and that in itself changed my life in terms of how I would go into battle. I would never have fear for my opponent, but love for the people I was fighting for. That's why, if you look at the picture [of Carlos and Smith with their raised fists], Tommie has his jacket zipped up, and [Australian silver medalist] Peter Norman has his jacket zipped up, but mine was open. I was representing shift workers, blue-collar people, the underdogs. That's why my shirt was open. Those are the people whose contributions to society are so important but don't get recognized.

What kind of support did you receive when you came home?

There was pride, but only from the less fortunate. What could they do but show their pride? But we had Black businessmen, we had Black political caucuses, and they never embraced Tommie Smith or John Carlos. When my wife took her life in 1977, they never said, "Let me help."

Did your being outcast play a role in your wife taking her life?

It played a huge role. We were under tremendous economic stress. I took any job I could find. I wasn't too proud. Menial jobs, security jobs, gardener, caretaker, whatever I could do to try to make ends meet. We had four children, and some nights I would have to chop up our furniture and make a fire in the middle of our room just to stay warm.... I was the bad guy, the two-headed dragon spitting fire. It meant we were alone.

Many people say athletes should just play and not be heard. What do you say to that?

Those people should put all their millions of dollars together and make a factory that builds athlete-robots. Athletes are human beings. We have feelings too. How can you ask someone to live in the world, to exist in the world, and not have something to say about injustice?

What message do you have for the new generation of athletes hitting the world stage?

First of all athletes—Black, red, brown, yellow, and white— need to do some research on their history; their own personal family. They need to find out how many people in their family were maimed in a war. They need to find out how hard their ancestors had to work. They need to uncloud their minds with the materialism and the money and study their history. And then they need to speak up. You got to step up to society when it's letting all its people down.

As you look at the world today, do you think athletes and all people still need to speak out and take a stand?

Yes, because so much is the same as it was in 1968, especially in terms of race relations. I think things are just more cosmetically disguised. Look at Mississippi, or Alabama. It hasn't changed from back in the day. Look at the city of Memphis, and you still see blight up and down. You can still see the despair and the dope. Look at the police rolling up and putting twenty-nine bullets in a person in a hallway, or sticking a plunger up a man's rectum, or Texas where they dragged that man by the neck from the bumper of a truck. How is that not just the same as a lynching?

Do you feel like you are being embraced now after all these years?

I don't feel embraced, I feel like a survivor, like I survived cancer. It's like if you are sick and no one wants to be around you, and when you're well everyone who thought you would go down for good doesn't even want to make eye contact. It was almost like we were on a deserted island. That's where Tommie Smith and John Carlos were. But we survived. ◆

Grilling Big George

George Foreman was born January 10, 1949, in Marshall, Texas. He was the heavyweight boxing gold medalist at the 1968 Mexico City Olympics, the same Olympics at which John Carlos and Tommie Smith made their stand. A former world heavyweight champion, Foreman lost his title to Muhammad Ali in 1974 and recaptured it twenty years later at age forty-five with a ten-round knockout of world champ Michael Moorer, becoming the oldest man to win a heavyweight crown. Here, Foreman discusses his impressions of the sixties.

Dave Zirin: You wrote in your autobiography about growing up in Houston, "On some nights, I stood in the dark on neighbors' porches, looking into their kitchens, amazed that families had leftovers at each meal.... I always hoped they would find me and ask me in." How did your upbringing shape your view of the world?

George Foreman: To say it honestly, I was hungry most of the time. The only question I would ask myself about the world was, "How do I get something to eat?" I was trying to supply for my needs. Growing up poor, I didn't even have a lunch to take to

Boxing great George Foreman appears at a signing for his new book *George Fore-man's Guide to Life, How To Get Off The Canvas*, **on January 7, 2003, in New York.**
(AP/Jennifer Graylock)

school. Lunch was 26 cents and we didn't even know what 26 cents looked like. I didn't love school because I wanted to disguise that I was poorer than everybody else. So when I was a teen, I reached out in a wrong way. I started to be a mugger, to rob people in the streets, just to supply for my needs.

You were born in 1949 in the South. What were your thoughts on the Civil Rights movement growing up?

I didn't know anything about anything except being hungry until I went in the Job Corps in 1965. Once I went in the Job Corps, I was awakened to what was going on with the Civil Rights struggles. I was awakened by a young Anglo-Saxon boy from Tacoma, Washington, named Richard Kibble. He was a young man like myself, but he was twenty going on twenty-one, and I was sixteen. He would have these old records, these old Bob Dylan records. And he would always play me Bob Dylan. I would hear those lyrics, "Well, they'll stone ya when you're walkin' 'long the street/They'll stone ya when you're tryin' to keep your seat/They'll stone ya when you're walkin' on the floor/They'll stone ya when you're walkin' to the door." I hope I didn't get that wrong. He had a lot of knowledge. He explained to me about things I had never thought about before, about civil rights. I had a thing about those Bob Dylan songs, boy. "How many roads must a man walk down before you can call him a man?" He was always talking about that stuff.

In 1965 one of the most prominent and controversial leaders was Malcolm X. What did you know about him at the time?

In 1965 I didn't know Malcolm X. I didn't even know there was another world. I was so ignorant I thought Lyndon Johnson was president of Texas because every time I saw him he was wearing a cowboy hat! I think it was the end of 1966 or the beginning of 1967 where I first learned about Malcolm X. I knew nothing about his life until I was given his book, *The Autobiog-*

raphy of Malcolm X. It was the most amazing thing to me. I was excited about his first life. He was trying to be a pimp and a hustler and he found peace. I was trying to lift myself at the time out of a life of mugging and robbing, and I loved that he could turn around his life. It was the first time I ever read a book about a person from the front to the back. It was amazing.

What about another political lightning rod of that time, Muhammad Ali? What did you think about him as a young man in 1966?

I knew about Ali way before 1966. I knew him earlier than most. It was 1962 on the radio before his first fight with Sonny Liston. My brother and his friend and I would run all around looking for a radio to hear him speak, just to hear him talk. Everyone was talking about this boy from the Olympics [Ali won the gold medal in the 1960 Olympics], and here's Ali shocking the world every time he opened his mouth.

What about when he changed his name soon after the Liston fight from Cassius Clay to Muhammad Ali. What were your thoughts?

When I first heard about it, all I ever heard anyone saying in the fifth ward was, "How could that boy change his name? What is that boy doing?" Then we heard he was a Black Muslim. My community was afraid of that word.

The word Muslim?

No, the word Black! The word frightened everybody. No one had heard the word Black in Texas to describe a so-called "Negro" at that time. Everyone was saying he was crazy. Then there were some people who said, "I would like to meet him, to talk to him, to hear what he had to say." I just had admiration for him at the time. You would hear about him being on the radio and you would just tear home no matter what was going on. We all liked him because he said he was pretty. None of us thought we were pretty. Then here is this man saying, "I'm pretty! I'm pretty!" And we thought, We're good-looking too!

What about seeing Ali as someone who was standing up to racism?

I didn't think about it like politics. Stand up to something? We didn't even know there was something to stand up to. Politics didn't even exist. I lived in a world where I was striving to get a scrap of food, striving to get a job. And the newspapers didn't report on Ali as much as you would think. Even the Black newspapers wouldn't talk about him. So we didn't know everything that was going on around him.

In 1968, you won the gold medal at the Mexico Olympics, and then famously waved a small American flag and bowed a few short days after Tommie Smith and John Carlos made their Black power salute on the medal stand. Tell us about the 1968 Olympics.

I'm living in the Olympic Village at the time with all the other athletes. And I was loving it. And Smith and Carlos and [Bob] Beamon loved it too. The track and field guys back then were the celebrities, the rock and roll stars, the beautiful guys at the village. Everywhere they walked people said, "There's Smith and Carlos!" They loved it too. We were like a family. And we were all focused on trying to win our own gold medals, so we didn't feel the outrage, the controversy after they raised their fists. So when they were immediately sent home and sent packing we were all like, "How can they do that?" And they were just dismissed. I thought about going home myself. We all did. I'll never forget seeing John Carlos walk past the dormitory when he was sent packing, with all these cameras following him around, and I saw the most sad look on his face. This was a proud man who always walked with his head high, and he looked shook. That hurt me, and it made us all mad. Forget about the flag. This was our teammate…. We loved each other, and it made us mad. It made us shook.

When you waved the flag and bowed it was seen as a reaction, a rebuke of Smith and Carlos. Were you asked to do that?

No way. It was spontaneous and had nothing to do with them. I always carried a small American flag—red, white, and blue—with me so people would know I was from America. Also it was tradition to bow to each judge after a fight so the next time you get points. And I wanted the world to know where I was from. I wanted to say to the world, "We gotcha." America gotcha.

What was the reaction back home?

Most people thought it was great, but then something happened that caused me more pain than I had ever felt as an individual. I was a happy nineteen-year-old boy, and some people came up to me in the 5th ward and said, "How can you do that when the brothers [Smith and Carlos] are trying to do their thing?" They thought I betrayed them. That people would think that caused great pain.

If you had to do it all over, would you still wave the flag?

If I had to do it all over, I'd wave three flags! I feel that I had been rescued from the gutter by America. One day I was under the gutter, chased by police, thinking dogs were going to get me. I laid there listening to the dogs and the gutter. The next day there I am standing on the Olympic platform and you hear the anthem. I was proud. Thanks to the Job Corps, I had a chance. I had three meals a day and a chance. LBJ started this war on poverty from 1964 and that's why I would wave three flags. I know there are a lot of guys who had to do their thing to make a political stand. But some of us felt very separated from that. In 1968, there were people organizing to get us to boycott the Olympics. Did you know [the boycott organizers] only approached the college guys? The guys who competed in college? Not one of us high school dropouts were ever asked to be part of what they were doing. They never asked the poor people to join. And I didn't like being called or set apart as a "Black athlete." I was an American athlete.... I got a chance from this country, and when I go to Africa or Germany, or anywhere else in the world, people don't see me as Black, but as an American (laughs). Not that that is always a good thing.

You have spoken about your positive experiences in the Job Corps. Right now many of these kinds of government programs are being cut from state budgets. What do you think about that?

That Job Corps, what a great thing. I think it was great because so many of us were victims of the times. No one was teaching us in schools. I remember in school once the teacher gave us speech about how anyone can make it if they try, and then she looked at me and said, "I don't know what you are going to do, Georgie." When you were in junior high school. You heard that. Today is different. You have Head Start, tutoring programs, you don't need a Job Corps because there is opportunity.

But Head Start is one of the programs that is being cut right now.

There shouldn't be budget problems. There is so much money that goes untapped. If every athlete gave 5 percent of what they earned, there wouldn't be any budget problems.

What do you think about athletes using their position to talk about politics, for example, some like Felix Trinidad speaking on Vieques?

I think once you are established, then you should talk. I try to sell George Foreman, and we all try to sell ourselves. Our time as athletes is so short—like an NFL player or a boxer, you only have so much time. You need to make all you can, and then you can speak all you want. Our problem as a people is that we celebrate before we emancipate.

Before we stop, I have to ask you about the "Rumble in the Jungle." Why do you think the people there responded to Ali so strongly?

He wanted them to love him. When you go somewhere and want people to love you, they will love you. Ali made them love him. That's why I couldn't beat him. He heard them chanting his name and said, "I'm not going to lose." That's where the stamina and taking my punches came from: They loved him, and I love him too. He's the greatest man I've ever known. Not the greatest boxer—that's too small for him. He had a gift. He's not "pretty," he's beautiful. Everything America should be, Muhammad Ali is.

Does boxing need a union?

I think we need unity but I don't think we need a union. The unions saved this country back when, but we've already been saved. Yes, boxers should unite, but I don't know about unions. We should understand that we make sure our money goes into a trust, that we watch out for our health. It's crazy that we have a cup downstairs but not on our heads to protect our brains! No headgear. Let's put the cup from down below to up top. Do we need a union to get this? I don't know. Do we say union, or do we just need to unite?

Do you think there needs to be a new civil rights movement in this country?

I think there needs to be a new awareness of what rights we have. We have so many freedoms and people have no idea. These are rights that people died for and somehow we need to make the new generations aware. More rights? Let's use the rights we have. Defend, appreciate, and use them. ◆

I Wish My Brother George Was Here: The Evolutions of George Foreman

You could not reproduce a character like George Foreman—unless Madeline Albright had a love child with Bernie Mac. Foreman's life's journey took him from "the gutter" of poverty and hunger to the apex of the heavyweight ranks. As a heavyweight champion, he snarled his way through fights, his face an expressionless mask, his punches unprecedented in their power. Then he left boxing in his prime to start a ministry and preach the gospel, causing one commentator to call him "the first heavyweight champion who didn't hang on too long."

But after a decade in the pulpit, Big George came out of retirement and boxed into his late forties. His Afro shorn, his once muscular frame buried under a jiggling cushion of fried foods and sweet tea, he was Buddha as drawn by Aaron McGruder. The boxing cognoscenti moaned that Big George was heading for a violent fall, but the "Punching Preacher," employing a new boxing style influenced by martial arts, had an impenetrable defense and only had to land one big punch per fight to put a new generation of heavyweights to sleep. His return culminated in winning the heavyweight title against Michael Moorer, a fearsome opponent rumored to have punched a racist police officer in the jaw so hard that his spine snapped backward and broke. And yet, with just one punch, Moorer was splattered on the canvas like a freshly painted Jackson Pollack. As Foreman became a new-old sensation inside the ring, on the outside he went global selling anything not nailed to the floor. Defined by his bulbous girth, a living-breathing Michelin Man, Foreman has made millions of dollars selling dietary grills—which is as counterintuitive as John Kerry and Al Gore hawking motivational tapes. Foreman is now an industry unto himself, his name a brand as trusted as Xerox or Kleenex.

The question arises: why was Foreman permitted to recreate himself with panache and abandon while John Carlos, a man of talent, intelligence, and strength, of courage and principle, was blackballed from the sporting world, denied rewarding employment, and consigned to total obscurity? As James Baldwin once wrote, "America is a country devoted to the death of the paradox." In other words, we live in a world that exalts individuality as long as it is superficial and nonthreatening. In every other instance, conformity is not only encouraged but enforced. You are what you do, and if you transgress, a slap in the head awaits. If you are an athlete, you better not have political opinions. If you dig ditches, you better not write poetry. If you work at Wal-Mart, you better not talk union. If you raise a black-gloved fist at the Olympics, don't bother looking for a job when you come home.

Foreman has been able to pretzel himself into more shapes than your Aunt Trudy's challah. But he has never broken the mold of the successful, acceptable, and digestible patriotic athlete. This tendency can be traced back to that moment in 1968 when he chose to wave a tiny flag instead of standing with his persecuted Olympic teammates. Foreman made a choice that day. He sent a message that he would play the game of sports American style—and play it he has. In our interview, he made his priorities clear when asked about athletes who speak out on issues, saying, "Our time as athletes is so short—like an NFL player or a boxer, you only have so much time. You need to make all you can and then you can speak all you want." If Muhammad Ali and John Carlos were role models for political courage and telling bitter truths, Foreman is perhaps the role model for, as he put it, selling himself—a more serviceable model in a capitalist culture dominated by the cult of self-promotion.

George Foreman acts as a red, white, and blue bridge between Muhammad Ali and Michael Jordan, and he wears those colors like a new suit. In America, Foreman sees a terrific system because he made it out of the gutter. He believes that if he could do it, anyone can. Foreman does not draw Martin Luther King's conclusion: that a system that produces gutters needs to be restructured. He is generous enough to say, "Everything America should be, Muhammad Ali is," but he doesn't take America to task for trying to tear Ali to shreds. He believes that sports provide a ticket out of poverty, even though, for the overwhelming majority, it's a ticket on a broken-down bus going absolutely nowhere. He believes that the ability to sell yourself is the key to success and survival in our society. He is correct. But such a strategy offers nothing to those—like John Carlos, like Lee Evans, like Tommie Smith—who choose not to be commodities. George Foreman is held up as a role model for the world we live in. Perhaps. But he's not a role model for a world worth fighting for. ◆

CHAPTER FIVE

"We Really Just Hate to Lose": Unions and Sports

When fans are asked what's wrong with sports today, most say, "I can't believe Alex Rodriguez makes $25 million a year" or "That Kevin Garnett! How dare he make so much money!" The commonly accepted view is that today's pro athletes are self-centered and grotesquely overpaid. This image isn't helped when basketball star Latrell Sprewell complains about a $27 million three-year contract, often saying, "I need to feed my family."

There is no question that the priorities of a world where A Rod pulls in 1,000 times what a teacher makes are obscenely misplaced (especially given the way he played against the Red Sox in the playoffs). But the real obscenity of riches is not on the field but in the owner's box. As the inimitably prickly Barry Bonds once said, "Nobody is complaining about the owners' salaries. So don't complain about us."

Pro sports owners are some of the filthiest of the filthy rich and no exception to the expression that behind every great fortune is a great crime.

There are the Seattle Seahawks and Trail Blazers, owned by multibillionaire (as in, he's worth $30 billion) Paul Allen, who made his fortune cofounding the rapacious monopoly also known as Microsoft with Bill Gates. There are the Detroit Lions, owned by the Ford family—as in Ford cars and trucks. The Ford name also crops up periodically in history book chapters that cover everything from anti-Semitism and the holocaust to union repression. And don't forget the former owner of the Texas Rangers, an amiable fellow with loftier ambitions than most named George W. Bush. Beau Turner—whose daddy Ted has owned his share of franchises—summed up the owner mindset when he said: "There is nothing better than going to a game, kicking back and saying 'I own a little piece of those guys.'"

Far less reported than the latest mega-salary contract, however, is the fact that the overwhelming majority of players toil in the minor leagues, on the fringes of their sports, barely making peanuts, let alone crackerjacks. Minor League Baseball players make less than $900 a month on average, which, as is the case with most U.S. workers, is less than they made thirty years ago. Arena Football League players make $30,000 a year and, amazingly, don't have health care. And, of course, college athletes produce billions and don't see one cent.

Without a doubt, the players in the major leagues of sport make serious bank. The average salary in Major League Baseball is $2.4 million. In football, the average is just over $1 million, far more than most people see in a lifetime. But this was not always so. In 1967, the average baseball salary was $19,000 a year. That same year, the average NFL salary was just $8,000. A typical athlete in 1967 worked in the off-season. Not in cushy jobs, but performing labor that reflected the hardscrabble background of many of the players. One crew of linebackers would work summers in a quarry. Take a second to imagine Peyton Manning crushing rocks and you can see how much things have changed.

So how did (some) athletes get where they are today? Yes, the industry expanded and created a bigger pie, but the periods of boom in the twenties and the fifties didn't automatically mean higher salaries. It took union power, exercised in the late 1960s and early 1970s, to change how the sports pie was cut. Pro athletes had to reject a tradition of company-run unions and fight to end the reserve clause, which tied players to the team that drafted them with no rights to go anywhere else. Athletes won the right of free agency and used their solidarity—and the power of the strike—to extract more wealth from the bosses.

The pioneer of this approach was Major League Baseball union leader Marvin Miller, a former United Steel Workers union official who headed up the Players Union in 1966. As Reggie Jackson said, "Miller had more influence on Major League Baseball than anyone ever," quite a statement from someone who might wish to reserve such a claim for himself.

Miller's genius was that he understood that a larger radicalization in society was thundering its way into the world of sports. The Black Power movement had radicalized African-American players, and he courted them to challenge the reserve clause. As Miller said, "After the Civil Rights movement, you now had players thinking in terms of what was wrong with the society, and what we could change."

Miller found a player willing to stand up in the St. Louis Cardinal's Curt Flood. Flood was born and raised in Oakland and was fighting mad after making it through a Southern Minor League system of segregated hotels and nights eating out of the kitchen on road trips. Miller remembers today, "To me Flood epitomized the modern player who began to think in terms of a union, to ask questions like, 'Why should we be treated like property?' 'Why am I a $40,000-a-year slave?' Basic questions that had gone unasked."

In October 1969, the Cardinals traded Flood to Philadelphia and Flood just said no. The All Star contacted Baseball Commissioner Bowie Kuhn in writing:

Dear Mr. Kuhn:
　　After 12 years in the major leagues I do not feel that I am a piece of property to be bought and sold irrespective of my wishes.

> I believe that any system that produces that result violates my basic rights as a citizen and a human being. I believe that I have the right to consider offers from other clubs before making any decisions. I, therefore, request that you make known to all the major league clubs my feelings in this matter, and advise them of my availability for the 1970 season.

It sounds polite but at the time this was TNT. Kuhn didn't take Flood seriously at all, replying: "Dear Curt: I certainly agree with you that you, as a human being, are not a piece of property to be bought and sold. That is I think obvious. However, I cannot see its application to the situation at hand." As the great columnist Red Smith put it, in a beautiful pro-Flood piece, "Thus the commissioner restates baseball's labor policy any time there is unrest in the slave cabins. 'Run along, sonny, you bother me.'"

The union stood with Flood and he won his freedom but paid a terrible price: Flood was shunned and cast aside. The lifetime .293 hitter and Gold Glove centerfielder found himself shut out of the 1970 season. The following year, Flood returned with the Washington Senators and quit after eighteen games of mistreatment by Major League Baseball and anti-union teammates. He was never to play Major League baseball again. Although Flood—who passed away in 1997—never achieved the financial gains of the next generation of players, his example surely stiffened their spines. One All Star said anonymously, "10 percent of Alex Rodriguez's check should go to the family of Curt Flood."

Now there is a tradition in baseball of labor solidarity that has remained firm through six work stoppages since 1972—the most recent in 1994 when the World Series was shut down and the Players Union is recognized as the strongest in the country because they never give an inch. Matt Williams, a recently retired, power-hitting third baseman summed this up well. He was on pace to break Roger Maris's record of 61 home runs when the 1994 Players Strike/Owners Lockout ended the season in August and cancelled the World Series. Williams was asked if he regretted missing the opportunity to pass the most hallowed record in the game. He said, "No. The way baseball players think about it is guys before us have sacrificed to enable us to have a healthy game. We're a strong union because we're all on the same page. We need to keep it that way." ◆

From Cowhide to Pigskin

Football union fights have been even more intense. A football player has a very short career, generally averaging less than three years, so any strike means closing off part of a fairly small earning window. In the early 1970s, players radicalized by the period—many of whom were among the 300 players who signed a statement in 1972 against the war in Vietnam— were at the heart of building the National Football League Players Association (NFLPA). The NFLPA steeled itself over the course of long, bitter strikes in 1982 and 1987. During the 1987 strike, players in the South even armed themselves on picket lines.

This tradition of sports labor unionism continues. The first boxers union—called Joint Action for Boxers or JAB—was recently launched and is part of the Teamsters union. It is being headed up by Eddie Mustafa Muhammad, a former light heavyweight champ who has vowed strikes if health care— which does not exist in boxing—doesn't become a standard part of contracts.

Of course, when these strikes happen, athletes are vilified as greedy brats being paid a fortune for playing a kids' game. Sports strikes are routinely described by sports radio—and by many on the left—as battles that pit "billionaires vs. million-aires." They say that athletes are "not real workers" and they don't have "real strikes." George Meany, the first president of the AFL-CIO, demonstrated this attitude when he said, "I have no use for ballplayers as union men. You'd never see the day when one of those high-priced bozos would honor a picket line set up around the ballpark by the beer vendors, would you?" Of course, it is true that ballplayers have a terrible reputation when it comes to rising to the defense of concession workers, or even umpires. But it is worth saying that this is true of the labor movement as a whole, and Meany himself, a labor leader, once bragged that he "never walked a picket line."

But as long as a union exists, there is always the potential for solidarity, regardless of past reputation; witness the baseball union publicly vowing not to cross the line or endorse the super-markets involved in the recent UFCW strikes in California. And if athletes make a tremendous amount of money playing their games, many also pay a terrible price. The average NFL player has a life expectancy almost a decade shorter than the average person. A truly tragic example is Johnny Unitas, who died in 2003 at the age of 69. His body was a wreck of scar tissue, and the great quarterback couldn't even grip a baseball because of joint pain.

It's certainly true that a layer of mega-salaried players de-velop a massive and distorted stake in the system. During the 1994 baseball strike, ballplayer Lenny Dykstra said, "Hey, I own a chain of restaurants, so I know how it is when you have to keep your workers in line." Bigger examples than Dykstra include Magic Johnson, who is worth upwards of $600 million and is part owner of both the Lakers and a healthy chunk of Harlem, and Michael Jordan, who runs a division of Nike and has been in negotiations to buy his own NBA team.

This is the sports equivalent of an aristocracy of labor with a vengeance. Sports players—like actors—have unions that deserve support and solidarity like any other. But they also have pay differentials between the lowest- and highest-paid workers that would make even the most corrupt union official blush. In this respect, sports unions are qualitatively different from other unions. Steelworkers' pay increases never got them the money to buy a chain of restaurants, let alone their own mills. Any honest look at sports unions needs to recognize this. But the bottom line is that athletes should extract whatever they can from their bosses. If the money from sports doesn't go into their pockets, it travels past the stands and right back into the owner's box. The solidarity and even militancy of sports unions is something to emulate, not dismiss. ◆

An Interview with Marvin Miller

Born in 1917, Marvin Miller never played the game, but he may have had more influence on baseball than anyone else in this half of the century. As executive director of the Players Union from 1966 to 1982, he brought a wealth of experience—garnered in the tough steelworkers union—to bear on baseball labor relations, and his knowledge, organizational ability, and resolve completely overmatched the owners and their representatives. During his tenure, the average player's salary increased from $19,000 to over $240,000 a year. Today, the Baseball Players Union is acknowledged as one of the strongest labor organizations in the United States. Here is Marvin Miller in his own words.

Dave Zirin: Who or what shaped your thinking as a young man?

Marvin Miller: Well, I guess a big part of what shaped me was that I entered high school in February of 1929. Several months later, boom, we have the Great Depression. All through the early 1930s, my father, who was a retail store salesman, saw how the businesses that employed him went downhill, and all through the Depression, my father got more and more anxious and concerned, and I was old enough to be aware of all of that.

How did the Depression affect where you grew up?

I grew up in New York City and, in that period, you couldn't help but observe the breadlines, the increase of the number of people begging in the streets, the people selling apples. The signs of economic hardship were easy to see. I am reminded of a question I was asked a couple of years ago. I was speaking to a group of young Black students in New York, talking about the Depression, breadlines, and so on, and one of the kids asked me if there were white people also on the breadlines and selling apples in the streets. Of course! In fact, most of them! In the New York of the early 1930s, there was a Black population, but it was largely ghettoized in Harlem, and unless you went to Harlem, you didn't see Black people on the breadlines.

How did the Depression move you toward trade union politics?

My father, who had never been in a union in his life, became active. He was a member in the wholesale clothing workers union in lower Manhattan, and I have a very early memory of going to a store where he was working and finding him on a picket line. Also, my mother was a teacher in New York City public schools, and she became one of the early members of the city's teachers union. As the thirties progressed and the CIO [Congress of Industrial Organizations] and industrial unions formed, everybody was aware of the ferment of the labor movement. All of these were influences.

When did you personally become involved?

I graduated college in 1938, and in that period, a good part of the country was seemingly coming out of the Depression. But New York City was not. New York just kept dropping until April 1940 after the rest of the country was moving. I can recall won-

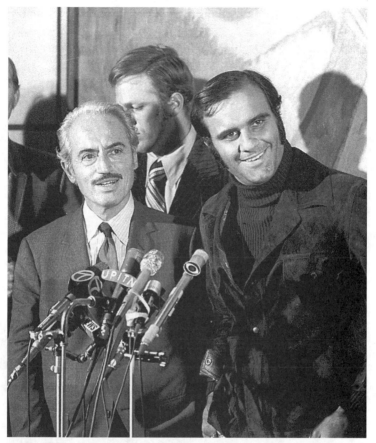

Marvin Miller, left, executive director of the major league players association, and future Yankee manager Joe Torre, then of the St. Louis Cardinals, talk to news reporters in New York City on April 13, 1972. Miller announced that the baseball strike had ended. Behind Miller is Wes Parker of the Los Angeles Dodgers. (AP)

dering if I was ever going to get a job. Unlike some friends and neighbors, my father did not own a business. I was in different straights. I had no affluent uncles. In those days, when you looked for a job, you would go to employment agencies and the situation was so bad you had to connive just to get an application filled out and handed in. Eventually, I got some meaning-less jobs here and there—a drugstore, a small wholesale gift outfit, working for a shipping broker, a customs broker, down at the foot of Manhattan.... I had other meaningless jobs, and I kept taking civil service examinations.

I finally got appointed, working with relief populations, which was an eye-opener, and an economist for the war production board, and, eventually, I moved to a brand new agency called the War Relations Board, and this was charged with a new function of hearing virtually every labor-management pursuit. This is how it formed. The labor movement had been asked to make a no-strike pledge for the duration of the war, and the Chamber of Commerce was asked to, in good faith, make a no-lockout pledge. The labor movement said, "OK, but we are still organiz-ing and there are conditions all over that haven't changed since the Depression, and how are we going to solve disputes?" And FDR created—by executive order—the War Labor Board. I was a hearing officer. With the War Labor Board, I dealt with arbitrat-ing steel, auto, women in the workplace, and some time later I found a job, first with the IAM [the International Association of Machinists] and worked with them, and I also had a short stint with the UAW [United Auto Workers], and then the steelworkers starting in 1950, and I became chief economist and assistant to the president and I was with them until 1966.

Were you a baseball fan before your work heading up the Players Union?

Oh yes. I was an old Brooklyn Dodgers fan, and I was going to Ebbets field by myself by the time I was ten, when there was a Saturday double header. I was a huge fan from way back.

How were you recruited to head up the Baseball Players Union?

The players had a search committee made up of three or four players, including Robin Roberts, Jim Bunning [two pitchers in the Hall of Fame], and Harvey Kuenn. Roberts was really the sparkplug of that committee, and what he did was call [former chairman of the War Labor Board] George W. Taylor, and he recommended me.

What were the players looking for in you?

They had an organization—a fake union—called the Players Association that had been formed by the owners. This was a company union in every sense of the word, the employers had formed it back in 1947 as basically a response to two things. One, there was a drive to organize players into a union, and two, there had been an attempt by two wealthy Mexican businessmen to start a major league in Mexico and they offered larger salaries. That was also the year of Jackie Robinson coming to the Dodgers and the year of a man on his own trying to organize the players. A man named Robert Murphy went from Spring Training site to site—and the owners saw this and said, "We need to head this off and form a company union."

Why were the conditions so ripe for a strong union?

I don't know that they wanted a real union [at first]. If I had to make an educated guess, the one thing the players had which they prized was their pension plan. It was called a benefit plan that had been put into effect also in 1947—once again, the owners saying, "Let's do something to prevent the union here." Eighteen years later, two things were concerning the players. One was that the pension had not kept pace over eighteen years of progress. Also, they picked up strong rumors that the owners were wanting to change it. Television, by 1965, had grown tremendously. [L.A. Dodgers owner] Walter O'Malley saw this and wanted to go after the benefit plan. But beyond that, I was also learning that it was like pulling teeth learning what else made them unhappy. This was because they were a workforce basically unschooled in working conditions. They had all undergone a bunch of brainwashing that being allowed to play Major League Baseball was a great favor. That they were the luckiest people in the world. They were accustomed never to think, "This stinks. We need to change this." You have to remember, baseball players are very young, and, with few exceptions, have no experience in these matters.

Did the other movements of the 1960s—the Civil Rights struggle, the antiwar struggle—help give people the confidence to think union?

There is no doubt there was a major connection. You now had a great many Black and Latin players. You now had a much more diverse sampling of the American people than in the 1940s. You now had at least some people who were able to think in terms of what was wrong with the society, what was wrong with the conditions, people much more accustomed to think about these things. You have to remember—before 1947, the ballplayer came in tremendous proportion from rural areas rather than from cities, from the South and Southwest and not from big urban areas. And, by and large, from anti-union areas.

Why was Curt Flood the player who stepped forward to challenge the reserve clause?

To me, Flood epitomized the modern player who began to think in terms of union, to ask questions like "Why is baseball an exception to how labor is treated in other industries? Why should we be treated like property? Why should we agree to have a reserve clause?" Basic questions that had gone unasked.

Was the fact that he was a Black player related to his challenging the reserve clause?

It was definitely related. Black and Latin players like Roberto Clemente were at the forefront. This was not just the color of their skin. Flood, for example, did not grow up in the South. He grew up in Oakland, California. He was an outstanding high school athlete, he was drafted to play in the majors, and was promptly sent to the South. He wasn't old, but he wasn't a child. What I am about to say is not a fact, but I have always felt that when a player of his temperament and pride was sent to the South, not being able to stay in the same hotels and motels, playing in Georgia and Mississippi, I think it made a very big difference in his outlook on the world.

How did Curt Flood come to decide to file his lawsuit?

Curt Flood came to me to discuss the possibility of a lawsuit, and I thought that it was a losing case; the chance of winning was terrible. How was he going to finance it? I felt that he would indeed need help, and I was concerned how easy it was to make bad law with a bad case—and I felt the union should back him. And I began to lobby his case with the executive board, and since we were going to meet in early December, 1969, in San Juan, I arranged with Curt to have him come to the meeting, and have Curt be questioned, and when it came time to bring Curt in, I had already briefed him, and maybe some of them knew Flood, but not in this context. I brought him into the board meeting and turned it over. And finally a board member asked Curt, "The motivation here—why are you doing this?" Was it to attack the reserve clause to stop the owners from trading a player where he didn't want to go? Or was this a sign of "Black Power"? And Curt looked at him and said, "I wish it was, but we are dealing with an issue that affects every player. Color has nothing to do it. We are all pieces of property."

Does Curt Flood belong in the Hall of Fame?

Absolutely. No doubt about it.

Is there still a need for a strong union?

YES! I have seen good conditions go bad. I think in labor-management relations there is no such thing as standing still. You either move forward or you go back. There is no standing still.

Are salaries wonderful? Yeah, but we must remember that it is unity and solidarity and the struggles of the past that made them successful. There is no guarantee that this will continue. And without a union as successful as it has been, I would predict a downward spiral. The labor movement never stands still. ◆

An Interview with David Meggyesy

David Meggyesy was an All-American linebacker at Syracuse University before playing for the National Football League's St. Louis (now Arizona) Cardinals from 1963 to 1969. He was active in the movements for civil rights and in opposition to the war in Vietnam. In 1970, he wrote his football autobiography, *Out of Their League*, which examined how big-time sports in the United States can dehumanize athletes. Today he is West Coast director of the NFL Players Association. Here, Meggyesy speaks about how he organized on an NFL team during the 1960s and the lessons his experiences hold for sports organizing today.

Dave Zirin: You were raised in what has been described as a "low-income household in Glenwillow, Ohio."

David Meggyesy: (Laughs) Is that how it's been described? Actually I was, literally, raised on a pig farm next to a dynamite factory in Glenwillow, Ohio. Before we moved to the farm when I was five years old, my father worked as a machinist and was a union organizer in Cleveland, Ohio. The dynamite factory was the Austin Powder Company, whose property was right next to our farm. The company owned about 1,000 acres of land, the whole Glenwillow Township, including the town. It was one of the last company towns in Ohio. They had company housing, a company store, a company farm, and this factory that was churning out explosives.

How did your Dad's politics shape your view of the world?

He never talked about it that much, but he would be considered a progressive. He viewed the world from a radical perspective. He was very critical of the capitalist system and the political economy that we have in place in this country. He was in the middle of labor fights in Ohio in the 1930s. A lot of those guys were fighting for basic workers' rights, and their battles led to the formation of the National Labor Relations Act in 1936. His line was that President Franklin Roosevelt saved the country from going socialist by pushing for the NLRA.

When did you first realize that there was such a thing as a Civil Rights movement?

I didn't have a clue about civil rights—or people of color for that matter—when I was growing up. I didn't see a Black person until I was thirteen or fourteen years old, and that was on TV. During high school, I competed against Black athletes and had Black teammates on the football team at Syracuse University. During my senior year at Syracuse in 1963, I became aware of the Civil Rights movement.

How did you get involved in the movements of the 1960s?

Initially, I came at it from a sociology seminar I took my senior year at Syracuse. During this seminar, we read about and discussed civil rights and various human rights issues. This seminar certainly opened my eyes. Then, during my first year in the NFL, I read Michael Harrington's book, *Poverty in America.* The book had a big impact on me. Remember, I grew up poor. Reading it made me begin to question our economic and political system. I asked myself, how is it the richest country in the world has one quarter of its population living in poverty? As I was asking myself these questions, the Civil Rights movement was starting to heat up.

My third year in the NFL, I formed a friendship with an anthropology graduate student at Washington University named John Moore. John was in Vietnam as a Special Forces soldier very early on, long before our government admitted we had military forces in Vietnam. I remember John had this beautifully made crossbow mounted on his wall. I asked John about it, and he told me a story about being in Vietnam on patrol and a Vietnamese farmer came up out of an irrigation ditch and shot at his patrol with this crossbow. It started John thinking: What would make this guy have the commitment to do that? John said that he started reading progressive writings, including Marx's *Capital* and he became a Marxist. John—he turned me on to more radical literature. At the time, I was a sociology graduate student at Washington University. John is now chairman of the Anthropology Department at the University of Florida.

What did people on the Cardinals think about you exploring these ideas?

Coaches and teammates would see me reading various progressive books and magazines on the away game plane trips, and sometimes they would ask me what I was reading, but it wasn't any big deal. We didn't have sit-ins or study groups reading Karl Marx. I was going through a process of my own self-education. Through these various influences, I got involved in the Civil Rights movement. I was reluctant, at first, to tell my African-American teammates about it. My feelings were that it would be embarrassing for them to have this white guy being active, and they maybe feeling like they should have been involved. A lot happened between 1963 and 1969. The Civil Rights and then the anti–Vietnam War movements just exploded in every city in this country. I don't think you could be a young person—or old person for that matter—and see on TV the civil rights marches, the police dogs, fire hoses, children being murdered and people gassed and not be moved to do something. It was unbelievable.

What was it about the war in Vietnam that so infuriated you?

Eventually, more than half the country was against the war. On the evening news, every night people were seeing battle scenes, scenes with American and Vietnamese people being killed and bombed, of kids burning with napalm. There were body counts and increasing American casualties. And the American people were just appalled. There was absolutely no reason to be in Vietnam. Why do you think we have seen nothing during this Iraq war about what is really happening on the ground? We are dropping one-ton bombs on people in Iraq, and we see the bombs launched but not the level of destruction or the bodies. We say we precision bomb this, or bomb that, yet we, the citizens who are paying for these bombs and vast military, don't see how many people were killed. We don't see and aren't allowed to see the destruction and bodies in the street. The political establishment and the military have sanitized every war since Vietnam. They learned their lesson, and the media is kept away from what is happening. We the people need to start connecting the dots and asking why are we occupying this country? And we need to connect the dots more than that. Why, in the most fabulously wealthy country in the world, do we not have a national health care system and universal basic health care for everyone? Most folks don't connect those dots. In the 1960s, we were doing that.

What are your memories of Muhammad Ali resisting the draft?

I thought it was great! His famous line, "No Vietnamese ever called me the n-word," made sense to me.

It is thought that the NFL is a bastion of right-wing, hyper patriotic ideas. How did the movements of the 1960s for racial justice and against the war affect the discussions on the team bus and whatnot?

Probably one of the moments that politicized me and a number of my teammates was when we had to play our game against the New York Giants the weekend after President Kennedy was killed. Athletes tend to hold their political views to themselves. But guys were really pissed about that. We all felt out of respect for the president, we should never have played. But the orders came down from Pete Rozelle with the bullshit reason that we had to play to save the country, that NFL football games would bring everyone together. The players heard that and said, "This is a bunch of bullshit." Believe me, it generated a lot of discussion among the guys.

What about later in the Vietnam years?

During the latter part of my career, I began looking at sports and football and began trying to figure out its relations to society as a whole. And I began wondering why other countries don't play this game. I was coming to the understanding that big-time football was more than a game, that it was a form of political expression and political theater. During that time there was this jingoistic, super patriotic use of football, particularly during the Super Bowl, to sell the war in Vietnam. Yet, there were a tremendous number of people against the war, including myself. My response was to get more serious and start organizing my teammates on the Cardinals. I started a petition drive on the Cardinals, which would be sent to our congressional delegation and senators, calling for an end to the war. My teammate Rick Sortun and I put it together. Rick was a Goldwater Republican in 1964, and he was my roommate on the road. We had many heated discussions. During the off season in 1967, he went back to the University of Washington, and when he came back for training camp in 1968, he had gone from Goldwater Republican to a member of the Young Socialist Alliance. I kid Rick and tell him he was my first convert.

The times they were a-changing. The next petition Rick and I put together, in 1969, we had thirty-seven teammates sign it. In the locker room, political discussion and debate was quiet because the coaches frowned on it, but if I would be reading *Ramparts* magazine or an interview with Malcolm X, other players, including our star running back Johnny Roland, would give me a power fist salute as if to say, "We're with you." It wasn't that difficult to do it. There were a whole lot of people against the war.

What happened with the petition? Did it ever go public?

When I asked the guys to sign the petition, I told them it would not be made public. It was a letter we all signed that would be sent to our congressmen. It was pretty milquetoast given what was going on in other places. We were calling for a negotiated settlement and to bring the troops home now. A reporter from UPI got a hold of it and went to Cardinals owner Stormy Bidwell, asking for a comment. Stormy was pissed livid. He pulled me out of a defensive players meeting, and said I had to get a hold of that letter immediately before it went public. So I went outside the stadium in my football uniform, hailed a cab and got the letter back from the chairman of the St. Louis Anti-War Committee.

The next day Cardinals head coach Charlie Winner said to me, "I want you to apologize to the team. This is a big distraction for the team, and you owe the team an apology." I got up in front of the team and said I was sorry the petition almost went public because I said it would be kept private and that was all I was apologizing for. I told them if they wanted to sign a new petition they could stop by my locker after practice and do it. Charlie almost had a heart attack.

So many athletes have been "blackballed" for their politics. Did you ever feel that pressure?

They tried to put the hammer on me to get me to stop my anti-war activities. In 1968, I was taken outside by one of the coaches and asked, "Do you want to play football? I have been told to tell you by the ownership that if you continue to do what you're doing, you are going to be thrown out of the League." A few days later, I wrote the Cardinal management and told them if they continued to threaten me this way, I would go public. I said in my letter that half the country is against this war, and my anti-war work doesn't impact my playing, and it is my right as a citizen to protest the war. Nothing happened. Later in the season, NFL Commissioner Pete Rozelle sent an order down to the teams that when the national anthem is being played, we, the players, would have to hold our helmets under our left arm, look up, and salute the flag. I found it repulsive that anyone would be telling me and my teammates that we had to salute the flag and how to do so. So I did a low-key "Tommie Smith" and held my helmet in front of me and bowed my head. The next week, a sports columnist wrote about how reprehensible it was that anyone would refuse to salute the flag. The team didn't know what to do. They thought that if they would be cool, maybe it would go away. So at the start of our next game, some fans unfurled a big banner that said "The Big Red [the nickname of the Cardinals] thinks Pink." It was their way of saying that I was a "pinko" (a communist), and we were a "pinko" team.

Midway through 1969 season, I got benched. That hurt as much as anything because the ultimate power management has over a player is whether you play or not. At the professional level, this is also your livelihood. When they benched me, I just couldn't believe it. Clearly, I was superior to my backup. On the plane ride back to St. Louis with Rick Sortun, after our last game in Green Bay, we decided were going to quit. We were tired of being part of what we saw as an American war game and political theater that was supporting the Vietnam War. Personally, what really hurt was not being allowed to play. During the trip, fellow linebacker Larry Stallings sat down beside us and said, "Dave, I don't know what went down with you and the coaches, but you not being in there really hurt our defense." When I was benched for "political reasons," all kinds of self-doubts began to creep into my mind. Because one of the core values in sports from the athlete's point of view is that it is a meritocracy: The best players play. An athlete has to believe this is true, or he can't play. When someone messes with that, it messes with everything that is great about sports. That's why it was so incredibly gracious for Larry to tell me what he did, and it showed his integrity. Larry's comment meant a great deal because I knew my teammates understood.

What do you think of people who say that athletes don't have "the right" to use their public profile to speak out on political issues?

I think that is absolutely wrong. Athletes probably have more of an obligation to do so, precisely because of their public position. Athletes are citizens too. In the 1960s, Tommie Smith, John Carlos, Muhammad Ali, and others stepped up and took principled positions on issues. Now athletes are either making the most milquetoast statements or shilling for corporations that exploit their workers. For instance, Michael Jordan, who was the public face and billboard for Nike while they made their money off of Asian sweatshop labor. A few years ago, Jerry Rice came out to the grand opening of Nike's San Francisco downtown store. When Jerry showed up, the press started asking him about child labor in Nike's Asian factories, and he was just blown away. He said, "What right do you have to ask these questions?" Well, if you shill for Nike, you should have to answer those questions. In a way, Jerry was an innocent man; he didn't understand the connections.

Can you see players today speaking out against the war in Iraq?

It's possible; I doubt if it will happen. I think all people need to be more political, including athletes, but we need a mass movement to raise our political consciousness and push the political establishment. It is a chicken-egg problem, but I see signs of it building because people are feeling the pain of the present administration's policies. In the 1960's, there was more of a mass movement that coalesced around civil rights, then rolled into Vietnam and the women's movement. You could not help but be exposed to those ideas of economic and social justice. Just as today, a lot of athletes were pretty traditional about the system back then. That "don't question authority" attitude was more entrenched back then, but it began to change when these movements began to build. Of course we had great national leadership during that era in Martin Luther King, Malcolm X, and Robert Kennedy.

I think a lot of people are opposed to the Iraq occupation, and if that goes on too much longer it will ignite people. I want to be clear. I think no one should be obligated to do anything. Freedom means freedom to choose how you want to live your life. But that cuts both ways. History shows that if the citizens do nothing or very little the elites will rob them blind. My position has always been that everyone has the right to be free to speak out on anything. That is the biggest stone in our country's foundation. Last season, Toni Smith, the women's basketball player from Manhattanville College, turned her back on the U.S. flag protesting poverty and injustice here in the United States. It was a courageous and remarkable act, exercising her right of free expression. In the 1960s, athletes saw how sport was connected to politics. Smith and Carlos wanted to open the world's eyes as to how African Americans were treated at home. They said that you can't just send us out to run and jump and represent the United States and say things are groovy.

Do you think we need a new revolt of the athletes?

I think we need a revolt only in the sense that fundamental change needs to happen in many sectors of society. In our major professional sports, athletes made tremendous positive changes via their unions during the past twenty-five years. At the NFLPA, we organized the players and built a strong union, and now we have power and equity, a seat at the table, and leverage and to get the compensation the athletes deserve. I think the professional sports unions are excellent examples, showing how unions can effect positive change, how people can use ideas and organization to change structures. That is what the 1960s were really all about. People say we need—and I think they are right—political mass movements to effect positive change in the major political and economic structures. I think right now, today, with Bush, the Iraq occupation, and what his government has planned for the country and the world, we are looking down the barrel of a gun. It is time to act. As we used to say, back in the day, "Don't mourn, America, organize." ◆

Jabbing Back: The Eddie Mustafa Muhammad Interview

Eddie Mustafa Muhammad is a former World Boxing Association (WBA) light heavyweight champion who retired in 1988 with a lifetime mark of 50–8–1 (39 KOs). Today Mr. Muhammad is taking on a far bigger foe: the entrenched exploitation of fighters in professional boxing. Muhammad is the president and founder of the Joint Association of Boxing (JAB). Affiliated with the International Brotherhood of the Teamsters (IBT), JAB is attempting, with success, to organize a union in the world of professional boxing. Mr. Muhammad talks about his efforts.

Dave Zirin: When did JAB get started?

Eddie Mustafa Muhammad: All this happened last year. A lot of people know I am the type of person who don't take stuff from nobody; I walk the walk and talk the talk. What you see is what you get. So when an attorney named Walter Kane contacted me to discuss JAB, I jumped in there. I went there to organize and let them know what a union is all about.

Are you finding an audience?

So far we have 300–350 fighters signed up on JAB union cards. I get calls from London to South Africa to Mexico. Some of the biggest promoters around the world want to contribute money to JAB. They say, "Champ you are doing a great job." But some want to see JAB destroyed because they want to keep stealing from the fighter. Boxing is corrupt; let's get that out front. Why so corrupt? The promoters. The fighters don't make it corrupt, the promoters do. Influencing judges to make crazy decisions. The fighters are just pawns.

A lot of us are not educated on legalities, and they want to keep us in that position.

The promoters are the reason that boxing is the last major sport without a union. They don't want these fighters to see what the networks are giving them. The promoter has his hand in the cookie jar and wants to keep it there.

What kind of response are you getting from the fighters for JAB, from club fighters to the biggest names?

The biggest names, they really don't need us because they can maintain on their own, but the other 99 percent, the four-, six-, or eight-rounders that don't make it, they need us. The Lennox Lewises, the Oscar de la Hoyas, the Roy Joneses don't need us. They have been blessed to be great fighters and take care of their own welfare. What I need from those guys is an endorsement that this is something good for fighters to be a part of.

JAB is affiliated with the International Brotherhood of Teamsters. Other sports unions are independent of larger formations like the Teamsters.

Being a Teamster means an extra sense of strength and soli darity. [IBT President] James Hoffa treats us with ultimate respect and sees, as we do, that there is a need for protection of fighters. People have learned what a union is all about.

You have said that you are proud to be a union man. What, in your mind, is a "union man"?

It means the blue-collar worker, the hard worker. Someone who stands up for rights and benefits, a pension, all those things that fighters don't have. A union man means you have purpose. The other 99 percent of the fighters that don't make it, that end their careers 8-16, we can make sure they are protected and keep their dignity. You are only as good as your last fight. The promoters are smart. They know the majority of fighters come from the inner city. They are not adept at understanding the intricacies and legalities of a contract, and the promoters exploit that. That's how it is. Whereas being in a union, that can't happen because unions stand up for the hardworking individuals and we can't be bought.

Why did you, Eddie Mustafa Muhammad, throw yourself into this organizing effort?

First of all, I was a world champion. Whatever I said, I've done. I can't be bought. I will challenge anybody that exploits the fighter or exploits the game of boxing no matter who it is. You can be the biggest promoter in the world. I really don't care. I'm coming after you. This is how I made my livelihood. This is how I got myself out of the inner city and made something of myself, so I'm not going to sit around like other guys do and say we should do this and we should do that. I am not going to talk. I am going to do it. After fighting I trained successfully six guys for world champion. I get calls every day, but I have to put that on the side to deal with the exploitation of the fighter. I have done everything in boxing. What more can I do, except try to clean this up? In boxing, your next fight can always be your last. You can have a great family and all of a sudden you step in the ring and something happens. Who is going to take care of your family? Not the promoter. I don't see anyone running to the aid of [disabled fighters] Gerald McClellan or Greg Page. Those guys gave their all—great fighters. Now who is paying their bills? They have the right to benefits. But if they had a union before their mishaps happened, they would be in a different situation.

When you see a Greg Page or a Gerald McClellan, do you ever think the sport should just be banned?

No. This is what we do. But at the end of the day, when our fighting career is over, let's have something to fall back on. Let's have a pension. Let's have medical benefits. Let's have a retirement package. Let's have a job waiting for us to keep our dignity. I don't want charity helping me out. I want to be able to sustain for my own, provide for my family, without throwing a benefit…. I don't need that. James Brown had a record: "Open the door and I'll get in myself." That's all I'm saying.

Have any promoters taken you on?

They're not man enough to say it to my face. But there is backbiting going on. No doubt about it. The doors are closed, they talk about Eddie Mustafa Muhammad like he's a dog, but when the door is open, and they take me face to face, they want to embrace me, but I can dig that because I can see right through them.

Do you see JAB as a union that would strike to win its demands?

You know what? We don't want to do that, but if promoters don't cooperate, we will have to take action. I don't want to strike. All I'm trying to do is create a union for the fighters and their well-being. If any promoter is against this union, then they are against a better life for the fighter. That's all it is. Clear and simple. I am not trying to turn the fighter against the promoter. I am trying to establish something for them to fall back on. What's wrong with that?

You guys would also have a most imposing picket line.

No doubt.

Other sports unions are notorious for not respecting the picket lines of service industry, low-paid workers. If the wait staff or custodians in a casino were on strike, would JAB respect their line?

We would have to honor their picket lines. The bottom line is that we are blue-collar workers. We are what is good for the fighters, and I have already been out there on the picket line with other workers. I know how it works. I was asked to take part in sit-downs and I have done that. We are a family. We are Teamsters and we have a lot of strength in numbers. ◆

CHAPTER SIX

In the Shadow of Ali:
Sports, War, and Resistance Today

Dwight Eisenhower once said, "Sports are perfect for preparing young men for war." And sure enough, as long as there have been organized sporting events, war and combat have both lurked in the shadows and stood out in plain view. In modern sports, this is most obvious in football, a game made up of advancing and retreating over patches of ground. The quarterback is known as the "field general," and the area around the line of scrimmage is called "the trenches." Also, the field general throws "bullet passes" or "bombs," depending on the situation. But it is during periods of actual war, like the one we are in now, when the synergy of sports and war takes center stage. A typical pro game includes F-14 bombers buzzing the stadium, multiple national anthems, everything but a mandatory loyalty oath and bombs bursting in air (although the fireworks come close).

The story of Pat Tillman, the NFL All-Pro turned Army Ranger turned casualty, encapsulates how craven the masters of war are in their push to claim useful symbols, while ESPN's broadcasts from a gunner's nest in Kuwait demonstrate just how willing and eager the corporate media is to project those symbols all over sports. But there are times when the rah-rah meets resistance. Like when All-Star Toronto Blue Jays Slugger Carlos Delgado refused to stand for "God Bless America," or when the Iraqi soccer team squashed President George W. Bush's efforts to turn them into extras in an election ad, or when Notre Dame basketball star turned army veteran Danielle Green started to speak out against a war that almost left her dead. The following chapter looks at recent moments when sports and war have stood arm-in-arm, as well as times when athletes have just said no.

The Utterly Un-Lonesome Death of Pat Tillman

When Pat Tillman walked away from the NFL to join the Army Rangers, pro-war politicians started drooling—veritable rivulets of saliva flowed from the White House to the Pentagon. Here was the Arizona Cardinals' record-setting safety turning his back on a $3.5 million NFL contract to "fight the war on terror." Immediately, Madison Avenue PR firms, hired by the Defense Department with our tax dollars, began churning out press releases exalting "The American Athlete at War," replete with stories of baseball hall-of-famer Ted Williams flying missions over the Pacific. The confederate confines of talk radio spoke of Tillman as "A Real American Hero" making "The Ultimate Sacrifice." One wonders if James Earl Jones was specially contracted to intone, "Pat Tillman: An Army of One."

There was just one problem. Tillman wouldn't play their game. He turned down "hundreds if not thousands" of interviews and photo ops. He refused to be in any recruitment videos or on a single poster. Soon the story of "NFL player Pat Tillman in the Army Rangers" faded into the next news cycle. A year went by without a mention. No one tracked the day when his shoulder length hair was shaved to the scalp. No one snapped shots of his time in the "Army Ranger Indoctrination Program." No one knew about his first tour in Iraq. But when

Despite knowing that Pat Tillman had died in friendly fire, the military didn't inform his family until long after the funeral service. Above, John McCain was one of several politicians to shamelessly see the funeral as an opportunity to praise a man in death who would have shunned their attention in life. (AP/Gene Lower)

Tillman was killed in Afghanistan by "friendly fire," the gears began to turn again. As Tillman's family and football fans grieved, the United States' war machine sprang into action. Death rendered Tillman helplessly compliant—and far more useful to the masters of war than he had been in life.

In "The Late Pat Tillman," the Washington establishment

finally had a dead soldier they could cozy up to. "Where do we get such men as these? Where do we find these people willing to stand up for America?" asked Republican Representative J.D. Hayworth, diving bravely in front of the nearest camera. "He chose action rather than words. He was a remarkable person. He lived the American dream, and he fought to preserve the American dream and our way of life." Senator George Allen of Virginia, son of the late pro football coach, George Allen Sr., sent a letter to NFL Commissioner Paul Tagliabue, asking the league to dedicate the season to Tillman and other U.S. soldiers "serving in the war on terrorism."

And, of course, former Texas Rangers owner George W. Bush jumped into the fray commenting, "Pat Tillman was an inspiration both on and off the football field."

At a time when the United States' "coalition of the willing" was starting to come apart as fast as the Iraqi resistance was growing, the folks at 1600 Pennsylvania Avenue saw Tillman's death as Christmas in April. The former seventh round draft pick became the symbol, as the White House commented, of "all we are fighting for."

Yet the late Pat Tillman is in no way representative of the typical dead U.S. soldier. And pretending otherwise is—like so much of Bush's global conquest—a bloody lie. The face of the typical dead U.S. soldier is not that of a twenty-seven-year-old man walking away from millions of dollars to make "the ultimate sacrifice." The typical dead U.S. soldier was far more likely to have gone into the military with hopes of finally getting an education, and was probably in Iraq or Afghanistan beyond his or her tour of duty. This dead soldier, chances are, was suffering from depression and crushingly low morale in the days before death. The dead soldier was making $18,000 a year and possibly living on food stamps. The dead soldier is disproportionately likely to be Black or Latino.

While one NFL millionaire served in "Operation Enduring Occupation," there are 37,000 noncitizens serving in the Iraq occupation alone, hoping to stay alive long enough to benefit from a new program that allows immigrant soldiers to apply for citizenship immediately without having to wait the usual five years. The typical dead soldier might have been recruited from the U.S. Army's new number one recruitment spot: Tijuana, Mexico. When we look at the actual faces of dead U.S. soldiers, and the growing anger of the families who will never see those faces again, we can understand why commander-in-chief Bush has boycotted all their funerals. We can explain why photos of flag-draped coffins had to be smuggled out on military cargo ships, and why the workers who took those photos were fired. With the distortion of Tillman's death, Bush is hoping to shore up support for his Middle Eastern slaughter, something the actual facts on the ground will never accomplish.

But not everyone is taking the bait. In fact, by "humanizing" the death of a popular ex-football player, Bush could be running right into some hard-core necessary roughness. Sports fans and scribes aren't the mindless patriots that the White House—and much of the left—tend to believe. The public parade of Tillman's remains has bred a variety of reactions. Nationally renowned—and dependably apolitical—sports columnist Mike Lupica wrote, "Pat Tillman got to live out his professional dreams for a little while. What about all the ones dying over there who didn't?" ESPN's *Sports Reporters* show commented, "The White House has no right to say anything about the death of Tillman since it doesn't want to show pictures of the dead. They can't have it both ways." And on what is possibly the most frat boy–driven sports radio show on the air today, *The Jungle with Jim Rome*, one caller identified himself as an ex-soldier from Arizona and said, "The president needs to take a long look in the mirror and try to figure out if this is worth it." He then paused and said, "War to no one. Fight for peace."

This feeling only intensified when people learned the truth—that the weapons that ended Tillman's life were fired by his own platoon. Like the war itself, initial reports of Tillman's last moments were shrouded in lies. As the *Washington Post* reported in a December 2004 exposé, "His superiors exaggerated his actions and invented details as they burnished his legend in public, at the same time suppressing details that might tarnish Tillman's commanders." Shamefully, the military did not shy away from manipulating family, friends, and teammates in its efforts to mislead the public.

As the *Post* article put it,

> It would take almost five more weeks—after a flag-draped coffin ceremony, a Silver Star award and a news release, and a public memorial attended by Sen. John McCain, [quarterback and best friend] Jake Plummer and newswoman Maria Shriver—for the Rangers or the Army to acknowledge to…his family or the public that Pat Tillman had been killed by his own men.

It is also significant that Tillman's April 22nd death was announced just days before the shocking disclosure of photographs of torture by U.S. soldiers working as guards in Iraq's Abu Ghraib prison. The photos ignited an international furor against the U.S. armed forces. The timing of this cannot be dismissed as coincidence and may have played a role in the suppression of the truth.

Tillman's last moments sting the ears. As a young Ranger recalled to investigators during the inquiry, "I could hear the pain in his voice…[as he shouted], 'I am Pat [expletive] Tillman, damn it!' He said this over and over again until he stopped." Being "Pat Tillman" wasn't enough to save his life. But dead, he is worth his weight in black gold. ◆

Hold the Booyah: *SportsCenter* Out of the Middle East!

Has it come to this? Did *SportsCenter* really broadcast a week's worth of shows from Kuwait? Did we really receive our nightly dose of baseball, banter, and "booyah" from a set designed by the U.S. armed forces? Was the *SportsCenter* stage really constructed to look like a bunker, complete with camouflage netting and anchors' desks made out of sandbags and a Bradley tank?

Ideally, *SportsCenter* should be safe space, a space beyond the reaches of the drumbeat of war, like "home base" in a game of tag. It should be the one spot on the cable dial where we are not having an immoral, and, according to Kofi Annan, "illegal" occupation shoved down our throats like a new line of Happy Meals.

But no.

As one newspaper in Virginia chortled with glee, "Booyah! ESPN joins the battle!" (Yes, Virginia, there is a military industrial complex.) *Baseball Tonight* commentator Rob Dibble accepted the perils of the mission to Camp Arfijan in Kuwait with the solemnity of Patton, saying, "I know [we ESPN talking heads] are risking our lives but it was the least we could do."

Who could possibly be behind such a shameless synthesis of sports and Scuds? Sing it with me: M-I-C-K-E-Y M-O-U-S-E. Leave it to ESPN's parent company, Disney, and rodent-in-chief Michael Eisner to spice up our sports with pro-war poison. The same Disney that hired that epitome of fitness and athletic accomplishment Rush Limbaugh to comment on the NFL; the same Disney that refused to distribute *Fahrenheit 9/11* because it was "too political"; the same Disney that never met a union it wouldn't bust—that very same Disney took ESPN's flagship show, and, before you could say "Pat Tillman," turned it into an ad for the Army of One.

But that wasn't enough for Eisner and company. With the subtlety of Zell Miller critiquing fellow Democrats at the Republican Convention, they kicked off their "Salute to Our Troops Week" on Saturday, September 11th. Leave it to this platoon of Pinocchios to carry on the tradition of Bush, Cheney, Powell, and Rice by attempting to establish yet another (entirely engineered and after the fact) connection between 9/11 and the Iraq Occupation.

Displaying all the journalistic integrity of a Frank Capra World War II film, *SportsCenter*-Kuwait also did features on armed forces flag football, former athletes or relatives of famous athletes in the service, and how quickly an ice cream cone [symbol of Americana] melts in the savage 120-degree desert heat. It was *Heart of Darkness, SportsCenter* style: Boo-YAH!

But the toy soldier sets and gauzy features looked like an Orwellian Epcot compared to the reality on the ground. *SportsCenter*-Kuwait played out in the context of a shocking rise in civilian casualties, as the U.S. military rained death on unarmed Iraqis. Meanwhile, U.S. troops were subject to eighty-seven attacks a day in August 2004—the month directly preceding these "special" broadcasts—more than double the average from the first half of that year. This surge of resistance forced the Bush administration to finally admit that whole cities in Iraq—including Samarra, Ramadi, Baquba, and Fallujah—were "no-go" zones for U.S. troops and Iraqi police forces alike.

Disney can cast more spells than the wicked queen in *Snow White*. But it would take a feat beyond the powers of animation to make a pretty picture out of this sick war. At a time when we should have been bringing the troops home, Disney brought them Stuart Scott. Tragedy became farce. Hold the booyah. ◆

Are We Ready for Some Football?

For two decades, I have celebrated the start of the National Football League's season. Yet this season I could not swallow it whole. Even in normal times, red, white, and blue bunting and all manner of other patriotic paraphernalia attach themselves to the NFL like barnacles on a boat. In normal times, a deft pressing of the mute button can block out the bluster. But these are not normal times. In these times, war is peace, occupation is liberation, and democracy has been reduced to voting for one of two pro-war Yalies and blaming the necessarily horrific results on progressives. Football has not escaped unscathed. The game's beauty has been swamped in a cesspool of warmongering impossible to ignore.

The stink was up my nose during the season's opening game between the New England Patriots and the Indianapolis Colts. Timed to coincide with the anniversary of 9/11, the heavy helping of patriotic hoo-ha that came with the game forced fans to cower under bomber jets, swallow our concern for the health and sanity of cheerleaders clothed in little more than red, white, and blue pasties, and listen to Hank Williams Jr. asking us if we were "ready for some football"—all before the opening kickoff.

Williams Jr. is, perhaps, a fitting choice to stand amidst the planes, pompoms, and patriotism. In his hit 1988 song, a historical epic called "If the South Would Have Won," he yodeled:

If the South would'a won, we would have it made
I'd make my Supreme Court down in Texas
And we wouldn't have no killers getting off free
If they were proven guilty, then they would swing quickly
Instead of writin' books and smilin' on T.V.
We'd put Florida on the right track, 'cause we'd take Miami back
[from who? Jews? Cubans? Haitians? Or will Hank go for the trifecta?].

I said if the South would'a won, we would'a had it made!
Might even be better off!

Disgusting. And yet—in a league that is 65 percent Black, but 80 percent of the coaches, 94 percent of the general managers, and 100 percent of the owners are white–a racist paean to plantation life seems disturbingly appropriate.

Given the flag waving, war posturing, and the swirling mists of sexism, I understand why there are courageous radicals who would sooner spoon Dick Cheney than watch the game, why there are heroic activists who would rather see Alan Keyes in Mel Gibson's *Othello* than join a tailgate, why there are principled vegans who would prefer to drink a mug of gravy and floss with gristle than do anything that involves John Madden.

But channel changers also missed a display of everything great about the gridiron—wild running by Corey Dillon and Edge James, sharp passing by Tom Brady and Peyton Manning, and a spine-tingling finish, with a Colt fumble and missed field goal in the final three minutes. The game had more suspense than anything since the scene in *Fahrenheit 9/11* when you wonder if George W. Bush is ever going to put down *My Pet Goat*.

Yet, when it was all over, the taste of right-wing sludge lingered, overwhelming the bright finish of the game. I now believe that it's time to be heard and I know I am not alone. We radical helmet-huggers want our game a-la-carte: sixty minutes of football, hold the militaristic pep rally. I'm tired of pressing the mute button on myself. If network honchos will exploit football for political gain, we should return the favor.

The next time we're at the stadium or in the sports bar, and the game is being used to push an agenda completely at odds with the kind of world we want to live in, let's open our mouths and speak out.

This might not make you the most popular person in the room, but if you scratch the surface with most folks, it's amazing what you can find. Fifty-five percent of this country thinks we are moving in the wrong direction and opposes the continuing occupation in Iraq. A lot of those folks spend their Sundays watching the patriotic hoedown thrown by the NFL. I say it's time to crash the party.

Are we ready for some football? Sure, but let's turn the question around and ask: Is football ready for us? ◆

Carlos Delgado Stands Up to War

Toronto Blue Jays first baseman Carlos Delgado is known throughout the baseball world as one of the most feared sluggers in the game. In 2003, the thirty-two-year-old All Star hit forty-two homers and drove in 145 runs. He has averaged almost forty home runs a year over the last six seasons. With his imposing physical frame, bald scalp, and gold earring, Delgado is one of the most recognizable figures in the game. And he has put the baseball world on notice that he will use his fame to fight the U.S.'s war on the world.

In a very sympathetic story on the pages of the *Toronto Star*, Delgado went public with his decision not to stand on the dugout steps for the seventh-inning-stretch singing of "God Bless America" that was added to the MLB program after 9/11. "I never stay outside for 'God Bless America,'" Delgado said. "I actually don't think people have noticed it. I don't (stand) because I don't believe it's right, I don't believe in the war."

Delgado also made clear that he couldn't abide the priorities of the U.S. military machine. "It's a very terrible thing that happened on September 11," he said.

> It's (also) a terrible thing that happened in Afghanistan and Iraq. I just feel so sad for the families that lost relatives and loved ones in

the war. But I think it's the stupidest war ever. Who are you fighting against? You're just getting ambushed now. We have more
people dead now, after the war, than during the war. You've been
looking for weapons of mass destruction. Where are they at?
You've been looking for over a year. Can't find them. I don't support that. I don't support what they do. I think it's just stupid.

Historically, athletes have paid a steep price for standing up
to the way sports is used to package patriotism and war. As we
have seen, Muhammad Ali was stripped of his heavyweight
title for refusing to go to Vietnam in the 1960s. In 1991, Bulls
guard Craig Hodges found himself blackballed from the NBA
after protesting the Gulf War during a visit to George Bush's
White House with the champion Chicago Bulls. A similar fate
befell shooting guard Mahmoud Abdul-Rauf in 1998 when he
refused to stand for the national anthem. Delgado doesn't care.

"Sometimes, you've just got to break the mold. You've got
to push it a little bit or else you can't get anything done," he
told the *Toronto Star*. Delgado, fortunately, is aided by both his
superstar status and the fact he plays in Canada where the
media is less likely to take orders from the Pentagon and slam
the slugger. But his resolve comes from a deeply personal
place. You might say that, for Delgado, the human toll of the
U.S. military hits home.

Delgado is from Puerto Rico and has campaigned for years
to end the U.S. Navy's presence in Vieques, an island that had
been a weapons testing ground for sixty years. The Navy recently left Vieques, but it has also left behind an area with ab-
normally high cancer rates, 50 percent unemployment, and
deep poverty. Delgado is now part of a movement to get the
U.S. government to clean up their mess. He sees the people of
Vieques as casualties—collateral damage—from the war on
Iraq because they served as guinea pigs for the weapons that
have wreaked havoc throughout the Persian Gulf. "You're dealing with health, with poverty, with the roots of an entire com-

munity, both economically and environmentally," Delgado has said. "This is way bigger than just a political or military issue. Because the military left last year and they haven't cleaned the place up yet."

The catalytic event for his activism was the killing of a Vieques man, David Sanes, by an errant bomb on April 19, 1999. Delgado wanted to act, so his father hooked him up with "an old Socialist Party pal" named Ismael Guadalupe. The high school teacher, "a leading figure in the island's protest movement," had spent six months in prison in 1979 for protesting on "Navy property" in Vieques. "He wanted to help out with more than just the situation with the Navy," Guadalupe, fifty-nine, said of Delgado. "He wanted to help the people there. He wanted to help the children." Delgado has done more than talk a good game. Together with singer Ricky Martin and boxer Félix "Tito" Trinidad, he took out full-page advertisements about Vieques in the *New York Times* and the *Washington Post*. The ads included the names of fellow Major League All Stars Roberto Alomar, Juan González, and Iván "Pudge" Rodríguez. Boxer John Ruiz and golfer Chichi Rodríguez also signed on. Delgado didn't fear reprisals for these ads, which were very critical of the Navy and ran in April of 2001. "What are they going to do, kick me out of the game? Take away my endorsements?"

Delgado has put his money where his mouth is for other causes as well, donating $100,000 to youth sports, schools, and activism on the island. He also travels to Vieques every January to run clinics for and give gifts to the children. "You'll need millions and millions of dollars to clean Vieques up. So, we try to make [the money] as effective as we can. We make it work for kids. I can't clean up Vieques by myself. It's going to take a lot of people." You get the feeling Carlos Delgado wants to see a cleanup far beyond the borders of Puerto Rico. ◆

The Iraqi Soccer Team Kicks Back

Once again we have been reminded that the Olympics can serve as an international platform not only for flag-waving and truck commercials, but also for resistance. In an incredible piece by Grant Wahl in *Sport Illustrated*, the Iraqi Olympic Soccer team issued a stinging rebuke to George W. Bush's attempt to use them as election year symbols.

Iraq's soccer squad was perhaps the biggest surprise of the entire Olympics, advancing to the semifinals despite the war and occupation that has gripped their country for the last seventeen months. Yet, amidst the cheers and triumph, they were infuriated to learn that Bush's brain, Karl Rove, had launched campaign ads featuring their Olympic glory as a brilliant byproduct of the war on terror. The commercial, subtle as a blowtorch, begins with an image of the Afghani and Iraqi flags and a voice-over saying, "At this Olympics, there will be two more free nations—and two fewer terrorist regimes."

Bush also exploited their successes in stump speeches. Much more comfortable talking sports than foreign policy or stem cell research, Bush brayed with bravado in Oregon, "The image of the Iraqi soccer team playing in this Olympics, it's fantastic, isn't it? It wouldn't have been free if the United States had not acted." This compelled the Iraqi soccer team, at great personal risk, to respond. Midfielder and team leader Salih Sadir told *Sports Illustrated*, "Iraq as a team does not want Mr. Bush to use us for the presidential campaign. He can find another way to advertise himself."

Sadir has reason to be upset. He was the star player for the professional soccer team in Najaf. Over the last year, Najaf has been overrun repeatedly by U.S. troops and the new Iraqi army as part of their efforts to uproot rebel cleric Moqtada Al-Sadr. Thousands have died, each death close to Sadir's heart.

"I want the violence and the war to go away from the city," said Sadir. "We don't wish for the presence of Americans in our country. We want them to go away."

Sadir's teammates were far less diplomatic. Midfielder Ahmed Manajid told Wahl angrily, "How will [Bush] meet his god having slaughtered so many men and women? He has committed so many crimes." Manajid understands Sadir's pain because he is from another Iraqi city that has been in a state of siege: Fallujah.

Manajid told Wahl that his cousin, Omar Jabbar al-Aziz, a resistance fighter, was killed by the U.S., as were several of his friends. Manajid even said that if he were not playing soccer he would "for sure" be fighting as part of the resistance. "I want to defend my home. If a stranger invades America and the people resist, does that mean they are terrorists? Everyone [in Fallujah] has been labeled a terrorist. These are all lies. Fallujah people are some of the best people in Iraq."

Usually when there is political unrest on Olympic teams, the coach tries to be a mitigating force in dealing with the media. But not here and not now. Iraqi soccer coach Adnan Hamad also went public with his outrage, saying, "My problems are not with the American people, they are with what America has done in Iraq: destroy everything. The American army has killed so many people in Iraq."

To be clear, Iraq's team is not pining for former Olympic head Uday Hussein, notorious for torturing athletes who underperformed. Yet they don't feel their choice has to be between Uday's way and the bloodbath that has been visited upon their country. As Hamad said, "What is freedom when I go to the [national] stadium and there are shootings on the road?"

The ideas expressed by the Iraqi soccer team are by all accounts commonplace in Iraq, yet they find little expression in the mainstream media here at home. It is critical that their words be heard. ◆

"D" Was Never So "Smooth"

"Coach, you know how you were always on me about working on my right hand dribble. Well, I'm going to start." With this line, delivered amid laughter and tears, former Notre Dame basketball standout, southpaw Danielle "D-Smooth" Green, told the horrifying news to her ex-Fighting Irish coach Muffet McGraw: a grenade had blown off her left hand when she was—as Army MP Green—patrolling a Baghdad police station.

Like late NFL safety turned Army Ranger Pat Tillman, Green could easily be used as a symbol of patriotic resolve and sacrifice. She would fit neatly into that potent place where athletics meets war and produces pro-military demagoguery. Yet unlike Tillman, who cannot speak for himself, D-Smooth has foiled attempts to exploit her experience for pro-war purposes by speaking out against what she sees, from firsthand experience, as an unjust war. From her hospital bed, Green told the *New York Times*, "They just don't want us there. I personally don't think we should have gone into Iraq. Not the way things have turned out. A lot more people are going to get hurt, and for what?"

Secretary of State Colin Powell, confronted with her words on *Meet the Press*, could only mutter, "I hope she will see in time that her sacrifice was worth it." Green does not give him much basis for this hope. "I'm not going to lie, I didn't understand the mission, the purpose. If you understand what you're fighting for, then you've got something to hang on to. But we didn't even have that. I think if I hadn't lost my arm, I would have lost my mind. It was enough to drive you insane, and I think that's where I might have been headed."

If D-Smooth weren't so quick to speak her mind, she would be perfect fodder for a pro-war press desperately searching the rubble of Iraq for positive news about the U.S. occupation. Green would otherwise fit the bill. She was a decorated athlete at Chicago's Roosevelt High School, winning eleven letters in four sports. She was also sports editor for the school newspaper, a lieutenant colonel in Junior ROTC, treasurer of the student council, and a member of the National Honor Society. She accomplished all this while emerging from a childhood in which her prime adult role model was a mother addicted to drugs. "I was six or seven years old the first time I saw my mom smoke reefer," Green remembered. "Then it got to be an everyday thing. And then I saw her smoke out of a crack pipe. I went to my room and cried. But I also made up my mind that day what I was going to do with my life. I wrote down some goals. I wanted to go to Notre Dame someday, and I wanted to be GI Joe in the military."

Those dreams have been shredded, along with her illusions about why she enlisted. "The most disappointing thing about Iraq is that I thought I was going to change those peoples' lives. But in the four months I was there, I don't think I touched one life." But by not being silent, Green will touch more lives than she can imagine. "D" has never been so "Smooth." ◆

CHAPTER SEVEN

Gone with the Wind? Sports, Racism, and the Modern Athlete

We are told that the sports world is, as journalist Red Smith put it, "a true meritocracy," in which the color of your skin matters not, as long as you can produce on the field. We are told that racism—if it exists at all—is just a hangover from the days of Robinson and Ali, who fought the good fight and led us into a more enlightened age.

This is dead wrong. Racism in sports is alive and well. It is standing in plain sight at the University of Alabama, where the board of trustees passed on a chance to bury its racist past by hiring its first Black coach, choosing instead to perpetuate a racist present. It has been institutionalized—and emblazoned on hats—with the use of Native Americans as mascots, with team names like "Redskins" and the rotten histories behind them.

Sometimes, racism hides in the shadows, but if you want to see it emerge, just speak out against it—like when baseball slugger Barry Bonds called Boston a "racist city." He was told to "just shut up," but, as we will see, history is on his side. And right next to this same old same old racism, we have the "new" racism, which accuses young Black athletes of being more concerned with "posses," "boyz," and "bling bling" than with being serious athletes or even people.

But racism begets antiracism, as was the case when ESPN, rather inexplicably, hired Rush Limbaugh to talk football, and Limbaugh, after making ignorant and bigoted comments regard-

ing Black quarterbacks and the Philadelphia Eagles' own Donovan McNabb, found himself run out town on a rail. Here we look
at some of the more outrageous—and more covert—expressions
of racism in sports.

Barry Bonds vs. Boston

Last season, the media and sports radio establishment of
Boston called for the head of All-World baseball player Barry
Bonds. In an interview with the *Boston Globe*, Bonds was asked
a cream puff question about whether he would consider finishing his career in Beantown. Bonds shook his head and said,
"Boston is too racist for me. I couldn't play there. That's been
going on ever since my dad (Bobby) was playing baseball. I
can't play like that. That's not for me, brother." When the reporter countered that the racial climate has changed in Boston,
Bonds responded, "It ain't changing. It ain't changing
nowhere."

Boston is a city that treasures its image as a liberal enclave
of elite universities and tweedy baseball poets, so Bonds's
words went over like a Fourth of July Picnic in Fallujah. He has
been roundly criticized and won the coveted "Just Shut Up"
award from ESPN radio. By calling on Bonds to "just shut up,"
the media is just participating in a pastime that National
League pitchers have practiced to perfection: avoiding confrontation with the seven-time MVP.

To be clear, Boston has not cornered the market on bigotry.
Every city has its stories of both racism and resistance. Yet
Boston's history is particularly nasty. The most violent anti-bus-
ing demonstrations in America were not in Birmingham or
Biloxi but Boston. More recently, in 1989, when Charles Stuart,

San Francisco Giants' Barry Bonds points to the sky after hitting his 701st career home run off San Diego Padres' David Wells in the second inning on September 18, 2004, in San Francisco. (AP/Ben Margot)

a wealthy white businessman, murdered his pregnant wife and told police that "a Black guy" did it, the police believed him without a millisecond's doubt. They launched a vicious manhunt, fanning out through housing projects and sweeping the streets of Black neighborhoods. State politicians whipped up a further frenzy by calling for the reinstatement of the death penalty. When Stuart committed suicide after his brother blew the whistle on his crime, all police spokeswoman Margot Hill could say—and she said it without apparent shame—was, "[Stuart] took advantage of the environment he was in. He knew exactly what he was doing." It is precisely what Ms. Hill calls "the environment" that has found expression in the world of sports.

The Boston Red Sox were the last team in Major League Baseball to integrate. They waited so long to sign African Americans that the city's hockey team, the Bruins, actually beat them to it. In 1959, twelve years after Jackie Robinson broke through with the Brooklyn Dodgers, the Sox removed their color bar by begrudgingly bringing marginal infielder Pumpsie Green up from the minors. They could have broken the bar earlier, and with a better player, but racism got in the way. In April 1945, the Red Sox held a private tryout at Fenway Park for Robinson himself. With only management in the stands, someone yelled, "Get those niggers off the field," and the door was shut, the line unbroken. And again, in 1949, the Red Sox laughed off an opportunity to sign Bonds's godfather, the legendary Willie Mays, who would go on to hit more career home runs than all but one man before him and awe crowds with his speed and defense. As Juan Williams reports, "One of the team's scouts decided that it wasn't worth waiting through a stretch of rainy weather to scout the black player." That decision killed the possibility of Mays and Ted Williams playing in the same outfield. In the 1950s, as teams strengthened themselves immeasurably by signing players like Mays, Henry Aaron, Ernie Banks, Don Newcombe, Roy Campanella, Elston Howard, and others, the Red Sox stood pat with an all-white hand. So the next time you hear a Boston fan complain about "The Curse of the Bambino," inform them that "The Curse of the Racism" has had a much more adverse effect.

As the Civil Rights movement bloomed, New England's Black baseball fans would root for integrated clubs over their own home team. In other words, they practiced their own form of ABB—Anybody But Boston. Therefore, unlike other cities, such as New York and Chicago, where rooting for an integrated team actually helped advance people's consciousness and challenge racist ideas, the Red Sox proudly planted themselves on the wrong side of history. In the 1950s, if you were young and Black, Fenway Park was about as safe a space as Bull Connor's backyard.

But the racism in the Boston sports scene doesn't stop at the Green Monster. During the 1950s and 1960s, Boston was treated to the most successful run in the history of team sports, with the NBA's Celtics winning eleven championships in thirteen seasons.

The mainstay of that team was a player of immense skill, selflessness, and leadership: Bill Russell. Russell won five MVPs to go with his eleven championship rings. In 1967, he became the first African-American coach of a pro team. In 1974, he was elected to the Basketball Hall of Fame, and in 1980, the country's basketball writers voted him "The Greatest Player in the History of the NBA."

Russell also felt a deep desire to resist racism. Once in Marion, Indiana, he was given the key to the city during the day, only to be refused service that evening in his hotel's dining room. Russell went to the mayor's home, woke him up, and returned the key. His fierce pride (which the media called "a bad attitude") mixed about as well with Boston fans as would a "Strom Thurmond Remembered" concert at the Apollo Theater. The result was that the greatest player in Boston team sports history was the target of a constant campaign of racial harassment. When Russell tried to move from his house in the Boston suburb of Reading to a new home across town, neighbors filed a petition trying to block the move. When that failed, other neighbors banded together to try to purchase the home that Russell wanted to buy, according to Celtic great Tom Heinsohn, a close friend of Russell's. Once, vandals broke into Russell's home and defecated on his bed. Heinsohn said two white sportswriters from Boston told him they wouldn't vote Russell the league's most valuable player because he was Black.

Russell's achievements during his days in Boston, from 1956 to 1969, drew national acclaim, but never won local fans' hearts the way white Boston sports heroes did, from hockey player Bobby Orr to baseball player Carl Yastrzemski to basketball icon Larry Bird. Despite all the rings, the Boston Garden averaged 8,406 fans a game during Russell's playing career, thousands short of a sellout. "We always sold out on the road, but rarely when we played at home," said Satch Sanders, who played with the Celtics from 1960 to 1973. By contrast, the Celtics teams led by Larry Bird in the 1980s sold out the 14,890-seat Garden for 662 straight games, from 1980 to 1995. "I didn't play for Boston," Russell once said, "I played for the Celtics." Another time he called Boston a "Flea Market of Racism." Things haven't changed much from Russell's day. As recently as a decade ago, Celtics Slam Dunk Champ Dee Brown was roughly accosted by police while jogging in his Wellesley neighborhood for being the wrong color in the wrong place at the wrong time.

Despite this mountain of evidence that Bonds speaks truth, he is being told to "shut up." The few Boston writers, like the *Globe*'s Bob Ryan, who, to their credit, have chosen to actually engage with what Bonds is saying, have argued that, "there may be a bad history, but it has gotten much better." Has it? Last fall, WEEI Boston Sports Radio host John Dennis, after looking at a photo of a gorilla that had escaped from the Franklin Park Zoo and was lurking near a bus stop, said the animal was "probably a Metco gorilla waiting for a bus to take him to Lexington." Dennis was referencing the Metco program, under which more than 8,000 children of color from Boston and Springfield have attended suburban schools over the past thirty-seven years. Despite an outcry, he was neither fired nor disciplined.

And to think, Bonds dared say out loud that the Boston sports scene is racist. No wonder ESPN wants him to "shut up." I guess the truth hurts. ◆

Alabama's Crimson Past

The University of Alabama. The name is prominently etched in two very different chapters of U.S. history. In one chapter, there is the Alabama Crimson Tide football program: perched on the Mount Olympus of college sports, home to twelve national championships, twenty-one South Eastern Conference (SEC) titles, and legendary coach Paul "Bear" Bryant. In another chapter, far removed from cheerleaders, tailgating, and touchdowns, there is the university as it stood in the 1950s and sixties: a fortress of racial segregation, and ground zero in the movement for civil rights. In this chapter, the star is not Joe Namath passing the Tide to Sugar Bowl glory, but Governor George Wallace, standing on the steps, proclaiming "Segregation forever!" to rapturous cheers, and a young James Meredith needing a National Guard escort to walk through a very different kind of crimson tide just to get to class.

In 2003, the divergent themes of this tale of two Alabamas collided. After an "exotic dancer" charged $1,000 to his hotel

University of Alabama students burn desegregation materials during a demonstration in Tuscaloosa, Alabama on February 6, 1956, protesting the enrollment of a Black student. The student, Autherine Lucy, a 26-year-old Birmingham secretary, was barred from attending classes after rioting crowds stoned and egged her and school officials. (AP)

room, Tide football coach Mike Price was fired, and it was time to look for a new coach—and look quickly. Pulses raced and jaws dropped when Green Bay Packers assistant coach Sylvester Croom was interviewed for the top job. Croom was a star player under "Bear" Bryant, an assistant coach at Alabama for ten years, and had another seventeen years of coaching experience in the NFL.

But Croom was more than an accomplished candidate from the Alabama football family. He would have been the first African American to be a head coach in any team sport for the Crimson Tide. He also would have been the first African-American head football coach in the history of the South Eastern Conference.

Of course, hiring Croom wouldn't signal the end of prejudice and eternal harmony in a "New South." Perhaps it would have been merely symbolic, more show than substance, more pretense than progress. Yet what actually happened was just as symbolic. Croom did not get the job. Instead it went to thirty-five-year-old Mike Shula, a former Alabama quarterback in the 1980s, with less than half of Croom's experience. Articles praising the hiring of Shula and his "pedigree" (he is the son of coaching legend Don Shula) poured in from around the country. Croom was set to resume his role as an invisible man, returning to the shadows where all African-American assistant coaches are told to sit and wait.

But then a voice that you don't usually see on the sports page hit the print next to the box scores. The Reverend Jesse Jackson had something to get off his chest. At a hastily called press conference, the former North Carolina A&T football player's voice shook with emotion. "The SEC maintains a culture of excluding blacks beyond the playing field," he said. "White players, beyond the field, can expect to become coaches, athletics directors, and college presidents. Blacks have no life beyond the playing field. A hundred years ago, we were picking cotton balls and we couldn't grow in the cotton industry. Today, we are picking footballs and we can't grow in the athletics industry."

Moreover, Jackson pointed to milestones in the Civil Rights movement, saying, "Forty-nine years after the 1954 Supreme Court decision, thirty-eight years after the Voting Rights Act, and thirty-five years after the King assassination, Alabama is proving that old habits fall slowly." The national sports press has hammered Jackson for raising these concerns. As *USA Today* put it, "Who says Sylvester Croom is more qualified than Mike Shula to coach the University of Alabama football team? The Rev. Jackson, that's who. Interesting. I didn't know he was qualified to make that determination. Perhaps he feels social change is more important than winning football games. I doubt they think that down in Tuscaloosa, Alabama."

The insinuation that Croom, who—to repeat—is more experienced than Shula, would merely have been a candidate of "social change" and not equipped to "win football games" is insulting enough. But Jackson is not merely giving football tips any more than Dr. King was advising the Montgomery Bus Lines in 1955 how to run a more efficient transit system.

As Jackson said, "This issue is just suggestive that the culture of racial exclusion…is still prevalent in Alabama," he said. "It's not just in football coaches, it's in bank lending, mortgage lending, and the criminal justice system." In other words, Mike Shula was far more of a symbolic hire than Sylvester Croom ever would have been. Symbolic of a past that the History Channel tells us is "gone with the wind." Symbolic, as one athletic booster put it, "of preserving the real tradition of Alabama football."

What exactly is this tradition that the people at the University of Alabama are trying to preserve? In recognition of the fortieth anniversary of the historic desegregation of Alabama's capital, Birmingham, let's take a look. There is the Birmingham tradition of Sheriff Bull Connor, the water cannons, the attack dogs, and the ordinary people bleeding rivers in the streets as a result of asking for the most basic of human rights. There is the Birmingham tradition, from 1957 to 1963, of fifty cross burnings and eighteen racially motivated bombings—causing Birmingham to become known to many as "Bombingham."

This "tradition," which may be remembered in rosy colors by a booster on his fifth gin and tonic, inspired Dr. Martin Luther King to write his nationally published "Letter from a Birmingham Jail." With a pen borrowed from a prison guard, King wrote in the margins of a newspaper, "We know through painful experience that freedom is never voluntarily given by the oppressor; it must be demanded by the oppressed. For years now, I have heard the word 'Wait!'.... This 'Wait' has almost always meant 'Never.' We must come to see, with one of our distinguished jurists, that 'justice too long delayed is justice denied.'"

Croom has since been hired by SEC also-ran Mississippi State, but this neither dulls the slight nor changes the fact that he is now one of only three African-American head football coaches in all of Division I College Football. As reams of newspapers tell Jesse Jackson and like-minded people to "wait" and "mind their own business," there is no greater tribute to struggles past than to remember that justice delayed is absolutely justice denied. And our final victory does not occur with the hiring of the Sylvester Croomses of the world, but when their hiring is not a call for news. Only then can we start a new chapter in Alabama's history: a chapter not written in crimson. ◆

Redskins: Time to Change the Name?

Redskins. It's the name of D.C.'s cherished home team. It's also an ethnic slur as ugly as anything in the English language. Say it loud enough in a South Dakota Black Hills bar or a Salt River, Arizona Public Park, and you are leaving with a punch in the mouth—and for good reason. In the old days, trappers would kill a Native American, slice some bloody skin off the top of his head, and then put a "redskin" in their pouch with the deerskin, bearskin, and other nonhuman skins.

Redskins, of course, is more than a name. After years of wins, losses, and a trunk full of Super Bowl glory, following pro football is the closest thing to a common culture the city of D.C. has. Entire row houses in North East D.C. have been painted burgundy and gold. This team is the sun around which all other local sports revolve.

But it's past time to face the fact that the name is racist and has got to go.

In Washington, D.C., our nation's capital, where forty years ago Martin Luther King shared his dream of living in a world where the "color of one's skin" would be irrelevant, the moniker Redskins is a brand of shame.

I believe most fans would support a name change. But the campaign to protect the brand that is being conducted by the Redskins organization and their minions on talk radio is very organized and very real. "It's just a name," they say. "This is about preserving tradition." The sensitive New Age line from Redskins' vice president Karl Swanson is that the name was, "derived from the Native American tradition for warriors to daub their bodies with red clay before battle." This is their argument: that the name must stay because it was actually born of a deep cultural respect for "redskin warriors."

Since Swanson and company brought it up, it's worth examining the roots of this particular Washington football "tradi-tion." The great Redskin patriarch who brought the team to D.C. in 1937 was a man named George Preston Marshall. Marshall, in the words of late sportswriting legend Shirley Povich, "was widely considered one of pro football's greatest innovators and its leading bigot." Marshall's Skins were the last team to integrate in the entire NFL. Povich once wrote famously that "the Redskins colors are burgundy, gold, and Caucasian."

Marshall finally integrated the team in 1962, and only after the Kennedy Administration's Interior Secretary, Stewart Udall, issued an ultimatum: sign an African-American player or be denied use of the new government-financed 54,000-seat stadium. Marshall responded by making Ernie Davis, Syracuse's All-American running back, his number one draft choice. One problem: Davis's response was a forthright "I won't play for that S.O.B." Davis was traded to Cleveland, who in exchange sent all-pro Bobby Mitchell.

Marshall's racism was more than just bad ideas. It was the material foundation upon which the Redskins Empire was built. He brought his football team to Washington with a plan to make them "the South's team." He signed television contracts with stations in Southern cities, and mostly drafted players from Southern colleges. The team, once again to quote Povich, "became the Confederates of the NFL." In fact, in the original version of the ever-present fight song "Hail to the Redskins," the line "Fight for Old D.C." was "Fight for Old Dixie."

In light of this history, it is hard to imagine Marshall as a student of the cultural intricacies of Native American warriors and any real or imagined propensity for red clay. It is far more likely that he was marketing a minstrel show in shoulder pads, preying on bigotry for big bucks. Critics may call this "overly sensitive," but in 2002, when a group of Native Americans and non-Indians at the University of Northern Colorado turned the tables and named their intramural basketball team The Fighting Whites—complete with mascot: a stereotypical 1950s-style white man in a suit and tie carrying a briefcase—that same "anti-racial sensitivity" crowd freaked out. The Fighting Whites and their tongue in cheek slogan "Every Thang's Gonna Be All White" became a topic of national debate.

I don't know about you, but I think there always needs to be time, during periods of war and recession, for debates that involve intramural basketball. But then, it wasn't really about that. If you look closely, you'll see that this hullabaloo over The Fighting Whites was actually a function of the Redskins and their ilk feeling the heat. In 2003, a three-judge panel of the U.S. Patent and Trademark office ruled in favor of seven Native Americans who filed a complaint against the Redskins in 1992. The board ordered the cancellation of the federal registration of seven Redskins trademarks, under a 1946 law that says names cannot be protected if they are "disparaging, scandalous, contemptuous, or disreputable." This ruling has since been overturned on appeal, but one appellate court's ruling doesn't change the objective truth that "contemptible" and "scandalous" don't begin to describe this name or its true history.

It will take far more than a judge's ruling to exorcise the ghost of George Preston Marshall. It will take all of us. Washington football is Sonny Jurgenson, "The Diesel" John Riggins, Darrel Green, Doug Williams, Smurfs, Hogs, and the great Joe Gibbs. There is no reason why it also has to be Dixie, minstrelsy, and gutter racism. Let us, therefore, start a contest—with the winner receiving peace of mind and a small place in history—to rename the Washington, D.C. football team. ◆

The Results

Readers of *The Edge of Sports* came up with a stirring selection of new names for the squad, names that reflect the best of the people who live, work, and cheer in the District instead of the worst. After sifting through about 1,000 entries, I chose the following as the top five:

5. The Washington Dukes, from Bernard C. A tribute to immortal musician and local favorite son Duke Ellington. I would also have been open to paying homage to that other D.C. musical mastermind, Marvin Gaye, but that may be setting the bar a little high. One battle at a time.

4. The Washington Tecumsehs, from Suzette B. This entry is inspired. What better way to make up for years of racial mockery than a name paying tribute to the great Warrior Chief Tecumseh, who united various factions of indigenous tribes to build history's most successful liberation movement against the European Huns. A great idea, Suzette, but in Redskins owner Daniel Snyder's hands, the Tecumsehs would have cheerleaders called "The Squaws" and a mascot named "Chief Score-a Point-a" by week's end.

3. The D.C. Diesels, from Ryan in Hyattsville. I am very into this one: a nod toward the legendary John "The Diesel" Riggins, a player who once attended a state dinner drunk as a skunk and told Supreme Court justice Sandra Day O'Connor to "lighten up" before passing out under the banquet table. Also, Riggins used to have a mohawk and currently appears as "Mitch" on *Guiding Light*. The Diesels? This might have to happen.

2. The D.C. Go-Gos, from Keandra F. Love this name, a tribute to that distinctive musical hybrid of soul, funk, and bass, truly indigenous to the nation's capital. This was narrowly defeated because it was felt that, outside of D.C., people would think it was a tribute to Belinda Carlisle and that is

patently unacceptable.

1. The Washington Reds, from Joe D. We have a winner. Let's eject the word "skins" and make the Washington football squad a true people's team. Here are the stadium rules for the new Washington Reds: Everyone in a union will get full access to the luxury boxes, hot dogs will cost as much as an actual hot dog and not a month's rent, parking will be free, and seats will be equipped with voting boxes so fans can decide one play in every quarter. Also, during halftime, twenty people in the crowd will be randomly chosen to speak at midfield in front of 80,000 fans. The best speech will win a take-home version of our new mascot, a stuffed pig called "The Danny Boy." Sounds like a plan. Hey Snyder, are you ready for some football? ◆

What's the Matter With "Leon"?

It's now the hottest commercial since Clara Peller looked beseechingly upon the world and asked us for the location of "the beef." Thanks to Budweiser, the buzz is all about "Leon." "Leon" is Bud's big joke parody of the modern professional athlete. "Leon" won't do interviews unless his special dimple is on display. "Leon" is far more concerned about looking "pretty" than playing well. "Leon" is egomaniacal, lazy, and all about the bling-bling. "Leon" only speaks in the third person. Oh, by the way, "Leon" is Black. Well Dave Zirin thinks that the "Leon" commercials are pure, unfiltered racist crap, and Dave Zirin is going to tell you why.

"Leon" is supposed to be a harmless caricature, but of whom? Some say he's based on Philadelphia Eagles wide receiver Terrell Owens. But Owens, for all his celebrated end zone hijinks, is an MVP candidate who hasn't taken a play off since he entered the league. Others have suggested Minnesota Vikings wideout Randy Moss. The same Moss who has made multiple pro bowls and led the Vikings to two NFC championship games? Those cleats don't fit either.

So who is "Leon"? And if he doesn't have much to do with real any real players, then what is he doing? You can't answer this question without examining the place pro sports currently holds on the national agenda. Pro sports play two primary roles in our society: on the one hand, they are critical for the reinforcement of "values" like discipline, hard work, and patriotic obeisance. On the other, they represent one of the United States' biggest global cash cows—bringing in, according to *Business Week*, hundreds of billions of dollars a year. Players like Michael Jordan—who CNN once called "the ultimate global marketing tool"—have brought corporate values and profits together in one smiling red, white, and blue package. But in an increasingly polarized country, the public's acceptance of this package is coming apart. We live in the sports age of the "antihero." Young people are increasingly identifying with athletes who seem to want to tell everybody to go to hell. Or maybe not everybody. When Terrell Owens takes over the game with his bizarre touchdown choreography, risking thousands of dollars in fines, he is bypassing the No Fun League to make a direct connection with the fans. When Barry Bonds starts his own web site to stick it to reporters and "communicate directly with the people who support me," he earns popularity at the same rate he loses endorsements.

But the ultimate antihero—the poster child for everything that flies in the face of corporate America's frantic quest to rectify "values"—and retain wealth—is the Philadelphia 76ers' Allen Iverson. Iverson's nickname is AI but there is nothing artificial about him. When AI was a rookie, he schooled Jordan on a crossover dribble and said afterward "[Jordan] is not my hero. None of my heroes wear suits." Corporate America both drooled and recoiled as interest in the whip-fast, charismatic guard exploded. To this day, they love the way Iverson's jerseys and sneakers fly off the shelves, but can't stand the "baggage" that comes with him. They love his pedigree as a star Virginia high school quarterback and basketball guard and they hate his teenage prison stint for a bowling alley "race riot." (His conviction held such a strong taint of "southern justice" that it was highlighted on *60 Minutes* and the governor eventually pardoned him.) They want him on the cover of their programs and magazines, but despise his multitudinous tattoos so much that they have been known to airbrush them right off his arms. They market him as being "real" and "from the streets" but hate the childhood friends—referred to by fifty-year-old sports columnists as "his posse"—who watch his back. (Funny how it wasn't a "posse" when Mickey Mantle, Whitey Ford, and the crew went drinking and carousing at Toots Shor's.)

But the fans love AI's every transgressive move—especially when combined with his style of play. Iverson has been voted, year in and year out, one of the toughest guys in the league by his peers. He weighs 160 pounds soaking wet, and wouldn't top six feet in a pair of pumps, but never shies from contact, getting more bumps, bruises, and floor burns than any player alive. He is the only player under six feet tall in NBA history to be named the game's MVP and, along with Jordan, is the only player to ever lead the league in points and steals in the same season. Yet for all his on-court efforts, he also thinks nothing about blasting "practice" as a waste of time, saying over and over at a 2001 press conference, with an incredulous roll of his eyes, that he cut practices because "We're talking about practice." Saying "to hell with practice" is a shot at the very idea, pushed by the leagues, that hard work, discipline, and obedience are the parallel lanes of the road to success. Iverson also has never been too shy to state his belief that the notoriously racist Philadelphia police department is out to get him, an opinion that has merit considering the fact that a felony indictment against Iverson for handgun possession in a domestic dispute was revealed as an utter fabrication. League commissioners and corporate sponsors are flummoxed over what to do about Iverson. One answer: Leon.

So who is "Leon"? "Leon" is the personification of corporate America's hatred toward modern Black athletes and anti-heroes. They are striking back, not only at the players themselves, but also at us—the fans—for embracing these antiheroes. We shouldn't accept that. Let's load "Leon" on a bus with Stepin Fetchit, Mammy, Charlie Chan, and that damn Taco Bell Chihuahua—and push it off the pop culture cliff. Until Leon goes, home brew will suit Dave Zirin just fine. ◆

USA Basketball in Black and White!

The United States lords over the Olympics like Alexander the Great. Consequently, for people outside of the United States, rooting against the world's lone superpower has become as natural as cheering for Rocky Balboa. Our defeats are celebrated as dents in the armor. But the last Olympics saw an entirely new phenomenon: people *inside* the Unites States cheering against one U.S. team in particular. And for all the wrong reasons. The bronze medal winning U.S. basketball squad became the team fans in the U.S. loved to hate. According to a national poll, 54 percent of fans said they wanted to see the team of NBA superstars lose—with another 20 percent reporting that they "kind of" wanted to see them taken down.

Some of this animosity is more racist than a Bob Jones University course syllabus. As sports writer Jason Whitlock wrote, it is as if white America got a memo reading:

> [Y]ou do not have to support a group of Black American millionaires in any endeavor. Despite the hypocritical, rabid patriotism displayed immediately after 9/11, it's perfectly suitable for Americans to despise Team USA Basketball, Allen Iverson and all the other tattooed NBA players representing our country. Yes, these athletes are no more spoiled, whiny, and rich than the golfers who fearlessly represent us in the Ryder Cup, but at least Tiger Woods has the good sense not to wear cornrows.

Talk radio has been a fertile breeding ground for this anger. On one show, a caller who identified himself as a former member of the American military said he hates Team USA because they don't "represent the America I fell in love with." When asked to describe the America he fell in love with, he said, "It was a country where you could walk the streets without worrying about being mugged."

Another ESPN morning radio host—in an over-caffeinated frenzy—even called the players "uppity," the classic slur for Black people who "don't know their place." Generally the code is subtler: it is said that this team is "too hip-hop." They "don't care" or they have "too much attitude and swagger" are also popular criticisms. But either way, the meaning is clear to all who take a step back.

Perhaps racial slings and arrows are easier for the sporting public to take than the uncomfortable truth when it comes to explaining Team USA's loss. The straight dope is that the U.S. no longer owns a patent on the game of basketball. Unlike their predecessors of 1992, when the first Dream Team of Magic, Bird, and Jordan posed for pictures and signed autographs for opponents and then won by forty, the teams of Argentina, Italy, Spain, Lithuania, and even Puerto Rico, now play an equal or superior brand of basketball. They weave around the court like they're playing a beautiful game of soccer, with backdoor cuts, infectious flair, and unrestrained emotion. It's no coincidence Argentina won the gold in both basketball and soccer. They play both sports with joy and teamwork that is a wonder to behold.

But instead of analyzing why Argentina won, we get a self-absorbed analysis of why the U.S. lost. Forgotten is the fact that the U.S. team was playing against international teams that have been together for a dozen years. It is also forgotten that these so-called "lazy" players agreed to come while the top NBA stars refused to play. Forgotten is the fact that the NBA is now an international league, with players from Puerto Rico's Carlos Arroyo to Argentina's Manu Ginobli to China's Yao Ming having great success. Most importantly, it is forgotten that international basketball bears about as much resemblance to the NBA as tai chi does to judo.

International ball is a game of constant passing, three-point bombing, sharp-shooting goliaths, packed-in zone defenses, and a paint that is shaped like a geometrician's nightmare—some sort of trapezoid or maybe a rhombus. As former NBA coach Dr. Jack Ramsey wrote, "It may be just about impossible to teach the international game to a group of NBA players in the span of a couple weeks. Coach Brown, and assistants Gregg Popovich and Roy Williams, are among the top coaches in the game today. And they haven't gotten the job done."

The U.S. lost because the organizers of Team USA Basketball—not the players—were arrogant enough to think they could just roll the balls on the court and other teams would genuflect in front of the NBA's marketing might.

Count me as someone who is glad the U.S. was toppled—it's always good to see William "Braveheart" Wallace stick it to Longshanks—but the racist scapegoating reveals all that is bankrupt about the so-called Olympic spirit. Face the facts: Argentina is on top of the basketball world because they can pass, shoot, and run better than anyone in the world. It's a style of play that rests on the basic principle that no individual is superior to the team, a lesson USA basketball has yet to learn. ◆

Rasheed Wallace: The Messenger and the Message

Rasheed Wallace has earned more technical fouls than a Dennis Rodman with Tourrette's syndrome. He has smoked more weed than tailgaters at a Cypress Hill concert. But to truly earn the ire of NBA Commissioner David Stern, you must speak your mind. In a wild, free-ranging interview last year with the *Portland Oregonian*, the man then called the leader of the "Jail Blazers" blew the doors off the New York league offices.

Wallace expressed his view that the NBA is basically a sweatshop with fluffier towels. "I ain't no dumb-ass nigger out here. I'm not like a whole bunch of these young boys out here who get caught up and captivated into the league," Wallace, then twenty-nine, said. "No. I see behind the lines. I see behind the false screens. I know what this business is all about."

Wallace also took a shot at NBA commissioner Stern and his $8 million a year contract. "I know the commissioner of this league makes more than three-quarters of the players in this league," Wallace reported. He then articulated in no uncertain terms that the NBA banks on drafting the young and the ignorant to keep the league afloat:

> In my opinion, they just want to draft niggers who are dumb and dumber—straight out of high school. That's why they're drafting all these high school cats, because they come into the league and they don't know no better. They don't know no better, and they

don't know the real business, and they don't see behind the cha-
rade.... They look at black athletes like we're dumb-ass niggers.
It's as if we're just going to shut up, sign for the money and do
what they tell us.

Stern shot back:

Mr. Wallace's hateful diatribe was ignorant and offensive to all
NBA players. I refuse to enhance his heightened sense of deprivation by publicly debating with him. Since Mr. Wallace did not direct his comments at any particular individuals other than me, I
think it best to leave it to the Trail Blazers organization—and its
players and fans—to determine the attitudes by which they wish
to be defined.

The press was quick to jump on this as the "latest in a series of embarrassing episodes for the 'Jail Blazers.'" Wallace's
words have been lumped in with the team's long list of arrests
for things like marijuana possession, sexual assault, and illegal
possession of pit bulls. Never mind that a reasoned critique
and an arrest record are two completely different things.

Yes, there is no doubt that some of the Blazers make
Cheech and Chong look like Donnie and Marie. Power forward Zach Randolph's high school coach, Moe Smedley, was
quoted as saying, "I just don't want the day to come where I
pick up that paper and it says [Zach] shot someone, or that he
was shot. Every day that goes by that I don't see that, I feel
good." But Stern's smear only proves Wallace's point: the folks
who sign the NBA checks don't really care what these young
men have to say as long as it comes out in saccharine clichés.
Stern didn't speak to why a player making millions of dollars
would feel like he is little more important than the backboard
supports. He didn't explain what the league is doing to educate
eighteen-year-old rookies about handling their money. He did-
n't comment on why so many players, living under a micro-
scope and feeling like targets in public, would not just prefer
but feel absolutely compelled to stay home and smoke weed.

Instead he called Sheed out as being a lunatic and basically instructed the Portland franchise, under fire for a variety of recent episodes, to do something about it. Clearly they did, because before they finally sent Wallace packing to Detroit, he was in front of the cameras apologizing to everyone in the free world. It was almost like he was reading from a telephone book until you realized that the one name he wouldn't single out for apology was David Stern.

Bashing Wallace is a favorite pastime for more than a few writers. I don't know the man. Maybe he is a big, misunderstood teddy bear; maybe he is meaner than Dick Cheney at a solar energy convention. But we should ask why Stern and his ilk are going after the messenger instead of taking on the message. For certain, by going to the Detroit Pistons and helping them win a championship by playing hurt and being a selfless part of a team, Wallace had the last laugh. ◆

Fight Night in the NBA

I don't think we'll be hearing the "NBA Action Is Faaaantastic" slogan revived anytime soon. The aftermath of the most violent player/fan brawl in U.S. sports history has met with the kind of hand-wringing we have come to associate with Janet Jackson's right breast. The fight between several members of the Indiana Pacers and a garrison of Detroit Pistons fans veered wildly from the frightening to the ridiculous.

Representing the frightening were Pacers forwards Ron Artest and Stephen Jackson swinging haymakers at anyone with a potbelly and a Pistons jersey. On the side of the ridiculous were their 5-foot 9-inch, 220-pound combatants, throwing punches at Artest like he was Joey from the block and not a 6-

foot 8-inch pro athlete who could cave in their faces. There was Rick Mahorn of all people—the tough guy of the 1980s Pistons teams, getting up from the broadcast booth and pulling people apart—like an "old timers brawl," of sorts. (I kept waiting for Charles Oakley to emerge from the crowd and hit Mahorn with a folding chair.) And there was that moment when tragedy truly became farce when Rasheed Wallace stepped in as "peacemaker."

What started it? A Pistons fan pelted Artest with a cup of ice. But the minute Artest hurdled into the crowd and started throwing haymakers like Clubber Lang, you knew where NBA commissioner David Stern would bring down the hammer, and he did not disappoint. Artest, the reigning NBA defensive player of the year, received a seventy-three-game suspension, the longest in NBA history. Also getting nailed with historic time away from the court were the Pacers' Stephen Jackson, who got a thirty-game vacation, and All-NBA forward Jermaine O'Neal, who was not only pegged with twenty-five games, but also faces charges for coldcocking a fan off camera in full view of several Auburn Hills' cops.

Whenever an event this out of the ordinary occurs, the sports establishment, ever fearful of a black eye, treats it like an imminent epidemic, and this time, true to form, it has offered PR solutions ranging from banning beer sales to circling armed cops around the court (that is exactly what Friday needed amid the chaos: guns).

What this approach ignores, besides logic, is the opportunity to confront a new phenomenon in U.S. sports: the simmering animosity between ticket-holding (emphasis on ticket-holding) fans and the players. Here, whether Stern and the NBA brass want to discuss it or not, we have a mulligan stew of race, class, and grievance that says a great deal about the uneasy place of pro sports in U.S. society. The first ingredient in this bitter recipe, as columnist Jason Whitlock commented after the brawl, is the fact that "...fans love the sport but just hate pro athletes." Athletes, in the eyes of a minority of fans, are too spoiled, too loud, too "hip-hop," too tattooed, too corn-rowed—all of which translates to players as "too Black." (A New York Black radio station actually said of Artest, "You can take the nigger out of the projects, but you can't take the projects out of the nigger.")

Also, in this era of fantasy leagues, yipping, high-testosterone sports radio, high-ticket prices, and league-sponsored EA Sports video games that wallow in computerized bench-clearing brawls, fans more than ever see themselves as participants and not observers (the EA sports slogan actually is "get in the game"). Those fans in Auburn Hills, $50 tickets in hand, believe it is not only their right but their duty to throw punches at opposing players if the opportunity presents itself. One striking scene from the Auburn Hills fight was when a man clearly on the gray side of forty appeared to be pulling at Artest to break up the fight, and then threw three straight rabbit punches to the back of the 6-foot 8-inch forward's head.

This man also happened to be white, which brings us to the other element in the fan/athlete resentathon. NBA players, the overwhelming majority of whom come from poor, inner city backgrounds, don't look at the stands and think, "Hey! What a terrific group of forty-year-old white guys I'm going to be dunking for this evening!" As one player said to me, "I look at the seats and don't see anyone from my old hood or anybody that looks anything like me. It's like you're a monkey in a cage." So we have angry white fans trying to punch out angry Black players with the players returning the favor. This animosity is very real and not going anywhere.

And we will pause a moment to note that although these were Detroit fans, the brawl did not happen in Detroit proper;

it happened in Auburn Hills, an upper class suburb made famous in Michael Moore's *Bowling for Columbine*. Those of you who saw the film may remember the woman from the impoverished city of Flint, Michigan, whose six-year-old son shot and killed his classmate while his mother was struggling to keep a roof over his head by working two jobs under the auspices of Michigan's welfare-to-work program. She was bused eighty miles roundtrip, according to Moore, to "mix drinks and make fudge for rich people." And what was the site of her indenture? Auburn Hills.

This cauldron is also heated by the violence that engulfs U.S. society more broadly—not street violence, but the state-sanctioned variety. ESPN has replayed the "horror" of the fight ad nauseam, in color, in black and white, with all kinds of slow-motion effects and from countless revealing angles. They have reveled in this fight, crying all the way to the ratings bank. But as the "World Wide Leader" cries over thrown punches, remember that this is the same network that shot a week's worth of *SportsCenter*s in Kuwait, on a set made up to look like a machine gun nest. Ask the people in Fallujah what violence really looks like, and what role a network like ESPN plays in promoting the acceptance of such carnage. One NBA players union rep quite correctly tried to place the brawl in context, commenting that "Yes it was violent. But there is violence everywhere. There is violence in war." This is a thoughtful comment with at least a dollop of perspective. He will probably be fired.

Because the main players in the debate over what to do about violence in sports seem to be allergic to trying to look at any broader context. Discussions are raging across ESPN and the talk radio spectrum asking if "the NBA should disassociate with hip hop" (whatever that means) and whether the influx of players straight out of high school has led to a "thug life" mentality in the league. Of course, no one is saying that seventeen-year-old Yugoslavian players like Darko Milicic shouldn't be adopted (I mean drafted) by teams—just players named Qyntel, Kwame, and LeBron. Like so much in this barely coded discussion of athletes, fans, and violence, it comes down to race. When very Caucasian Yankees pitcher Jeff Nelson and utility infielder Karim Garcia pulled a heckling special-ed teacher out of the Fenway Park stands in the 2003 playoffs and pummeled him, it was a "brawl." When Roger Clemens, also white, threw a splintered bat at Mike Piazza in the World Series, Clemens' behavior was ascribed to his being overly competitive and "wound too tight." But when it is Black athletes throwing the punches, all the language changes. The Pacers/Piston fans brouhaha becomes—as ESPN is now routinely calling it—a "riot."

None of this is to excuse what broke loose in Auburn Hills. Without question, the assaults were as ugly as anything seen in an NBA arena since Paul Mokeski. Artest is a troubled young person who recently took the number ninety-one as a tribute to Dennis Rodman. But, unlike Rodman, who in his spare time took part in World Championship Wrestling shows and cheesy action flicks with Jean Claude Van Damme, Artest has never seen basketball as entertainment or spectacle and has had real issues with rage. *Washington Post* columnist Michael Wilbon has said for years that Artest's much talked about on court "antics" and flagrant fouls were not funny and that someone in Pacers management needs to step in and get him professional help before "something terrible happens."

But instead, league commissioner David Stern and his corporate backers are satisfied with kicking dirt on Artest—saying he will need to reapply to even rejoin the league next year. Yet fans are starting to show up in stadiums with Artest jerseys. This show of solidarity stems from a broader anger: anger at racism, anger at poverty, anger at the hypocrisy of a value system that cries out against violence on the court while imprisoning millions at home and bombing cities to the Stone Age abroad. This anger must be addressed, or there will be no end to Fight Nights in the NBA. ◆

Out of the Darkness: From Miners to Fab

In the early 1990s, college basketball was turned on its head by five freshmen from the University of Michigan. Before the arrival of the "Fab Five," it was believed that seniors or at the very least "mature" juniors were critical for any team wanting to reach the Final Four. But then five first-year blue chippers— Chris Webber, Juwan Howard, Jalen Rose, Ray Jackson, and Jimmy King—made history by starting for consecutive finals teams. They scowled through all conventional wisdom about the limitations of underclassmen and brashly stalked the court in shorts baggy enough to take flight on midwestern winds. Each player had a role: Webber was the talented throat-slashing leader and Rose his swaggering sidekick. Howard was the low post rock in the middle, while King and Jackson rounded out the picture. They became legends of March. But then the brass at the University of Michigan, scurrying under the floorboards to avoid the harsh light of NCAA sanctions against the Fab Five, took down the Final Four banners and literally expunged the players' names from the record books. The Fab Five have now officially never existed.

It was not the first time that Black players of infinite confidence crashed head-on into a college basketball establishment girded in conservatism. The victory of the 1966 Texas Western Miners also exploded notions of what champions were supposed to be. The 1966 Miners were the first all African-American starting five to win the NCAA championship game. Their legend was burnished further because they vanquished a Kentucky team led by fabled coach and arch segregationist Adolph Rupp. But the Miners of Texas Western have been grossly misrepresented over the years. The story has been that by using "urban" Black players, Texas Western's "athleticism" overwhelmed the Kentucky farm boys—as story that shows about as much respect for the truth as disappearing the Fab Five.

The short-lived glory and ultimate erasure of the Fab Five—almost forty years after the Miners schooled Adolph and Kentucky—indicate both how far college basketball has come and how much further it still has to go when it comes to judgments based on merit. Understanding Texas Western's success helps us to understand why the Fab Five were thrown to the wolves. In fact, a thread of connection stretches between the two teams like deep-sea fishing line, strong but so clear that it doesn't immediately catch the eye.

Major League Miners

The official story of the 1966 NCAA championship, in which Kentucky's "fundamentally sound and intelligent" (read white) five were jumped over by the "high flying" (read athletic and brainless) Blacks of Texas Western has, of course, very racist roots. "Hot" Rod Hundley, the former West Virginia and Lakers star, said at the time about Texas Western, "They can do everything with the basketball but sign it." James H. Jackson of the *Baltimore Sun* wrote, "The Miners, who don't worry much about defense but try to pour the ball through the hoop as much as possible, will present quite a challenge to Kentucky. The running, gunning Texas quintet can do more things with a basketball than a monkey on a 50-foot jungle wire."

In fact, as columnist Frank Fitzpatrick analyzed in a brilliant breakdown of old game footage, the Miners were far from flashy.

They more accurately fit their moniker, playing a lunch-pail style brand of ball that stressed defense and rebounding. The Miners gave up a scant sixty-two points a game, and in the pre-shot clock era, didn't so much walk as trudge the ball up the court. "We played the most intelligent, the most boring, the most disciplined game of them all," said Texas Western guard Willie Worsley. This approach put shackles on a Kentucky team that tried to turn the game into a track meet. In reality, the roles were the reverse of what appeared in the sports pages; in reality, it was the white Kentucky team that relied on athleticism—and lost.

Yet the one thing the mythmakers can't obscure is the psychological importance of the contest for the emerging civil rights movement sweeping the south. The Black freedom struggle, which would explode on the athletic scene during the 1968 Olympics in Mexico City, was still in its infancy. The young Muhammad Ali was speaking out on war and racism, but beyond, or perhaps because of, Ali, the dominant attitude was that sports should be kept hermetically sealed from politics. Yet the walls that upheld this separation were starting to crack due to bombardments from both sides. Before the game, Kentucky coach Rupp allegedly vowed that "five Negroes" would never beat his team. Whether Rupp said it or not, Texas Western coach Don Haskins told his team of Adolph's promise. This was not something to say in 1966 when Blacks were being stoned and beaten across the south for demanding civil rights. Texas Western players made their own locker room vow that Rupp would eat his words.

On the Miners' second possession, Miners center David Lattin slammed a forceful dunk over Kentucky's Pat Riley. "[Lattin] said, 'Take that you white honky,'" recalled Riley—the future Hall of Fame NBA coach. "It was a violent game. I don't mean there were any fights—but they were desperate and they were committed and they were more motivated than we were." In the end, Rupp choked on the loss.

This was a proper capstone for a man who can be likened without exaggeration to George Wallace with a clipboard. When school president John Oswald ordered Rupp to desegregate, he reportedly let out the plaintive whine, "That son of a bitch is ordering me to get some niggers in here. What am I going to do?"

Unlike other legendary southern coaches, like Alabama's Bear Bryant, who recanted any role he might have played in buttressing the system of Jim Crow, Rupp was unrepentant, and the bitterness of that 1966 loss ate him alive. "[He] carried the memory of that game to his grave," wrote his biographer, Russell Rice. Friends noted that, even as he was dying from cancer in a Lexington hospital in 1977, the old coach lamented to visitors about the loss.

"No one will remember him without remembering us," said Texas Western's Harry Flournoy. "And I guess there is a certain justice to that."

The contest's symbolic magnitude, occurring in the eye of the Black freedom struggle, transformed it into far more than just a game. Over time, the contest's aura has only grown, taking on the feel of a bygone era, aided both by the fact that Texas Western no longer exists (having renamed itself the University of Texas El Paso), and that, in those days of pre-Vitale innocence, the finals, far from the billion-dollar spectacle they are today, were played on tape delay with the grainy production values of an amateur stag film. Seen past the stereotypes, Texas Western versus Kentucky is the athletic equivalent of the march on Selma Bridge, or a confrontation at a Greensboro lunch counter.

Miners to Fabulous

When the Fab Five—Webber, Rose, Jackson, King, and Howard—came onto the Michigan campus in the fall of 1991, they never had to face Bull Connor, attack dogs, or burning crosses. Instead, they were confronted with people's preju diced perceptions of youth, rebellion, and hip-hop, as well as a certain resentment over their elation at being young, gifted, and Black. The talent was obvious. Within two months of their freshman year, *Sports Illustrated* even suggested Webber for the NBA-led 1992 Olympic Dream Team.

The Fab Five took a squad that went 14-15 the season before they arrived and grabbed it by the throat. Their freshman year, Michigan improved to 25-9. Their sophomore season, the Wolves went 31-5. The Fab Five didn't lose in the 1992 NCAA Tournament until the final against Duke and were victorious in the 1993 tournament until the unforgettable championship game against North Carolina when Webber, with seconds remaining and pressured by Tar Heel defenders, called a timeout Michigan didn't have, perhaps costing Michigan the victory.

Those games remain the two most watched in College Basketball history. And these finals defeats didn't affect their standing in the eyes of a growing fan base. The Fab Five had an outlaw image their fans embraced. "Michigan was one of the first anti-establishment programs in college," says former Wolverine and NBA player Tim McCormick. "It gave them a freshness." Not unlike the then newly emerging gangster rap music being consumed in mass quantities by both urban and suburban youth, the Fab Five came to represent everything street-tough and badass. And the Michigan administration rode the chest-thumping squad right to the bank. Wolverine gear royalties more than tripled, from $2 million in the pre-Fab year of 1990–1991 to a peak of $6.2 million in 1993–1994.

"Kids could relate to the 'Fab Five' and wanted to emulate them. Wearing Michigan merchandise became a way that you could transform yourself into being as 'cool' as the 'Fab Five,'" says Derek Eiler of the Atlanta-based Collegiate Licensing Co. Not surprisingly, the Fab Five's profile and success attracted leagues of social parasites, willing to slip them walking-around money at a moment's notice. But NCAA players aren't allowed to make money—only have money made off them. Sanctions followed, and now that these scandals have come to light and the Michigan brass has safely laundered their millions, they are scrambling to literally erase any mention of the Fab Five or their legacy. Why go to this extreme? In an echo of 1966, their old coach Steve Fisher has an explanation for the backlash that may bridge the distance from Ann Arbor to El Paso "Five black kids starting at the University of Michigan, that might have offended some Michigan people. Not many would admit to that fact, but it might have."

Fisher's words raise the question of how much progress has actually been made since 1966. Black students no longer have to stare down the dogs and hoses. We no longer see Adolph Rupp sneering across the court. But our March Madness heroes still toil in indentured servitude, are still prey to a new breed of racist stereotypes. The Final Four is a billion-dollar industry built on the backs of players who don't see a dime. The Miners of Texas Western kicked open a door—the sin of the Fab Five was daring to act like they owned a piece of the house. ◆

When Chickens Roost: Why Rush Was Flushed

Even in Rush Limbaugh's loneliest grade-school dreams— dreamt while waiting in vain to be picked to play during recess—he probably never imagined the coverage he would get in the nation's sports sections in the fall of 2003.

Limbaugh ignited a sporting world inferno by wheezing on ESPN's NFL pre-game show that Eagles QB Donovan McNabb is "overrated" because of the "media's social concern" to see a successful Black quarterback.

Before you could say "big fat idiot" three times, the man who says he has "talent on loan from God" was in the eye of a media hurricane. Never one to defend his rancid ideas publicly, Limbaugh refused an opportunity to respond on ESPN, and chose instead to play martyr and resign. I don't want to say Rush is a coward, but he would sooner sing "We Shall Overcome" in a pink thong than debate outside the friendly confederate confines of right-wing talk radio.

It's understandable why some would say that skewering Limbaugh for this is like prosecuting Capone for tax evasion. No one in power said a peep when Rush told an African-American caller to "Shut up and get the bone out of your nose," or when he once asked, "Why does every criminal composite photo look like Jesse Jackson?" One anti-Rush local named "Steve" called into a national sports radio talk show furious that it took a quarterback controversy to call out Limbaugh. "We've got black folk in jail and in the army because they can't get a job, with HIV, and no one gets mad about that," he shouted, "but you insult a quarterback and all of a sudden all hell breaks loose!"

But to me, the outcry over Rush, even for this relative misdemeanor, was quite welcome. When people like him are allowed to spew it gives all bigots license. Reverend Pat Robertson of the *700 Club* recently said,

> There is, without question, an incredible effort on the part of the media to elevate these minorities into positions of prominence, at least if nothing else in fictional stories. You look at Morgan Freeman who is a tremendous actor. He started off playing a chauffer in *Driving Miss Daisy* and then they elevated him to head of the CIA and then they elevated him to President and in his last role they made him God. I just wonder, isn't Rush Limbaugh right to question the fact, is he that good an actor or not? And was there a preference given? The same thing with the quarterback, did they give him a break?

Hello? The good Reverend doesn't get it. Rush did more than insult a quarterback. He applied his apartheid view of the world to the NFL, using McNabb to jab at affirmative action and raise the question of whether the new wave of Black quarterbacks is just a creation of politically correct media hype.

Columnist E.J. Dionne of the *Washington Post* thinks this ticked everyone off because people don't want politics in their sports. Dionne argued, "Most of us who love sports want to forget about politics when we watch games. Sports, like so many other voluntary activities, create connections across political lines. All Americans who are rooting for the Red Sox in the play-offs are my friends this month, no matter what their ideology."

Dionne believes that people love sports precisely because they are divorced from politics. But Dionne is, as per his custom, dead wrong. Of course, you don't have to believe sports are political—just as you don't have to believe, as the saying goes, in gravity to fall out of an airplane. But in an era in which professional football stadiums are shamelessly spun as community development programs, siphoning off millions of dollars in public money into commercial enterprise while the public school budget is cut—one can hardly say that sports exist in a separate world from politics.

But what Dionne, and on another level, Rush, don't get is that, in sports, we see our own dreams and aspirations played out in dynamic Technicolor. Politics are remote and alien to the vast majority of people. But the playing field is where we can project our every thought, fear, and hope. We want to believe fiercely that it's the one place where ability alone is how we are judged. If you can play, you *will* play, no matter your color. This is why boxers like Joe Louis and the great Ali, Olympic stars like Tommy Smith and John Carlos, tennis players like Billie Jean King and the Williams sisters, and even golf's Tiger Woods (although he would never want the title) are viewed as political beings—carriers of the dream that all doors are open to all people.

The job of NFL quarterback has been one of the final athletic frontiers for the African-American athlete. This year, more than twenty Black QBs were on NLF rosters, an all-time high. The racist tune has always been that African Americans just aren't "smart enough" to play quarterback. And if they did play quarterback, they would be the "running and athletic" as opposed to the "thinking" variety. A reporter asked Randall Cunningham, when the Eagles drafted him in 1984, "What makes you think you are smart enough to read NFL defenses?" Doug Williams was asked, "How long have you been a Black quarterback?" before the 1988 Super Bowl. But, fortunately, this stereotype has not been able to survive the play of QBs McNabb, Michael Vick, Daunte Culpepper, Byron Leftwich, and 2003 NFL co-MVP Steve McNair, who proved definitively that it was racism, and not any lack of ability, that kept Black players out of the quarterback position.

When Rush attempted to resuscitate the old minstrel tune, he stepped on the third rail of our collective illusions. He ignited fury by reminding people that open doors could always be shut. The unholy hypocrites like Limbaugh and Robertson, in my view, are barreling toward a golden age of comeuppance. People in power should take heed: if you spit on people's dreams, you will be flushed just like Rush. ◆

CHAPTER EIGHT

Taking Care of T-C-B: Sports, Sexism, and Gay Bashing

Scholars examining the role of women in sports have produced enough books, studies, and analyses to stock the Library of Congress—and for good reason. On the one hand, sexism of stomach-turning proportions prevails both within and surrounding professional sports, from the cheerleaders to the beer commercials. But sports have also provided a critical place for women to challenge sexist ideas about their abilities and potential. In the 1960s, Olympic athlete "Racey" Lacey O'Neal learned what it was like to be a star athlete in an era when women were still expected to be on the sidelines. Tennis player Billie Jean King, a leading icon in the 1970s women's rights movement, defeated "chauvinist pig" Bobby Riggs and not only scored a symbolic victory but also led a fight for material gains for women.

Despite these and other examples of progress, there is no denying the persistence of sexism in sports today. Katie Hnida, a former University of Colorado student, attempted to become the place kicker for the school's football team, and was attacked every which way for her trouble. And in sports, oppression operates on more than one level: a combination of sexism and homophobia produced chromosome checks for women, while the recent rape trial of Kobe Bryant demonstrates how racism and sexism can intersect with fame and fortune. Homophobia, as prevalent in sports as sexism but discussed far less often, is still largely accepted in the macho world of big-time athletics. Attitudes are beginning to

shift, and that should be recognized, but the openly gay male athlete remains a lasting taboo.

...in Numbers Too Big to Ignore?

What does the most watched basketball game in ESPN history
have in common with Michael Jordan, Shaquille O'Neal, or
Kobe Bryant? Not a damned thing. The most viewed basketball
contest in the network's history was a women's game. Five million homes tuned in to see the University of Connecticut
Huskies trounce the Tennessee Volunteers 70-61 in the 2004
NCAA championship. In front of a raucous, sold-out crowd,
UConn's three-time All-American guard, Diana Taurasi, played
her last collegiate game and went out in style. Taurasi, for those
basketball fans who have either missed or avoided her and the
women's game, is like Pete Maravich with a ponytail, with a re-
lease on her shot so fast it looks like she's setting a volleyball.

The success of this game would seem to bode well for the
professional Women's National Basketball Association
(WNBA). Without question, the WNBA has developed a core
of fiercely devoted fans—like Norma Havranek of Rockville,
Maryland, who hasn't missed a Washington Mystics game
since their debut in 1998. "I'm 75 years old, and I've waited for
women to get something for a long time," she told the *Washington Post*. "I really don't want this league to disappear because I
think if it did, I would go with it."

But while some franchises have found success, others have
folded faster than a rib joint in Tel Aviv. WNBA TV ratings are
microscopic, with little hope for improvement. There are many
reasons for this, from the overexpansion of the league to an
NBA-style marketing strategy that focuses on individual (and,

not coincidentally, telegenic) players—despite the fact that the women's game tends to be more team oriented, similar to the way men play basketball in Europe and South America, with an emphasis on cutting, passing, and a motion offense. Many franchises also suffer because it has become fashionable to hold the league up to constant derision and ridicule. Just as the boundaries for sexism have expanded in other forums in recent years—from the idolization of Britney and the mainstreaming of "gentlemen's clubs" to the *Maxim* clones that wallpaper magazine stands—it seems that no shot is too cheap to be out of bounds when it come to the WNBA.

Syndicated national radio host Tom Leykis, for one, suggested that the WNBA should change team names to things like "Denver Dykes," "Boston Bitches," and the "San Francisco Snatch." While Leykis represents the worst of the worst, the jeers don't spew from men alone. As Stacey Pressman, a contributing writer for ESPN and the Rupert Murdoch owned *Weekly Standard* wrote last year,

> Women's basketball sucks [now *that's* incisive writing!].... Political correctness has crept out of the academy and into the sports establishment. No one is allowed to say anything negative about women's basketball in fear of coming across as sexist—or worse. [I love when right-wing hacks whine about not having a voice…in national magazines.] In men's sports, ratings are everything. With women's sports, no one cares so long as you're 'on message.' The WNBA is so political that its website has an entire zone devoted to 'Show Your Support for Title IX.' [Of course, without the women's movement and Title IX women sports journalists like Stacey Pressman would still be confined to writing about society teas and zinnia festivals.] They're going to jam women's basketball down your throat UNTIL YOU LIKE IT! [Her caps. I don't use caps when I write unless I am critiquing A RIGHT-WING HACK.]

Remarks like those of Leykis and Pressman—and the UConn game itself—show that while there is a huge audience for women's sports, we still have far to go before there is equality and fair play, on and off the playing field. Despite the massive steps forward since the landmark Title IX legislation of the 1970s, sexism still runs through U.S. sports on every level. Women's bodies are constantly used to sell everything from commercial products to the games themselves. Women are systematically marginalized at every level of play, and female athletes face routine and sometimes violent harassment. Fear of strong, confident women who don't need a push-up bra to be noticed at a sporting event persists to this day. According to the Women's Sports Foundation, the only women to grace the cover of *Sports Illustrated* magazine in 2001—apart from models posing for the swimsuit issue—were the Dallas Cowboy Cheerleaders.

From Title IX to Today

Yet despite this systematic backlash, more women than ever participate in organized sports. Title IX, the law guaranteeing equity in athletics won by the women's rights movement of the 1960s and seventies, has had a seismic impact on girls' and women's participation in sports, and the effects of these extended opportunities reach far beyond the playing fields: young girls who play sports are less likely to suffer from eating disorders, be involved in abusive relationships, or drop out of high school. According to the Women's Sports Foundation, one in twenty-seven high school girls played sports twenty-five years ago; one in three do today. Before Title IX, fewer than 32,000 women participated in college sports; today that number exceeds 150,000—nearly five times the pre-Title IX rate.

A recent study by scholars R. Vivian Acosta and Linda Jean Carpenter illustrates the impact of Title IX on the collegiate level. The average number of women's teams per school is at an all-time high of 8.34, compared with two per school when Title IX was enacted in 1972, and 5.61 in 1978, when schools were expected to be in compliance. In just one year, 2001 to

2002, 118 women's teams were added. Basketball, volleyball, and soccer are the three most offered sports for women, followed by tennis, cross country, and softball.

Despite these gains, women and girls continue to face a very unlevel playing field. Across the country, girls get 1.1 million fewer high school sports participation opportunities than boys. Women also get 133 million less college athletic scholarship dollars than men and 58,000 (38 percent) fewer opportunities to participate than males at the college level.

This disparity goes right to the top. Of the sixteen schools that made it to the NCAA "Sweet Sixteen" of men's basketball in 2004, only one had a woman Athletic Director—the University of Nevada at Las Vegas (UNLV). None had women as head coaches or assistant coaches, which shouldn't surprise anyone since only 2 percent of male collegiate teams are headed by females. Even within women's collegiate sports, only 44 percent of the coaches of women's teams are women, the lowest level ever recorded. When Title IX was enacted in 1972, that number was more than 90 percent.

There are no women at all on the coaching staffs of NBA teams, and even in the WNBA, the majority of teams have male head coaches. But at least the WNBA provides a place for women to play professional basketball. The only other professional league for women is the temporarily defunct professional women's soccer league, the WUSA. Within these leagues, women face astounding disparities when it comes to pay. WNBA players average $55,000 per season while the men make $4.5 million. There is also pressure on women to take pay cuts—to "sacrifice" in order to maintain the profitability of the league. WNBA players were encouraged during their 2004 contract negotiations to mimic the actions of famed soccer player Mia Hamm, who was paid $60,000 instead of her rightful $94,000 in order to support the WUSA. This strategy proved its bankruptcy as the WUSA still went under financially. Of course, WUSA's bad business practices could not dim Hamm's brilliance—though they did help to ensure that said brilliance was ignored. ◆

"Mia Culpa": The All-Too Quiet Retirement of Mia Hamm

Washington Post columnist Michael Wilbon called Mia Hamm, "Perhaps the most important athlete of the last 15 years." This may sell her a bit short. Hamm, with little fanfare, retired recently at the age of thirty-two. She and her signature bobbing ponytail walked away from the U.S. National team that signed her up at the age of fifteen. Hamm departs as the all-time leading goal scorer, male or female, in the history of international soccer competition, with 158 scores. She also leaves the field of play with the one-name stature accorded a select few: Magic, Peyton, Michael, Shaq, Mia.

Mia Hamm's retirement should have been *Sports Illustrated* cover material. We should be able to wallpaper the halls of Congress with tributes to her greatness. Instead, the broad media silence that greeted her departure—beyond the ghettoes of soccer sportswriting—was deafening.

It would be tempting to just say that Hamm, always quiet, always humble, never the one to rip off her shirt after a goal or criticize teammates who did, left with the same reserved dignity that defined her play. It would be tempting, but as Samuel L. Jackson said in *Pulp Fiction*, "That shit just ain't the truth."

The testosterone-addled talking heads of sports always moan and groan about the lack of role models, difference makers, and dignity in sports. Yet when faced with the opportunity to highlight a career defined by these ideals, they looked the other way. Instead, we had another week about what Barry Bonds was or was not ingesting, whom Ron Artest did or did not punch, and what Ricky Williams is or is not smoking.

The lack of response to Hamm's retirement is yet another example of how women are forced to sit in the back of the athletic bus. Call it the "Kournikova effect," (named after Anna Kournikova, who made it to the cover of *Sports Illustrated* without ever having won a single tournament.) It's not enough for a woman to have blistering athletic talent. She also has to date cheesy celebrities, strip to her skivvies, and basically become Paris Hilton with muscle tone to generate any attention. If Mia Hamm was shtupping Justin Timberlake, or had appeared in *Playboy*'s September 2004 "Women of the Olympics" issue, her retirement might have generated some more ink. Good thing she married shortstop Nomar Garciaparra, a fact that forced its way into every story written about her decision to leave the league.

The shame of it is that—even absent paparazzi puke—Hamm's story justifies thorough examination. At thirty, she is roughly the same age as Title IX. Like all the 1960s reforms that improved the lives of women, people of color, and the poor, Title IX has been subject to a well-organized and well-funded backlash. Mia Hamm, who can be painfully shy, has carried, through her play, the symbolic weight of everything about Title IX that is indomitable and will not be turned back.

She bears this burden because, of all athletic programs affected by Title IX, the most profound impact has been on soccer. Women's soccer is now offered on nearly 88 percent of college campuses compared to only 2.8 percent in 1977. Through these openings, denied to women of previous generations, Hamm dazzled and became the first superstar that U.S.

Mia Hamm, forward on the U.S. National Women's Soccer Team, gets ready to un-leash a shot on the net against the Russia National Team during first half action in the 1998 U.S. Women's Cup at Frontier Field in Rochester, New York. (AP/Don Heupel)

women's team sports ever produced. She starred for the U.S. squad that won the 1991 World Cup championships and Olympic gold medals in 1996 and 2003. She was also the focal point for the national team that beat China in the historic 1999

World Cup final, which drew a crowd of 90,000 to the Rose Bowl and attracted a television audience of 40 million. Throughout her brilliant career, in the words of one writer, Hamm "undoubtedly inspired more girls to step onto a playing surface than all other female athletes combined."

In honoring the retiring Hamm, along with teammates Julie Foudy and Joy Fawcett, U.S. national team coach April Heinrichs said, "Think of it this way: Imagine that Magic, Larry Bird, Michael Jordan, Shaq, Kobe, and LeBron were all on one team for 15 years. That's what we have had with our women's national team."

Their play was so inspired, and the attention they received so profound, they were harnessed with the ultimate "compliment" when Bill Clinton joined the players' husbands and partners in a special stadium box for the game against China. Women were perhaps for the first time deemed a worthy vehicle for the ugly side of international competition: the kind of nationalism and saber rattling usually reserved for men's contests. It was the success against China that spawned the WUSA, and the failure of the league says more about the limits of corporate sponsorship and fan frenzy when not playing the "evil Chinese" than it does about the potential popularity of women's soccer.

The folding of the WUSA undoubtedly dimmed the light on Mia Hamm in recent years, but her last game was fitting material for an athletic epitaph. Hamm racked up two stellar assists that defy description. On the first assist, Hamm took a pass in the right corner of the box, started dribbling to her left, then to her right, faked back to her left, then raced around an off-balance defender. With goalkeeper Pamela Tajonar sliding to her left to cut off the angle, Hamm rolled a well-paced pass across the center of the box, and a hard charging teammate crushed a shot into the net. Hamm recorded another assist on a corner kick that sent the ball curling just over the goalie's outstretched hands and into the center of the box, where a teammate headed it into the goal. "Scoring is fun," she said. "But it's also fun to watch your teammates enjoying the game."

Hamm made a point of going to the stands to sign autographs, with some of the young fans lingering for more than an hour after the game. This is the way of life for an athlete who never shirked the responsibility to tirelessly promote her sport, or personify the athletic hopes and dreams of a generation of young girls. Mia Hamm earned this place by showing through her everyday play that women could equal or exceed a man's blood, sweat, and tears. She exhibited in practice that men do not own exclusive rights to the wicked dynamism that is athletic greatness.

As Heinrichs said when the retirement celebration drew to a close, "They had an impact on America's consciousness, on women's sports, on women's voices."

Having an "impact on women's voices" won't get you in *People* magazine, but it means a legacy for Mia Hamm that is richer and more resonant than yesterday's tabloids. Her legacy is one that will echo in our demands for women's equality in the generations to come. ◆

Harassment and Violence Against Women: The Case of Katie Hnida

In early 2002, George Bush, with grinning wife Laura at his side, announced that the U.S. would commit billions of dollars and thousands of troops to "liberate" the women of Afghanistan as part of the "war on terror." Maybe the Bush gang should have taken a practice run in Boulder, Colorado.

In March 2004, Colorado University, the home of the Buffaloes, was revealed to be ground zero in a campaign of sexist terror designed to recruit high school football athletes. Buffaloes Football coach Gary Barnett oversaw a program where escort services, strippers, and "alcohol-fueled sex parties" were just another part of "big-time football." Barnett and his staff brewed an atmosphere of sex and entitlement that finally exploded in their faces. Seven women came forward with allegations of rape and sexual assault at the behest of the football program. In the eye of this storm was a young woman who tried to be nothing more than a teammate to Barnett's Buffs—Katie Hnida.

Like Mia Hamm, Lisa Leslie, or Sue Bird, Hnida is a child of Title IX. Thanks to the women's movement she had athletic opportunities unimaginable to her mother's generation. But Hnida strived to do more than star for the women's soccer or softball teams: she wanted to be a placekicker and play football with the boys. As an All-World kicker in high school, Ms. Hnida thought she could make history by walking onto the Colorado football team.

If Barnett's Buffaloes so blithely abused women in their frat houses and classrooms, you can imagine what it was like for Katie Hnida on the practice field. First, she was told to go to hell. When that didn't work, footballs were whizzed at her head. Her body was grabbed at, her face slapped. Coach Barnett looked the other way as every practice became informally designed to drive her off the team. The abuse escalated until, according to Katie Hnida, she was raped. I say "according to Katie Hnida" because she decided not to press sexual assault charges—for now. Despite what the university has said, she reserves the right to press charges in the future and promises to do so.

Coach Barnett's response, when confronted with Ms. Hnida's allegations of rape, was to smear her playing ability, saying she was "only a girl" and a "terrible" player. This has earned him a suspension—with pay. Barnett damns himself as a coach, not only because of his lack of sensitivity or contrition, but also because of his pathetic inability to judge character—especially the character of the "terrible girl." The fact that Katie Hnida got out of bed every day to endure whatever the football team had in store shows her to be an athlete with far more determination and courage than Barnett could ever hope to appreciate.

Barnett knows "the bottom line" is wins, losses, and revenue, not the well-being of his players—especially any female ones. Big-time universities, especially state schools like Colorado, are becoming more dependent than ever on the cash that a mega-football program can provide. There is tremendous pressure to secure the "best" talent, and since the NCAA insists they truck only in "amateur" athletes, services cannot be secured with money. Therefore, sex—the warped version of sex the Barnetts of the world traffic in—is presented as payment. When the Katie Hnidas of the world step into such a situation, the very presence of a three-dimensional woman—nobody's girl—throws the whole system into question, forcing the Barnetts to either change or attack. He chose to attack because it required no courage and that's where the money is. As Colorado professor Ira Chernus has written, "Here in Boulder, they got private millions to enlarge the football stadium and deck it out with skyboxes. Every game day, those boxes are filled with corporate executives who stay warm and drink the game away at exorbitant rents—as long as the team is winning."

Although Katie Hnida chose not to press sexual assault charges, she did decide to move on. Now she kicks for the New Mexico Lobos. She recently said, "I have been able to play a game I love so much and also be part of a team that is like a family." Her experience has been so rewarding that she is petitioning the NCAA for a sixth season of eligibility. After all she has been through, Katie Hnida wants nothing more than more time on the field and more time as part of the team. Pity Barnett and the Buffs. They pushed away the toughest jock on campus. ◆

Homophobia: Navratilova's Chromosomes Are Just Fine

Women's participation in sports has always been a threat to the gender roles prescribed from on high. From the beginning, talented female athletes have faced taunts of acting—or being—male. As female athletes defy stereotypes of physical limitation, they undermine society's notions of women's abilities, destabilizing gender roles, and producing in many a response of fear and hatred rather than an admiration of athletic greatness. Some of the sharpest expressions of this fear are homophobic attacks on lesbian athletes and the depiction of all female athletes as "masculine."

To this day, women are forced to comply with mandatory "sex testing" in the Olympics, which was instituted by the International Olympic Committee (IOC) in 1968. Most find the testing to be demeaning and intrusive to say the least. Olympic heptathlete Jane Frederick, quoted in Susan Cahn's *Coming on Strong*, describes the effect: "I think they are saying, you are so good, we can't believe you are a woman. So prove it."

By 1985, tennis star Martina Navratilova had racked up millions of dollars in tournament winnings and earned international celebrity for her towering talent. She won six consecutive grand slam events, a feat never achieved before or since. At the time, she had made more money playing tennis than anyone in tennis history, male or female. While Navratilova had her share of admirers, she also faced a barrage of criticism for being "too good." Much of this criticism was shorthand for looking, playing, and acting "manly." Rather than being allowed to enjoy her celebrity, Navratilova constantly had to ward off homophobic attacks—like the comment by a player she defeated who said Navratilova "must have a chromosome loose somewhere." But Martina did not shy away from the issue. Instead, she helped push the discussion forward by coming out as a proud lesbian and giving her partner a prominent spot in the "family section" of matches. By confronting the homophobia around her, Martina has transcended the pantheon of great women players to earn a place among those like Ali and Jackie Robinson who were not content to let only their play do the talking for them.

Looking Back to Move Forward

Fear of women's "intrusion" into the world of sports is as old as the games themselves—but so is struggle against every barrier put in their place. This can be seen by going back to the dawn of our recently completed "sports century." The period around 1900 was a boom time for quack medicine. A fetid stew of doctors, phrenologists, and social Darwinists were busy devising theories about African Americans and other brown people's predisposition to laziness and criminal activity. Any ethnic group that attempted to assert itself was immediately analyzed, dissected and, lo and behold, discovered to be inferior to the well-to-do folks funding the studies.

As women became involved in athletics, the quacks turned their attention to the "weaker sex." They expressed a deep alarm that competitive sports would cause women everything from "harm to their fragile nervous system" to "collapsed uteruses, contracted vaginas, and unwarranted menstruation."

These studies did not appear because women started dribbling basketballs. They were part of a backlash directed at the rising movement for women's suffrage. This struggle was giving women the confidence to demand equality in all walks of life, and athletic achievement was a stirring symbol of all that could be achieved. Women, primarily middle- and upper-class women, entered the field in certain sports, such as cycling and archery. In 1895, nineteen years before women won the right to vote, suffragette Elizabeth Cady Stanton wrote "Many a woman is riding to the suffrage on a bike."

But by the 1910s, in workplaces around the country, industrial leagues for women flourished with women's bowling, basketball, softball, and track. Factory owners promoted the leagues as ways to "boost morale and foster teamwork," but in fact they were little more than transparent efforts to redirect energies away from unionization after years of labor unrest, much of which involved women workers. Nevertheless, leagues in female-dominated industries like textiles, sewing, and light manufacture offered working-class women an opportunity to play sports, travel, and get out of the sweatshop.

The most famous female athlete of the first half of the twentieth century came out of a factory: Mildred Ella "Babe" Didrikson. Didrikson rose to fame as a multi-sport star, first representing the Dallas-based Employers' Casualty Company team as an eighteen-year-old. She went on to win three medals in track and field in the 1932 Olympics and became the standard for all women golfers. Yet, rather than being celebrated for her athletic versatility, Didrikson was denounced as "mannish," "not-quite female" and a "Muscle Moll" who could not "compete with other girls in the very ancient and time honored sport of mantrapping." While Didrikson herself would blow off these remarks, women's participation in the sport she made famous, track and field, sustained a series of sexist attacks. ◆

Track and Field, the Color Line, and "Racey" Lacey O'Neal

In the early 1950s, International Olympic Committee president Avery Brundage aimed to eliminate women's track and field competition from the Olympics altogether, claiming that IOC members wanted to be "spared the unaesthetic spectacle of women trying to look and act like men." As white women left the sport in significant numbers, African-American women stepped into their places and quickly dominated the international scene. In 1960, when African-American track star Wilma Rudolph won three gold medals at the Olympics in Rome, she was nicknamed the "black gazelle" by the mainstream press. As women's sports historian Susan Cahn put it, "Like other black athletes, she was represented as a wild beast, albeit a gentle, attractive creature who could be adopted as a pet of the American public." While such treatment was common, many Black athletes did not accept it. One shining example of such resistance was Olympic runner "Racey" Lacey O'Neal.

Lacey O'Neal was a member of both the 1964 and 1972 U.S. Olympic Track teams. A former world record holder in the 200 meters, she was the first person to win a professionally sanctioned track meet in 1973. She competed at the top of her sport during a period of unparalleled change for women and African-American athletes. Like many top athletes of her day, O'Neal came into sports from a background of dire poverty. Born on the south side of Chicago, O'Neal had to overcome endless obstacles on her way to world-class status. "I had so many stigmas," she says with a smile:

> I'm black, I'm a female, I was an athlete. I had to overcome all of these "isms" as I called it. I heard, "You're not supposed to get muscles" and "Girls shouldn't be running—they're not going to have babies," or they would call us—you know we were beyond

tomboys—they were calling us "dykes" and all kinds of things. We got all of that. That was the athletic scene. So I had to make every effort to be as effeminate as I could be.

O'Neal made the 1964 Olympic team and went to Tokyo. Although there were sparks of the anger among African-American athletes that would explode in 1968, there was little opportunity, according to O'Neal, for women athletes to express themselves. "Within our own organization—you have to understand that with women's sports, especially track and field, we were always fighting to even get money to train, so we weren't about to start anything to take away from that. In other words, we kept very quiet. Back then we just took what they gave us."

But the evolution of the Black freedom struggle affected O'Neal even when she followed her coach to the University of Hawaii. Though far from the heart of the movement, geographically speaking, O'Neal still found something to do:

I helped start the first Black Student Union at the University of Hawaii. I was a part of that movement and I was also able to hold hands with Dr. Martin Luther King for three minutes. The university sponsored a symposium and allowed Dr. King to come over and speak. I shook his hand, and I asked him what could I do because we were over in Hawaii. And he says, "Well when you graduate come over and join us. Join the struggle, join the march." My teammate was saying, "Let me hold his hand!" and I just kept holding it, I couldn't let his hand go.... [It was] like if you just put your hand in the oven. He was so warm and strong. It was like a spiritual moment, now that I think about it. Just to hold his hand and look in his eyes and for him to just really talk to me. And I felt that I had to do something, so when he left we started the Black Student Union.

When the first rumblings of a 1968 Olympic boycott were heard, O'Neal, like many Black female athletes, balked at the idea.

I was quoted by the *Washington Post* on this one. I told them there would not be a "girlcott" for the mere fact that we were still in the infancy stages of trying even be recognized as female athletes. So when they came to me to ask me what my opinion was on it I said no there would not be a girlcott. I said that, as women, we have struggled too hard to win a measure of acceptance to throw it all away.

Despite her stance on the boycott—which not coincidentally was the position of a majority of Black athletes male and female—she stood resolutely with Tommie Smith and John Carlos when they made their Black Power salute from the 200-meter medal stand.

I was proud because that was their only way to be heard and I think they did it with dignity.... I think the message was that we're not just going to lie down and let people just do what they want to us. And by the mere fact that they got on the podium, they wanted to also say that we want the world to know that we have power. Period. And we're just not going to lie down. They got in trouble after that, yes. They felt the heat and they felt it for a long time.

As the 1960s became the seventies, O'Neal was able to see the situation for women change for the better, and she is very clear about the reason why. "We were more accepted because what happened was, there was a revolution. The women's movement meant a lot. We rode that momentum and we piggybacked on women's lib toward a better day."

Today—while acknowledging all the progress that has been made—"Racey" Lacey O'Neal sees the need to fight again. "Everything is seemingly going back," she says.

It's like a pendulum. It's trying to swing back to where we started from...instead of going forward, instead of being progressive. We just need to keep reminding people that the old hatreds are finished. We can't go back to old America. We're a new America. Too much has evolved. You cannot go back. You have to keep going forward. So somebody, some other movement has to happen— and has to be on a larger scale than just Black folk talking about civil rights. It has to be something that affects all of us. When I say us, I mean everyone: white, Black, Hispanic, all. ◆

The Legend of Billie Jean

Women's athletics have been around for a long time. As researcher Jacquelyn Hall wrote,

> I was struck by the way women's sports came into the story. Women's basketball, just to take an example of another kind of women's involvement in sports which we think of as something's that's very new and that it's only happened because of the Title IX and the women's movement and so on. But the reality is that women's sports of all kinds, especially basketball was a major, major sport in the south beginning in the 20's.

Fair enough. But it is also fair to say that women's sports have always been pushed to the margins whenever doing so served the powers that be. In the 1950s, as men came back from World War II and women returned to the home, women's sports—like the women's professional baseball league, highlighted in the Penny Marshall film, *A League of Their Own*—were cast aside. As images of June Cleaver and Donna Reed came to rule the newfangled TV screen, athletic aspirations were thwarted.

This was the terrain upon which women competed (or didn't compete) until the late 1960s, when a growing women's movement made demands for equality in society and in the world of sports. Their roar was demonstrated in utterly dramatic fashion when Billie Jean King faced off against Bobby Riggs in their "Battle of the Sexes," a tennis match called by the *London Sunday Times,* "The drop shot and volley heard around the world."

Riggs, a 1939 Wimbledon champion, had already beaten women's champion Margaret Court on Mother's Day in 1973. King, who previously had rejected Riggs's dare to play, finally accepted his challenge. "I thought it would set us back 50 years if I didn't win that match," the twelve-time Grand Slam

Billie Jean King watches her return to Bobby Riggs in the "Battle of the Sexes" match at the Houston Astrodome on September 20, 1973. Billie Jean King accepted the challenge of Bobby Riggs and beat him with a 6–4, 6–3, 6–3 wipeout that was a bold statement for a whole generation of women. (AP)

winner said. "It would ruin the women's tour and affect all women's self-esteem."

The "Battle of the Sexes" captured the imagination of the country, not just tennis enthusiasts. On September 20, 1973, in Houston, King was carried out on the Astrodome court like Cleopatra, in a gold throne held aloft by four muscular men dressed as ancient slaves. Riggs was wheeled in on a rickshaw pulled by tightly outfitted models bearing the name "Bobby's Bosom Buddies." Their entrances turned out to be the most competitive part of the match as King, then 29, ran Riggs ragged, winning 6–4, 6–3, 6–3.

As Neil Amdur wrote in the *New York Times*, "Most important perhaps for women everywhere, she convinced skeptics that a female athlete can survive pressure-filled situations and that men are as susceptible to nerves as women." The great Frank Deford added, in *Sports Illustrated*, "She has prominently affected the way 50 percent of society thinks and feels about itself in the vast area of physical exercise…. Moreover, like [golfer Arnold] Palmer, she has made a whole sports boom because of the singular force of her presence."

King was far more than a symbol, or an athlete. She was a participant and activist in the women's movement for equal rights. In the words of Martina Navratilova, she "embodied the crusader fighting a battle for all of us. She was carrying the flag; it was all right to be a jock." King fought for a women's players union and forged the Women's Tennis Association. She was elected its first president in 1973. King, who received $15,000 less than the men's champion, Ilie Nastase, for winning the U.S. Open in 1972, called for a strike by women's players if the prize money wasn't equal by the following year. In 1973, the U.S. Open became the first major tournament to offer equal winner's purses for men and women.

It was for her role in the movements of the day that *Life* magazine named her one of the "100 Most Important Americans of the 20th Century." She was the only female athlete on the list, and one of only four athletes. Of the other three, two— Jackie Robinson and Muhammad Ali—are also strongly associated with social movements (Babe Ruth was the fourth).

Today we are in a highly contradictory situation. Women's

athletics have never been more prominent, but the "Maxim-ifi-cation" of women continues unabated. *Playboy* can get away with its "Women of the Olympics" issue and the PR hacks of sports call this progress because they claim that, in posing naked for money, women are projecting an "image of strength." That's garbage.

Movements to both defend and extend women's rights and athletic participation must be rebuilt. It is no exaggeration that the future of women's sports—and women's rights in general—hangs in the balance. ◆

Kobe Bryant and the Price of Freedom

Eight to ten million dollars. That's how much Kobe Bryant shelled out to his legal team to avoid four years to life in a Colorado maximum-security prison. That's how much it costs for a young Black man to evade a rape trial by a jury pool that is less than 1 percent African American. That's how much it costs to get out of Dodge.

By some counts, it was a small price to pay. If convicted in Eagle County, Kobe would not have shared a cell with Martha Stewart in the Michael Milken Wing of some country club prison. Instead, he would have been ground through the sick machine of Colorado's sex-offense "rehabilitation" system.

Frankly, "sick" doesn't begin to describe it. First, Kobe would likely have been denied bail—the standard Rocky State result of a Class A felony conviction—and then spent sixty days in a county cell waiting to be sentenced. During the sixty-day waiting period, the NBA All-Star would have been given what is called a "penile plethysmograph test" or PPT. The PPT, which plays a determining role in sentencing, involves fitting an electric measuring band around the penis and connecting this apparatus to a computer. The subject is then shown films of graphic sexual violence and illegal pornography as the computer gauges his level of "arousal and deviancy." Former head of the Colorado Criminal Defense Bar Dan Recht described this "program" to *Sports Illustrated's* Rick Reilly as "kind of Clockwork Orangish." That's a bit of an understatement. At sentencing, the judge's only option is the state pen because of mandatory minimum sentencing guidelines.

For Bryant, raised in Italy, the son of a globe-trotting professional basketball player, taking up residence in a Colorado maximum-security prison would give new meaning to the phrase "culture shock." For the first year, "He [would] be in a cell 23 hours out of 24," explains Denver trial attorney Bob McAllister. "He's famous so the guards will make sure there's no appearance of favoritism. They'll probably be harder on him, full-body cavity searches, just to show him he isn't anything special." After the first year of near total isolation, Bryant would have gone through a mandatory rehab program that takes "five to eight years." According to the program's web site, the rehab would have included group therapy, anger management, admission of guilt, and a listing of "distorted core beliefs about self, men, women, children, sex, family, and the world."

With such a painstakingly detailed program in place, one would think that Colorado must be the safest place for women outside Vatican City. Hardly. According to the Colorado Coalition Against Sexual Assault, one out of every six American women has been the victim of an attempted or completed rape in their lifetime. In Colorado, the number is one in four.

Just ask Katie Hnida, the University of Colorado female football player who was physically abused by teammates and eventually leveled accusations of rape, only to suffer further abuse at the hands of her coach and a school administration that first ignored her, then mocked her, and finally smeared her name. As Hnida's experience shows, Colorado's penalties for sexual assault are not a by-product of heightened concern over violence against women any more than the U.S. armed forces are now aiding the Women's Liberation Front in Afghanistan. Instead, they are a result of the 1990s racist crime hysteria, which bred one unjust policy after another across the United States. "Three strikes" laws, zero tolerance policies, and mandatory minimum sentencing have left more than two million people—disproportionately Black and brown people—rotting in this country's prisons.

What about those who don't have ten-figure salaries to spend on attorneys? Get convicted, and punishment, torture, and twenty-three-hour lockdowns become your new life. That'll give you some "distorted core beliefs about self, men, women, children, sex, family and the world." As for women who suffer from violence, don't expect anything in the way of counseling or safe haven. The state has money for the latest in deviant pornography and erection testing computers, but not for you; in fact, there are currently more animal shelters than battered women shelters in the United States, with cuts occurring in every state and federal budget. That's because the priority is repression, not the rights of women.

This was obvious in the treatment of Kobe's accuser, who was clearly pressured by an overly ambitious and incompetent district attorney named Mark Hurlbert, and then dragged through hell by Kobe's attorney, Pamela Mackey, and Judge Terry Ruckriegle. They created a maelstrom around her nineteen-year-old life, trashing every rape shield law ever written in the process. Her name and picture—even her home phone number—are on thousands of Internet sites. Her medical records were leaked to the press. Her sex life in the three days prior to and following the alleged rape were ruled as admissible. She has also received "countless death threats."

No matter what "really happened," women will without

question be less inclined to come forward in cases of abuse in the future. As Mike LoPresti of *USA Today* wrote, "Whichever side one falls on the Kobemeter—believing he should be a pro or a con—everyone surely understands the latest cautionary tale here, of just what a woman must plan on enduring if she yells rape. Her life will be turned over with shovels. Unless the suspect is wealthy, and then it will be turned over with earthmovers." Unfortunately, the conductors of this tragic mess, Hurlbert, Mackey, and Ruckriegle, will not be forcibly compelled to come clean about their "distorted core beliefs."

So what did we learn from the putrid event known as the Kobe trial? We now know more than ever that prison is the destination of the penniless. We know that the wealthy have about as much chance of ending up in a SuperMax as Jenna and Barbara Bush have of seeing combat duty in Najaf. We know that women in 2004 are still put on trial when they are sexually assaulted. And we know that the criminal justice system in this country is rotten and racist to its core. Frankly, we knew all this before. Now if you'll excuse me, I need to delouse. ◆

Out at the Ballgame:
Sports and the Gay Athlete

In a world where *Will and Grace* is "must-see" TV and straight yuppies want a Queer Eye to help them choose their creature comforts, George W. Bush coasted to victory in the 2004 presidential elections on a shameless wave of antigay bigotry. With John "The Altar Boy" Kerry offering no resistance and mainstream Gay Rights groups covering for their candidate, Bush could wave the same-sex marriage fear flag unchallenged and rally his right-wing base to the polls.

Former Minnesota Vikings and Carolina Panthers football player Esera Tuaolo poses after an interview in 2002 in New York. Tuaolo recently came out of the closet because he was "tired of leading a double life."
(AP/Tina Fineberg)

But this same week, a new survey came out suggesting that one of the strongholds of homophobia, American men's sports, was starting to crack. In a Major League Baseball study sponsored by the Tribune Company, a shocking 74 percent of players said they would accept having a gay teammate. Former New York Met and Yankee All-Star Robin Ventura commented, "I'm sure I've had one at some point." Texas Rangers pitcher Doug Brocail chimed in, "I had [a gay teammate], Billy Bean, and I didn't have a problem with it." (After retiring, Bean famously wrote a book about his experiences as a closeted gay athlete titled *Going the Other Way*.)

These comments by players mirror those spoken by former New York Mets manager Bobby Valentine. "I think most clubhouses could handle it," said Valentine. "They're mature people who understand all the situations we live with in our society and this is obviously one of them.... It's just time to catch up and I think it can be done seamlessly if it's the right person or people.... Let's get rid of the whispers and let's be real about this.... There will be some distractions and we'll have to get through with them."

Both the numbers and the comments are welcome but it will probably be some time before they have any positive effect. No active player in the Big Three men's sports—baseball, basketball, and football—has ever come out of the closet. It's no wonder why. Players—who tend to come from poor to working class backgrounds—feel that they would risk financial, if not physical, ruin.

Former NFL tackle Esera Tuaolo wrote after he retired, "The one thing I could never do was talk about it. Never. No one in the NFL wanted to hear it, and if anyone did hear it, that would be the end for me. I'd wind up cut or injured. I was sure that if a GM didn't get rid of me for the sake of team chemistry, another player would intentionally hurt me, to keep up the image. Because the NFL is a super macho culture. It's a place for gladiators. And gladiators aren't supposed to be gay."

It's difficult to imagine a more oppressive atmosphere. Anti-gay slurs are as ingrained in pro sports as racism was fifty years ago. Players routinely get away with blithe homophobic comments. Most recently, it was All-Pro receiver—and All-World Mouth—Terrell Owens claiming that his former quarterback Jeff Garcia is gay, saying, "Like my boy tells me: If it looks like a rat and smells like a rat, by golly, it is a rat."

Other examples abound. Jeremy Shockey, the gimpy part-time Giants tight end and full-time jackass, called coach Bill Parcells a "homo" and said he "wouldn't stand" for a gay teammate. John Smoltz the Atlanta Braves pitcher—whose two favorite movies are (seriously) *The Passion of the Christ* and *Dumb and Dumber*—gave his view of gay marriage to the Associated Press with a pithy, "What's next? Marrying animals?"

But it was another Braves pitcher who made the comment by which all slurs are measured, tying his homophobia to a score of other prejudices. In 1999, John Rocker earned the ire of most of New York City's eight million or so inhabitants by saying, "Imagine having to take the 7 train to [Shea Stadium in New York] looking like you're [in] Beirut next to some kid with purple hair, next to some queer with AIDS, right next to some dude who got out of jail for the fourth time, right next to some 20-year-old mom with four kids. It's depressing."

In this atmosphere, players like Mets future Hall of Fame catcher Mike Piazza, quicksilver Falcons quarterback Michael Vick, and recent Terrell Owens target Garcia, have all felt the need to hold press conferences just to tell us that they are not gay.

If a gay athlete did come forward while still in uniform, the impact would be seismic. As former Vikings receiver—and Esera Tuaolo teammate—Cris Carter said, "Once you put a human face on the situation, it's hard to maintain those stereotypes. There is no doubt many on the team would try to run a gay player off, but I also believe the majority would support his right to be a member of the team."

The *Advocate* magazine, in an interview with Tuaolo, asked him why he didn't take the opportunity to be "the Gay community's Jackie Robinson." Not a bad question, but we have to remember that Jackie Robinson did not appear in a vacuum ready to take abuse, steal bases, and win our hearts. He emerged after years of agitation against Major League Baseball's color ban by Black and communist papers all over the United States. He also had a base of support in every city made up of Black Americans returning from World War II and demanding a share of the democracy they were supposedly fighting for overseas.

Given the current context, we cannot make demands on gay athletes to come out and risk their necks unless we are willing to hit the streets and do the same. Bush and Kerry have unleashed a homophobic backlash on this country. If we aren't willing to stand up right now for our gay brothers and sisters, then we shouldn't expect an athlete to do it for us. Many of us want a gay Jackie Robinson—someone to do for gay rights what Robinson did for the struggle for Black freedom. But before we can reasonably ask an athlete to step forward, we need to fight to create a climate in which such a decision will be seen as anything other than a potentially career-killing mistake. ◆

An Off-Field Obituary: The Death of Reggie White

NFL legend Reggie White passed away in his sleep at the age of forty-three. The 6-foot, 5-inch, 300-pound "Minister of Defense" was a football immortal. He played in thirteen consecutive pro bowls and retired as the all-time NFL leader in sacks.

In 1997, White led the hapless Green Bay Packers to their first Super Bowl victory in more than thirty years. Packers QB Brett Favre said that White was "the best football player I ever played with or against."

White's premature death unleashed a torrent of testimonials about his off-field work as well. He set up countless charities and got his hands dirty in the lives of gang members, drug addicts, and convicts. As former NFL great Cris Carter said, "Reggie made a far greater impact off the field than he did on it."

But there is another side to White that deserves exploration—and certainly more exposure than it has received. White's political ideas spanned the gamut from the noble to the wretched, and were rooted in the best and worst of his deep evangelical Christian faith. Religion is never static, either in its beliefs or uses. Black slaves in the U.S. transformed the religion that was at first imposed upon them into a weapon against oppression, while slave owners used what was ostensibly the same religion to justify their barbarism. "The religion of the slave" and "the religion of the slave owner" are two entirely separate belief systems, even when they use the same book as a reference. One set of beliefs helped to forge Martin Luther King Jr., a moral giant, and the other helps to sustain the cruel small-mindedness of George W. Bush. Reggie White embodied and voiced both sets of beliefs. And it is wrong to celebrate either his on-field successes or his off-field works of charity without denouncing his homophobic bigotry.

Burn

During the epidemic of Black church burnings that swept the South in 1995, Reggie White brought the issue national attention after one of his own Tennessee parishes was torched. "I think it's time for the country to take this stuff seriously," White told the *Boston Globe*. "It's time to stop sweeping this stuff under the rug because progress in race relations has not been made."

He then stood up to authorities shamefully trying to blame African Americans for torching their own churches. White put the focus squarely on the white supremacist hate groups everyone outside southern law enforcement could see were responsible. "When is America going to stop tolerating these groups?" White asked the *New York Times*.

> It is time for us to come together and to fight it. One of the problems is that the people financing and providing the resources for this type of activity are popular people with money who are hiding under the rug. Some of them may be policemen, doctors, lawyers, prominent people who speak out of both sides of their mouths. That makes it difficult to stop but not impossible. Not when we come together as one force against hate.

There was a joy in hearing someone like Reggie White speak the truth and make it plain in his signature raspy voice. When this mountain of a man sifted through the wreckage of his church, shaking with anger, we seethed alongside him. Maybe in another era, White would have embarked on a path of antiracist struggle, fighting the tide of oppression. But in the absence of a mass movement, the ugly side of Reggie White's politics and beliefs found voice. He became a confident and proud voice for an antigay agenda, and in the process became a spokesperson for organizations fanning the flames of the very bigotry that gutted his church.

The Wheel Turns

White's journey began in 1998 when he was invited to address the Wisconsin state legislature. White was expected to speak for roughly five minutes about his charity work. Instead he delivered a rambling hour-long rant in which he said the U.S. had "turned away from God" by allowing "homosexuality—one of the biggest sins—to run rampant." He also said, "People from all different ethnic backgrounds live in this lifestyle. But people from all different ethnic backgrounds also are liars and cheaters and malicious and back-stabbing."

He pointedly rejected the idea of civil rights protections for gays and lesbians (first enacted by the state of Wisconsin), claiming to be "offended" by any comparison between the struggle for gay rights and the Civil Rights movement. Afterwards, White was utterly unapologetic, saying that if anyone found his remarks offensive, "that was their problem."

In the commotion that followed, *CBS Sports* withdrew their contract offer to White to become a pre-game show announcer after his retirement. White and his wife Sara, on the television show *20/20*, blamed this on "sodomites" within and outside the network.

White continued to speak out against gays and lesbians, and in doing so, allied himself with a rogue's gallery of bigots and hatemongers. He hired a "family spokesman" named Bill Horn, president of the vociferously antigay organization "Straight from the Heart Ministries." Soon White was getting support, well wishes, and speaking engagements from the likes of the Reverend Donald Wildmon's American Family Association (AFA), Gary Bauer's Family Research Council, and the Christian Coalition. Unlike Bauer, who resembles a Kermit the Frog Shrinky Dink, White could successfully articulate the "Pro-Family agenda"—equating gays with child molesters and drug addicts—to a Black audience. His Blackness was also a plus for the nearly all-white groups trying to shake accusations that their antigay, "pro-family" agenda had kissing cousins in both racist and white supremacist ideas.

White spoke at one rally in Iowa protesting Governor Tom Vilsack's executive order banning antigay discrimination in state agencies. "Straight from the Heart's" Horn said the order "is a big political payoff to the governor's transvestite and cross-dresser supporters." At the rally, Horn wept as he introduced White to the crowd, saying "Reggie doesn't hate homosexuals; he loves them so much he is going to be honest with them and tell them that what they are doing is destructive." White followed Horn by preaching, "Every black person in America should be offended that a group of people should want the same civil rights because of their sexual orientation." When several gay rights advocates attempted to question the speakers, they were escorted out by force. "They were promoting anger and violence tonight," expelled activist Tina Perry told the *Des Moines Register*. "They slammed anyone who did not agree with their agenda."

According to the Minnesota Family Council, White became someone who "defends the family the same way he defended the goal line." This is a lie. As a player, Reggie White never ran away from a battle and worked to inspire his teammates to greater heights, liberating the Green Bay organization from decades of futility. As a "defender" of family values, he stood for bigoted ideas that keep humanity in chains. He supported the vilification of gays and lesbians instead of bringing people "together as one force against hate," as White himself so eloquently put it as he sorted through the burnt remains of his church.

I will miss Reggie White. He was a force of nature who changed the game with an unholy combination of speed, strength, and smarts. But more than that I will miss seeing if there would have been another chapter in his life down the road, in which he would have devoted his body and soul to standing against the moneyed bigots of this country instead of alongside them. ◆

CHAPTER NINE

Games That Bosses Play

The plutocracy loves sports first and foremost because they mean mega-profits. Hosting the Olympics or building a publicly funded stadium may translate into misery for the ordinary folks in a community, but it's champagne wishes, caviar dreams, and a king-sized "ka-ching" for the folks who collect the revenues. The "games that bosses play" can wreak havoc on the communities that they use sports to pillage. For example, when the havoc-wreaking pillager-in-chief, President Bush, receives enthusiastic support from Major League Baseball's billionaire owners, it is because they are backing one of their own—a former MLB boss who laid the groundwork for the stadium heists occurring around the country. This includes the recent, publicly funded, $550 million stadium plan for Washington, D.C.—a half-billion-dollar ballpark to "serve," over the wishes of its citizens, a chronically underfunded city that doesn't even have a public hospital. Such plans become even more ridiculous when we consider the death of D.C. high school football star Devin Fowlkes, a casualty of the priorities that have been imposed on the city.

Athletes are also casualties in the games that bosses play, high-priced pieces of equipment to maintain until they break down. That is why the "steroid controversy" in Major League Baseball is impossible to understand through the current media lens. Players who buck the smooth running of this profitable machinery can pay quite a price. That's why athletes like Barry Bonds and

Kareem Abdul Jabbar can end their Hall of Fame careers punished and in a state of purgatory for the sin of a strong will. Professional sports have also provided a home, recently, to what is the greatest labor swindle since Reconstruction: the NCAA's billion-dollar business. Here we look at Ohio State's star running back Maurice Clarett's futile efforts to take it on. And no discussion of sports today would be complete without an accounting of the workers who died making Athens "worthy" of hosting the 2004 Olympics.

Olympic-Sized Horror in Greece

You knew it was Olympic season in the USA because *Playboy* released its "Women of the Olympics" issue, in which world-class female athletes are shown performing pole vaults, long jumps, and backstrokes, completely in the air-brushed buff. Swimmer and photo subject Haley Cope accompanied her display with this inspiring message to young girls across America: "I vote Republican, I worship Martha Stewart and I don't mind being naked."

Lovely. And they say sports and politics don't mix.

We are also getting bombarded with stories about how Athens is "a city transformed" by the Olympics' Midas touch. As International Olympic Committee Chairman Jacques Rogge put it, "At Athens the legacy will be a new airport, new metro, new suburban train...this is a legacy the Greeks will be proud of."

But this is just more airbrushing; don't let it fool you. The Greek Olympics arrived bathed from head to toe in blood and dust. You didn't hear about it in NBC's gauzy coverage, but Amnesty International estimates that anywhere between forty and 150 construction workers died in workplace accidents building Olympic facilities. The center-right government of

Costas Karamanlis preferred sustaining these casualties to suffering the international embarrassment of not having a modernized infrastructure and put pressure on crews to finish facilities by any means necessary.

In the last push of round-the-clock preparation alone, no less than thirteen laborers were killed in the interest of making Athens, in the words of one Olympic official, "habitable for a global audience." As Andreas Zazopoulos, head of the Greek Construction Workers Union said, "We have paid for the Olympic games in blood."

Construction workers' deaths weren't the only cause for local anger. The Karamanlis government scuttled Greek law forbidding foreign personnel from carrying weapons in the country by allowing hundreds—perhaps thousands—of American, British, and Israeli Special Forces soldiers to be armed to the teeth throughout Athens. City authorities were also guilty, according to *Democracy Now!*, of "rounding up homeless people, drug addicts, and the mentally ill, requiring that psychiatric hospitals lock them up. Also affected by Athens Olympic cleanup are refugees and asylum seekers, some of whom are being targeted for detention and deportation in the days leading up to the games."

But none of this went unchallenged. A movement grew around those sickened by Olympic fever. Five hundred people, amid an atmosphere of tremendous repression, rallied on behalf of the dead, placing olive wreaths on thirteen crosses planted in the earth outside Greece's parliament. Inmates of Korydallos Prison and five other penitentiaries protested against the government's decision to stop authorizing parole during the games.

A Greek-based organization with the name, "Revolutionary Struggle" set off bombs in uninhabited buildings, releasing the following statement after blowing up an empty police station:

"With regard to the Olympic games we say that Greece's transformation into a fortress, NATO's involvement, the presence
and activities of foreign intelligence units show clearly that
[the Olympics] are not a festival like Games organizers say, but
it's a war."

They're absolutely right. We know it was a war because
there were casualties. Dozens of hard-working people are
dead. Just like the dissidents slaughtered before Hitler's 1936
Olympics in Berlin, or the protesting students massacred before the 1968 games in Mexico City, or those who died in Daryl
Gates's police custody in the leadup to the 1984 Los Angeles
games, they have joined the ranks of the Olympic martyrs.
They died so world dignitaries and CEOs could bask in the
light of athletic achievement—not unlike the Greek and
Roman Emperors of old.

May their blood forever stain every flag that's unfurled. ◆

Stadium Swindles

In the weeks before a legislative vote on a new stadium, the
Minnesota Twins ran a TV commercial featuring a ballplayer
visiting a boy in the hospital. A voiceover announced, "If the
Twins leave Minnesota, an eight-year-old from Wilmer under-
going chemotherapy will never get a visit from [Twins in-
fielder] Marty Cordova." It later turned out that the boy had
already died by the time the commercial aired. Whoops. Of
course, lying about a cancer-stricken child is small potatoes
when it comes to pro sports owners' drive for publicly funded
stadiums.

Pro arenas paid for on the public dime now dot the country
like monuments to extortion and corporate welfare. These

days, publicly funding a stadium is a simple process: A major sports owner threatens to move his or her team to another city and demands that taxpayers put up hundreds of millions of dollars to build a stadium that would be owned not by the city, but by the team's owner. Imagine if you wanted to move to a new town and demanded that your neighbors build you a home for the privilege living next to you and you begin to see the insane logic at work.

Public stadium deals have arisen alongside the broader trends of wealth polarization and stagnating wages in the United States. Over the last twenty years, working people in this country paid over $500 million a year in stadium construction and upkeep with more than $7 billion to be spent on new facilities by 2006. This does not include the $600 million that Washington, D.C. just pledged to build a baseball stadium for the newly named Washington Nationals (formerly the Montreal Expos). D.C. also just laid off 300 public school workers, closed its only public hospital, and has the second worst infant mortality rate anywhere in the Western hemisphere, bested only by Haiti. Converting the proposed site, an impoverished section of the city called the Anacostia Waterfront, will involve the destruction of low-income housing and homeless shelters under what is called, without irony, "fair use." The D.C. stadium swindle moved forward even though 70 percent of the city's inhabitants oppose public funding, and more than half strongly oppose it. These numbers cross all ethnic and racial lines in this heavily segregated city.

Opposition has remained consistent even though Major League owners, and their shill, D.C. Mayor Anthony Williams, continue to sell the fiction that the stadium will provide major economic benefits for the city. This is pure folly, not only in D.C. but around the country. According to the Brookings Institute, "No recent facility has earned anything approaching a reasonable return on investment. No recent facility has been self-financing in terms of its impact on net tax revenues.... [T]he economic benefits of sports facilities are de minimus."

As Roger Noll, co-author of *Sports, Jobs, and Taxes: The Economic Impact of Sports Teams and Stadiums* put it, "Any independent study shows that as an investment, it's silly. If they're trying to sell it on grounds of actually contributing to economic growth and employment in D.C., that's wrong. There's never been a publicly subsidized stadium anywhere in the United States that had the effect of increasing employment and economic growth in the city in which it was built."

Take Cleveland as an example. This former industrial city was once used as an example for how publicly funded stadiums could turn cities around. In 1990, full-page newspaper ads purchased by Cleveland's Central Market Gateway Project promised that a new sports complex would generate "$15 million a year for schools for our children." Instead—according to the calculations of the Cleveland Teachers Union—tax breaks given to the project have drained $3.5 million a year from the Cleveland school system, which is now in receivership. Cleveland was also recently named the poorest city in the U.S. with a poverty rate of 50 percent and unemployment hovering at 33 percent.

The truth is that stadiums help nobody but the sports bosses and their political cronies who make out like bandits while we are left holding the bill. Baltimore Ravens owner Art Modell, after securing funding for his free $300 million playpen, could only laugh, and in a rare moment of candor told reporters, "The pride and presence of a professional football team is more important than 30 libraries." Maybe for Modell, but growing legions of people disagree.

Bush and the Billionaire Owners

They didn't think he was good enough to be their baseball commissioner and follow in the immortal footsteps of people like Bowie Kuhn and Ford Frick, but the MLB's owners cabal is ponying up the dough to keep George W. Bush in the White House.

A recent Associated Press review found that the former Texas Rangers owner has had his palm greased by over half of the thirty Major League teams. Seven owners even hold the distinction of being "Bush Rangers," meaning they raised at least $200,000 each, and six are "Bush Pioneers" signifying a contribution of $100,000 a piece.

Bush's most ardent supporters in the owners' box are a rogue's gallery of right-wing ideologues. They include Detroit Tigers owner Michael Ilitch, who has his own Republican electoral ambitions, San Francisco Giants owner and Safeway union buster Peter Magowan, Minnesota Twins owner Carl Pohlad, best known for trying to contract his own team, and the New York Yankees' George Steinbrenner, another figurehead of a decaying empire.

The owners' ardor for Bush is more complex than that of your typical billionaire toward the tax-cutter-in-chief. Baseball owners all yearn for the same brass ring: They want municipalities and taxpayers to cover the tabs for new state-of-the-art stadiums—and no one ever fronted a stadium swindle better than George W. Bush.

The sad dreams of billionaires are projected onto Bush, who set the standard for large-scale extortion when his ownership group got the state of Texas to pay for The Ballpark in Arlington. Dubya, after an early adult life of incompetence and failed business ventures, finally got his dream job as managing partner of the Rangers. For an initial investment of $600,000—borrowed of course—the then president's son had to endure the toil of attending home baseball games and smiling a lot for the cameras.

But while Bush smirked his forties away, the owners behind him (think a dozen Dick Cheneys in ten-gallon hats) threatened to move the team if the city of Arlington did not foot the bill for a new park. The local government caved, and in the fall of 1990, they guaranteed that the city would pay $135 million out of an estimated cost of $190 million. The remainder was raised through a ticket surcharge. In other words, local taxpayers and baseball fans footed the entire bill. This plan was sold to Arlington voters with Bush's glad-handing help. At the end of the day, the owners of the Rangers, including Bush, got a stadium worth nearly $200 million without putting down a penny of their own money. But the scam did not end there. As part of the deal, the Rangers' ownership was granted a chunk of land in addition to the stadium. The land, of course, increased in value as a result of the stadium's construction. To make this happen, Democratic governor Ann Richards signed into law an extraordinary measure that set up the Arlington Sports Facilities Development Authority (ASFDA), which had the power to seize privately owned land deemed necessary for stadium construction. As Joe Conason has written,

> Never before had a municipal authority in Texas been given license to seize the property of a private citizen for the benefit of other private citizens.... On November 8, 1993, with the stadium being readied to open the following spring, Bush announced that he would be running for governor. He didn't blush when he proclaimed that his campaign theme would demand self-reliance and personal responsibility rather than dependence on government.

Bush held onto his stake of the team as governor and, by the time he cashed out in 1998, Bush's return on his original $600,000 investment in the Rangers was 2,400 percent—a cool $15 million. The next time someone complains about the "greediness" of pro athletes, tell them that if they are that bent out of shape about someone's undeserved wealth, they should make a detour to the upper deck and boo outside the owner's box.

We Can Fight Back

When sports owners and their media prizefighters are confronted with the mountains of statistics that show publicly funded stadiums to be fool's gold, they say "Well people want their sports and we are just giving it to them." Yes, sports are insanely popular in the U.S., but people have shown time and again that loving a team doesn't mean they want to be taken to the cleaners by the billionaire bosses. Polls show that up to 80 percent of everyone opposes public subsidies for stadiums. Stadium funding referendums have been defeated in states both "red" and "blue" ranging from California to Minnesota to Virginia.

But since polls and public opinion have not been enough to shut the gaping maw of the ravenous stadium beast, organizations have popped up around the country of people fighting to stop these temples of corporate greed. These groups range from lobbying operations to grassroots protest movements, but all are there for activists to enter and engage for the purposes of turning this into a national movement. The organizations (courtesy of the website fieldofschemes.com) include: Save Fenway Park! (Boston); People for Fair Development and Develop Don't Destroy (Brooklyn); No Jones Tax (Dallas); No Stadium Tax Coalition (Minnesota); Taxpayers Against an Anoka County Vikings Stadium (Minnesota); hellskitchen.net (New York); Hell's Kitchen/Hudson Yards Alliance (New York); New York Association for Better Choices (New York); Coalition Against Public Funding for Stadiums (St. Louis); No D.C. Taxes for Baseball (Washington, D.C.). Fighting stadium givebacks can raise big questions for people about the priorities of a system that will spit-shine sports arenas while schools and hospitals crumble. All people who believe in human need over corporate greed should join the fight. ◆

Why Did Devin Fowlkes Have to Die?

His friends and football teammates called him "Lil' Midget" because he was built so low to the ground. At 5 feet, 5 inches, and 155 pounds of solid muscle and wicked energy, he looked more Greco-Roman wrestler than running back. But as with "Mighty Joe" Morris or Lionel "Little Train" James, sixteen-year-old Devin Fowlkes carried himself like a football player and, also similar to those two gridiron gnats, he backed it up. "Lil' Midget," in fearless fashion, had paced the Anacostia Senior High School Indians with 476 yards and four touchdowns in 2003. Now he's dead.

The games stopped on October 30, 2003, when Devin was gunned down after school. He was the casualty of a fifteen-year-old gang member's stray bullet. The tears have not stopped since. Assistant Coach Philip Morgan told the media that Devin was "on the brink of becoming somebody to watch."

But Devin didn't believe that the cruel lottery of sports would be his only ticket across the Anacostia River. "He wanted to go to college," said his uncle Patrick Michael. "He wanted to really excel, to do well, not only for himself but for his mother and the rest of the family."

A young man, an athlete in the bloom of youth, cut down by a fifteen-year-old kid with a gun. As Indians head coach Willie Stewart told the press, "I'm just so tired of that scene." Coach Stewart then gave a roll call of the players who have been shot and killed since he started at Anacostia in 1983. "Lashon Preston. Anthony Butler. Donald Campbell—he had a great future. Robert Archie. Rodney Smith..." Stewart having a personal roster of heartache and funerals is difficult enough to swallow. But the latest news really sticks in your throat. Devin Fowlkes was shot, but he did not have to die.

Violence in Ward 7 is not new. Stray bullets have become

as tragic a part of the landscape as chop shops, liquor stores, and unpaved streets. Devin's friends even thought he was clowning when the shots rang out and he doubled over. The violence may be old hat to Ward 7 youth, but new was the absence of D.C. General Hospital. D.C. General had for years been a four-minute drive from Anacostia High. Mayor Anthony Williams (a Democrat) changed all of that. Williams made the decision to downsize D.C. General in 2001 over the objections of thousands of protesters and a unanimous opposition vote by the D.C. City Council.

After Devin was loaded onto a gurney, the EMTs, despite his shallow breathing, had no choice but to enter the early rush hour traffic on New York Avenue. By the time he arrived at Howard University Hospital on Georgia Avenue, fifteen minutes had passed. His stomach, normally tight as a drum from sit-ups and football practice, had begun to balloon and distend from internal bleeding. Little more than an hour later, Devin was dead.

"Maybe it would have made a difference if D.C. General was open," said one EMT, Rodney West. "He was very viable. His life probably could have been saved."

Mayor Williams, who spoke at Devin's funeral, bristled fiercely when asked if the closing of D.C. General contributed to his death. "You can always argue that you can have a trauma center nearer to someone, and it could make a difference," Hizzoner huffed to the *Washington Post*. "Is it horrible that he lost his life? Absolutely. But some states have one [center]. Many cities have far fewer trauma centers than we have."

Problem: The bevy of trauma centers Williams mentions is far from where most of the city's trauma and drama takes place. In the western part of the city, where D.C. magically becomes Washington, and K street lobbyists slide on their own trails of slime from saloon to state dinner, there are three trauma centers. In East D.C., the former home of Devin Fowlkes, there is presently not one. No trauma center in an area where, if the street crime doesn't get you, heart disease and high blood pressure will. No trauma center in Trauma Central.

One can only hope that the death of Devin Fowlkes will be a call to action for the people of this area. Here was a young man wanting to do everything right, trying to be, as Tupac Shakur once said, a "rose that grew from concrete." He took on challenges the same way he played football: fearless and undaunted by the size of the odds. The "Lil Midget" stood tall despite coming from a part of the city drowning in neglect, an area that seems to swallow young African-American men whole. We can debate until sunrise about the root causes of this tragedy. We can wring our hands about how we have created a country where kids kill kids.

But the rest of this story is not complicated. Devin Fowlkes was shot. He could have lived. He died. No wonder a fifteen-year-old could think that life is so cheap. He learned it from the Mayor. ◆

Maurice Clarett and the NCAA

Author Eduardo Galeano writes that we live in an "upside down world," a place where self-described "war president" George W. Bush is nominated for a Nobel Peace Prize, a place where investigations into Janet Jackson's missing bra led the news over missing weapons of mass destruction. We are gorged on lies until repetition becomes proof. As George Orwell predicted, war is peace, freedom is slavery, and ignorance is strength. The eternal truths of the moment hold sway in the sports world as well. We are told that the name "Redskins" is in fact a "tribute" to Native Americans. We are told that publicly funded stadiums benefit "all" even if "all" cannot afford tickets.

But the kings and queens of the upside-down sports world have to be the people in charge of the NCAA. Say what you will about Danny Snyder and George Steinbrenner: at least they wear their greed like pink carnations in their lapels. But the NCAA, a.k.a. plantation masters of unpaid athletes, will slam down their mint juleps and challenge you to a duel if you imply that they are anything but pure. That's why the initial court decision to allow Ohio State running back Maurice Clarett and others to bypass college and apply for the NFL draft was the sports equivalent of Fort Sumter, an opening shot at the NCAA's sweatshop of indentured servitude. "I was pleased with the judge's ruling," Clarett said. "It gives a lot of kids an opportunity to choose a different path. It wasn't me so much trying to take down the NFL, just having another option."

The NFL shot back, of course; the ruling has since been overturned on appeal, and Clarett is facing an uncertain future as a late-round pick. But Clarett and company shouldn't have to seek other options to be compensated for their sweat. The NCAA should pay them. For athletes who choose not to go to school, the NFL should fund a minor league. But why do that when, for a fraction of the cost, you can hire spokespeople, lawyers, and other professional dissemblers to tie up the courts for the foreseeable future. Why fund "The Topeka Tortugas" when you can hire NCAA "spokeswoman" Kay Hawes a.k.a. Scarlet O'Hara to say things like, "From an education perspective, we are disappointed with the decision...it clearly opens the door to more football student-athletes leaving college early and without degrees."

Frankly, Kay, your student-athletes don't give a damn. Yes, many college football players work hard in the classroom and on the field. But the majority attends classes as often as

George W. Bush attended drill duty for the National Guard. According to NCAA figures, Louisiana State University (LSU) graduates only 40 percent of its football players, and Oklahoma a shameful 33 percent. In fact, if teams were required to graduate 50 percent of their players to get in a bowl game, twenty-six of this year's twenty-eight bowls would have been canceled.

This should shock no one. If you were generating millions in profits for a school and practicing year-round for hours every day, meanwhile observing that your coach (say Miami's Larry Coker) is driving a Cadillac Escalade, that 8:00 a.m. class on Comparative Economics might look less appealing than a sing-along with John Ashcroft. If you were a "student-athlete" at LSU, one of the poorest state schools in the country, and you watched your coach Nick Saban re-sign for almost three mill a year while you were living in a dorm room with asbestos oozing out of the walls and no hot water, a shot at the pros before you tore your knee in eight places wouldn't look half bad.

Spencer Haywood, whose lawsuit paved the way for underclassmen to play in the NBA said, "I'd love somebody to explain to me how we can send an 18-year-old to war, but we can't to the NFL." Good question, Spencer. Just don't look to the NFL or the NCAA for honest answers. They will just roll their eyes and say, "Fiddle-dee-dee!" ◆

Maurice Clarett Gets ESPN-DED

Maurice Clarett finally dropped dime. The former Ohio State running back has come clean to *ESPN The Magazine* to reveal all that's rotten in one of the NCAA's premier programs.

Clarett unveiled all the perks of big-time college football, making Ohio State sound like an amusement park operated by

Tony Soprano. He detailed receiving construction site cash for "watching paint dry," quick money from boosters for "playing Sega with their kids," and free access to tricked-out SUVs—all under the watchful eye of Coach Jim Tressel. "I thought he'd give me the NFL," Maurice Clarett said of Tressel. "I thought he'd say, 'You took from me and you didn't tell on me, so here's the NFL.' He could have painted me as the first pick in the draft, as the world's greatest everything. He wound up selling me out."

This story is historic, a high-profile All-American coming clean. Clarett should be Valachi in a varsity jacket. Yet in the era of ESPN and the merger of big business and sports journalism, Clarett gets to disclose and be discredited in one fell swoop: with ESPN's college football cash cow safely spurting milk—but only into the mouths of its administrators.

The *ESPN The Magazine* story is Stop 1 on the Contain Clarett Express: a skillfully written piece with a dash of rhetorical relish by someone named Tom Friend. Clarett is described as a "football pariah, denounced by his own school, a school he carried to a national championship almost two years ago." Friend continues in this stylistic vein, explaining—as violin strings are massaged into sound—that Clarett has been smeared "by an Ohio State system that he says lined his pockets and then methodically tore him down."

Yet before the ink was even dry on Friend's friendly text, Clarett became the tackling dummy for eight hours on ESPN *Radio* as an "untrustworthy," "pathetic," and "wholly ridiculous" individual who should "just shut up." By the time the day was done, the scandal—for now—had largely been explained and contained.

To have ESPN—"your home for college football"—break this story is utter farce. This would be like Karen Silkwood exposing the truth about plutonium leaks in the Los Alamos corporate newsletter, or Deep Throat taking his tales of Watergate to the *National Review*, or Mordecai Vannunu revealing Israeli nuclear weapon secrets to the *Jerusalem Post.*

ESPN's disclosure and subsequent discarding of the Clarett story reveal far more about how corrupt college football has become than the allegations themselves. Once the NFL's poor Saturday afternoon cousin, college football—thanks to ESPN, or, should I say, thankfully for ESPN—is now televised every single day of the week. This serves to generate millions for athletic conferences, all of which negotiate individual deals with ESPN in the total sum of billions. Consider that the mid-major Conference USA's deal with the "World Wide Leader" is eight years for $80 million.

Yet while ESPN gets record weeknight ratings and universities rake in the bucks, the players who have to maintain the fiction of being student-athletes suffer. Will Rueff, a senior defensive tackle at Miami, has come forward to say, "After away games, it's terrible. When we played Marshall, we didn't get back until 4 in the morning. If you have an early class, it's almost impossible to get there. It's almost impossible to sleep on the bus. You're just worn out."

Allen Sack, who played on Notre Dame's 1966 national championship team and is a member of the Drake Group, a consortium of professors attempting to bring light to the exploitation of student athletes, says, "Schools playing midweek is incomprehensible to me.... The networks are in this to make money. The universities have decided to make money. Let's not put the responsibility on the network, but put the responsibility on the universities that have seen the technology and decided to exploit the athletes."

Which brings us back to Maurice Clarett. Clarett has attempted to break into the NFL since his stellar freshman season. He now finds himself on the outside looking in, losing court cases and watching his draft status sink like "Kerry in

2004" T-shirt sales. Because of its desire to keep college foot
ball as a free minor league, the NFL has moved heaven and
earth to fight Clarett's push for early entry. When athletes produce billions in revenue, don't get paid, and can't make it to
class, the label "student-athlete" rings awfully hollow. If the
NCAA doesn't pay these athletes for what they produce, the
graft and hypocrisy that stain college football will never end
and the athletes will continue to suffer for this fiction. As Maurice Clarett said to *ESPN the Magazine*, "Ohio State created
me. They created what they suspended." ESPN created Maurice Clarett as well. They'll recreate him as a malcontent if it
means protecting their cash cow. It's high time for the players
to seize control of this cow and make some steak. ◆

Steroids and the Glory of Competition

Steroid hysteria grips the world of sports with a fervor not
seen since the Salem witch trials. The buzz became a roar
when former baseball owner George W. Bush, in his 2004 State
of the Union address, took the time to sermonize about performance enhancers.

> To help children make right choices, they need good examples.
> Athletics play such an important role in our society, but, unfortu-
> nately, some in professional sports are not setting much of an ex-
> ample. The use of performance-enhancing drugs like steroids in
> baseball, football, and other sports is dangerous, and it sends the
> wrong message—that there are shortcuts to accomplishment,
> and that performance is more important than character. So
> tonight I call on team owners, union representatives, coaches, and
> players to take the lead, to send the right signal, to get tough, and
> to get rid of steroids now. (Applause.)

This time-out for tough talk on steroids seemed puzzling at best. No mention of AIDS or unemployment, yet the muscle mass of our nation's athletes demanded Executive Attention. Bush's steroid digression was like coming across a nude beach unexpectedly: odd, slightly embarrassing, and quickly forgettable. It appears we "misunderestimated" Dubya again. Bush's steroid talk was in fact the first opening salvo of a major political operation.

Because 2004 also saw former Attorney General John Ashcroft announcing that four very unknown men who front a fitness and nutrition company called Bay Area Lab Company (BALCO) were being charged with forty-two counts of conspiracy to distribute steroids, possession of human growth hormones, and distribution of banned drugs.

Ashcroft's press conference presence spoke volumes. Having the attorney general of the United States personally state charges of steroid pushing is like deer hunting with an AK47—overkill in the extreme. But the big guns were not really aimed at the proprietors of BALCO. They were trained on their clients: a collection of some of the most famous athletes in the Unites States. George W. Bush might not know BALCO from Sergeant Bilko, but he does know sports and the hold it can have on the 24-hour news cycle. BALCO's clients include Yankee first baseman Jason Giambi, track star Marion Jones, linebacker Bill Romanowski, and the big one, surely the Moby Dick to Ashcroft's Ahab, the home run king, Barry Bonds. Ashcroft made his real target plain when he said, "We have not limited prosecution in this setting to those who are being prosecuted today."

Putting the publicity-shy Bonds on a witness stand to explain, under oath, how he hit seventy-three home runs as a bulked-up thirty-seven-year-old surely made our former attorney general almost as happy as getting Strom Thurmond on a postage stamp. For Bush it meant a few days off from negative headlines during an election year—a media frenzy that temporarily jettisoned inconveniently dying soldiers and phantom weapons of mass destruction off the front pages. But while BALCO founder Victor Conte spilled his guts on *20/20* and his "associates" named names faster than Elia Kazan on May Day, the underlying pressures that led to the use and abuse of steroids went undiscussed.

I used to know a seventeen-year-old basketball player from Brooklyn who would do defensive slide drills at night holding a ten-pound brick in each hand until the blisters burst through his Nikes. My buddy, a high-school All Star, didn't even get a sniff at a college scholarship. Now he works sweeping those same Fort Greene courts with a herniated disk—the most lasting legacy of his years of practice. Every year hundreds of thousands of young people, like my old friend, push all their life's chips to the middle of the table in a bid to make it in sports, and the overwhelming majority doesn't even come close.

The pressure to make it at any cost means weight training, nutritional supplements, and performance-enhancing drugs. As sports have grown into a global Goliath, players have turned their bodies into chemistry sets. For perspective's sake, check out the famous 1988 World Series tape of injured Los Angeles Dodgers slugger Kirk Gibson crushing a home run on one leg off Hall of Fame reliever Dennis Eckersley. Gibson, who was a college linebacker at Notre Dame and an MVP power hitter, looks positively elfin as he circles the bases, his baggy uniform hanging loose as a poncho. Today, there are shortstops that stretch the seams of their jerseys and look like they could steal Gibson's lunch money.

In this bulked-up age, scores of players are producing eye-popping numbers. But they are also risking brutal health problems and even death. Former baseball MVP Ken Caminiti who died this past year of a drug overdose, was an admitted user. Coming clean in 2003, Caminiti told writer Tom Verducci, "Look at all the money in the game. A kid got $252 million. So I can't say, 'Don't do it,' not when the guy next to you is as big as a house and he's going to take your job and make the money."

> ...I got really strong, really quick. I pulled a lot of muscles. I broke down a lot.... I'm still paying for it. My tendons and ligaments got all torn up. My muscles got too strong for my tendons and ligaments. And now my body's not producing testosterone. You know what that's like? You get lethargic. You get depressed. It's terrible.

Caminiti's injury history is not unusual, according to a *Sports Illustrated* report. Major leaguers made 467 trips to the disabled list last season, staying there an average of fifty-nine days—20 percent longer than in 1997. And teams paid $317 million last year to players physically unable to play—a 130 percent increase from four years earlier.

"[Baseball] was always the sport for the agile athlete with the small frame," said noted sports orthopedist James Andrews of Birmingham, Alabama. "Over these last ten years, that's all changed. Now we're getting a bunch of these muscle-related injuries in baseball. You'd have to attribute that—both the bulking up and the increased injuries—to steroids and supplements." Former major leaguer Chad Curtis, who retired after last season, estimated that "40 to 50 percent" of major league ballplayers use steroids—sometimes supplemented with joint-strengthening human growth hormone—to become stronger and faster. As Curtis said, "If you polled the fans, I think they'd tell you, 'I don't care about illegal steroids. I'd rather see the guy hit the ball a mile or throw it 105 miles an hour.'"

Looking at trends around the majors, it would appear that most of the baseball establishment agrees. According to World Series hero and Bush shill, Curt Schilling, "We're playing in an environment in the last decade that's tailored to produce offensive numbers anyway, with the smaller ballparks, the smaller strike zone, and so forth. When you add in steroids and strength training, you're seeing records not just being broken, but completely shattered."

Steroids have also been linked to the deaths of prominent athletes including, among others, football stars John Matusek and Lyle Alzado. Alzado, a two-time All-Pro defensive end, admitted his abuse in a 1991 article in *Sports Illustrated*, three months after being diagnosed with brain cancer, a condition believed to be caused, if not exacerbated, by massive steroid use. He had been taking the drug regularly since 1969. "It was addicting, mentally addicting," Alzado wrote. "I just didn't feel strong unless I was taking something."

The deaths extend beyond the major sports to any sport in which athletes are set against one another to succeed or get booted. In the unregulated world of professional wrestling, where muscles are king, at least sixty-five wrestlers have died since 1997, twenty-five from coronary ailments. Wrestlers have been known to start betting pools on who will die next. Several of sports entertainment's biggest names, including Hulk Hogan and former Minnesota governor Jesse "The Body" Ventura, acknowledged using bodybuilding drugs years ago. "There was a joke: If you did not test positive for steroids, you were fired," former wrestler and broadcaster Bruno Sammartino told the *St. Louis Post-Dispatch* in 1991.

But beneath the cynical surface of pro wrestling is a core of cutthroat competition and desperate fear. Wrestling journalist Dave Meltzer got to the heart of the matter when he said, "No one is standing up. Either they don't know what's going on or they're terrified of being blacklisted." And while the owners are responsible for setting up a competitive environment in which destroying your body is accepted if not encouraged, maddeningly, the buck always seems to stop with the players. According to ESPN, "Athletes persist in taking [performance enhancers], believing that these substances provide a competitive advantage." This lets the owners completely off the hook. The hypocritical heart of the matter is that George W. Bush and the baseball owners who filled his campaign coffers get far more out of keeping the train moving than getting folks off.

Sports are first and foremost an avenue out of poverty for most players, a chance, as Henry Hill said in the movie *Goodfellas,* "to be somebody in a world of nobodies." Only 3 percent of high school athletes play in college and only 3 percent of college athletes play any kind of professional sport. But when 50 percent of young Black men are unemployed, like they are in New York City, or 60 percent of Black men are in the criminal justice system, as is the case in Washington, D.C., and the only places hiring pay $7.00 an hour with no benefits, 3 percent doesn't look like the worst odds in the world. It beats the hell out of the lotto. And as long as these conditions persist, we can expect more, not less, bad news about steroids.

Steroids to Heaven

Near the end of 2004, some genetically engineered chickens came home to roost for Major League Baseball. Grand jury testimony from the BALCO investigation was leaked to the *San Francisco Chronicle,* and the clucking began. We now know that former MVP and Yankee first baseman Jason Giambi admitted under oath to using all kinds of steroids. Reigning National League MVP Barry Bonds, in further transcripts, conceded to administering a "flaxseed oil cream" that he found out was a steroid after the fact.

Giambi, in particular, took grand jurors down a harrowing rabbit hole of steroid use. He testified to injecting human growth hormones in his stomach and testosterone into his buttocks during his 2001–2003 seasons. Giambi, in addition, rubbed an undetectable steroid known as "the cream" on his body and placed drops of another, called "the clear," under his tongue. He also admitted to ingesting a female fertility drug called Clomid, which some medical experts say can exacerbate pituitary tumors. Giambi suffers from such a tumor.

Without missing a beat, MLB Commissioner Bud Selig pointed a finger at the players and their union as the root cause of steroid abuse because they have the temerity to fight the strict unilateral testing Bud drools for. Selig said, "We're going to leave no stone unturned until we have [a very tough program] in place by spring training 2005." But as Selig attempts to use the scandal to turn the tables on the union he abhors, Big Bud and all MLB owners need to take a long, hard look in the mirror.

Steroids and their link to increased power numbers appear to be a fact of life in baseball's recent history. A player has hit fifty-six or more home runs in a single season only seventeen times. Eleven of those seventeen came between 1997 and 2001, including all six 63-plus campaigns. Adrian Beltre, in the first year of a relatively mild steroid testing program, led the NL in home runs with forty-eight. That number would not have made the top five in 2001 when Bonds set the all-time mark with seventy-three dingers. The moon-shots were epic, and Major League Baseball loved every minute of it.

It was Major League Baseball that hyped the hypo-using sluggers of the mid to late nineties. It was Major League Baseball that rode the 1998 home run battle between Mark McGwire and Sammy Sosa—commonly called "the home run race that saved the game"—to a popularity not seen since before the lockout/strike of 1994. It was Major League Baseball that approved Nike's "Chicks Dig the Long Ball" ad campaign. It was Major League Baseball that spent the nineties building ballparks the size of Hugh Hefner's hot tub to encourage high scoring and increased home run totals. It was Major League Baseball that advertised its Home Run Derby and All Star Game two years ago using cartoons of players with freakishly huge muscles slamming the ball out of the park. And it was Major League Baseball that rewarded the big bashers with eye-popping contracts.

I'm Sticking With the Union

Yet the brunt of the attacks, as Selig has signaled, will be aimed directly at the players union. The union has been attacked, slandered, and even brought in front of Senator John McCain's Commerce Committee for not walking lockstep with the Major League owners' draconian testing proposal. The union believes, quite correctly, that unless testing is done impartially, in other words not operated exclusively by Major League Baseball, the owners will use this power to request blood and urine samples on a whim to harass players and find ways to void burdensome contracts. If this sounds far-fetched to you, just take a look at New York, because it's exactly what the Yankees had in mind when "dealing" with Giambi—saving $80 million. The stakes are high and the union is rightly not signing off on anything that moves just because Selig and McCain are pressuring them to do so. (There is more than a little hypocrisy in McCain's concern about the health of players when he simultaneously cheerleads the use of chemical and biological agents, including depleted uranium, in Iraq. Let him grandstand for "healthy living" in the barely funded cancer wards of Baghdad.)

It's certainly true that steroids don't belong in baseball. They can destroy your body and even kill you. But as long as baseball pays the big money to the big bashers and glorifies the long ball, drugs will be ingested. And as long as players are pressured by agents and management to keep up with the guy in the locker next door, there will be more Giambis to come.

That's not the union's problem, or even the players' problem. It's on the owners, who see players as pieces of equipment, easily disposed of and easily replaced.

Steroid-mania: The Case of Barry Bonds

It was the ultimate slap in the face: Barry Bonds on the cover of *Sports Illustrated* with "The Asterisk" resting on his head. "The Asterisk" is the most dreaded of statistical addendums, marking a tainted achievement, emitting the scent of skulduggery. When Roger Maris surpassed Babe Ruth, smacking his sixty-first home run, AL Commissioner—and Ruth enthusiast—Ford Frick affixed an asterisk to the record because Maris had played in 162 games to Ruth's 154. Frick removed it after fans from the Bronx started bringing signs to the games telling Frick to "Kiss our Asterisks!" When the San Antonio Spurs won the NBA title in 2003, their second in five years, the play-by-play announcer yelped, "This one has no asterisk!" referring to their first title, which was won during the 1998–1999 strike-shortened season.

For *Sports Illustrated* to hang the asterisk on Bonds was to publicly call history's greatest baseball career into question. Throughout the 1990s, Bonds averaged thirty-four homers and thirty-six steals per season, but that was just a warm-up. At thirty-seven, in 2001, he hit seventy-three home runs; at thirty-eight he batted .370 with an ungodly .585 on base percentage; at thirty-nine, he won his sixth MVP, hitting forty-five home runs in only 390 at bats. At forty, he set a record by being the first person to have an on base percentage over .600.

In 2005, Bonds is poised to pass Babe Ruth and Henry Aaron and become the all-time home run champ. We should be marveling at his accomplishments, planning the tales to tell our children about how we got to watch the mighty Bonds. Instead, the Bush administration and MLB owners are leading an anti-Bonds PR campaign that Cubs manager Dusty Baker likened to

"McCarthyism." While Bonds and Yankee Jason Giambi probably won't be confused with Ethel and Julius Rosenberg anytime soon, the campaign has produced enough media and congressional hot air to steam a stadium-ful of dumplings.

Reports about Bonds' body—how wide his back is, how big his jaw is, how thick his legs are, basically dissecting the man like an animal—have peppered the papers. Never mind that Bonds has maintained that he has never taken any banned substance. Never mind that, except in 2001, Bonds—like Aaron—has never hit even fifty home runs in a season. Never mind that Bonds's trainer, indicted for steroid distribution, has maintained Bonds's innocence even though such a juicy snitch would keep him out of the clink. Never mind that Bonds has admitted to using a cream, once, that he later found out was a steroid. That's it. Never mind that, unlike Giambi, who showed up at training camp last year looking like Ally McBeal, Bonds has maintained his current physical shape for a decade, and even gained six pounds this off-season. Never mind how common it is for all athletes—take Michael Jordan and Shaquille O'Neal as examples—to thicken with age.

Never mind all that. The number one reason to stand with Bonds, to give this prickly character the benefit of the doubt, is his unparalleled middle-aged majesty. Steroids and rapid "unnatural" muscle growth put tremendous pressure on the joints and tendons. Admitted steroid users like former MVPs Ken Caminiti and Jose Canseco, Lenny Dykstra, and banned substance user Mark McGwire all saw their bodies break down as they hit their mid-thirties. In the end, they limped away from their careers, their bodies broken into pieces. To go by the rumors that surround him, Bonds's ankles should be snapping like toothpicks every time he jogs to first base. But instead, at forty, he thrives.

The media have been crushing Bonds without evidence because he has never played their game. If Michael Jordan was the Tom Hanks of the pro sports world, Bonds is Sean Penn, beating down the paparazzi and challenging their self-importance. I heard one sports radio chatterbox remark, "Even if Bonds isn't on steroids he is a freak, with his trainers, and supplements, and work-out regimens. The Babe would drink a keg, eat a steak, and hit three home runs. Let's see Bonds do that." According to this logic, Bonds's very commitment to his own health is a knock against him. This is also revisionist history. Ruth was known to have all kinds of 1920s home remedies injected in his system for increased potency (I assume in the field). And if they're so bent on assigning asterisks, how about one for Ruth? Playing in the era of segregation, Ruth never competed against Black players, nor did he ever venture further south of the Mason-Dixon line to play. I would love to have seen Ruth face Satchel Paige in a sweltering San Juan double header. Bonds, on the other hand, has produced in an era of global talent, cross-country travel, and intense media scrutiny.

Fraying Bonds

The Edge of Sports, to much derision, has defended Bonds and made the case for his innocence. As the story unfolds, I stand by my most basic assertion that muscles cannot substitute for the ability to hit a ball (although they can make a great hitter hit for more power) or there would be a potential All Star in every Gold's Gym across the country. Bonds is more than a basher. He is a lifetime .300 hitter with more than 500 stolen bases. He is not a lumberjack taking hacks at the plate. My belief that Bonds's continuing health and increasing strength argue against his being a habitual user also remains unshaken.

Therefore, until I hear more compelling information, I will stand with the 15 percent of people in a national poll who believe Bonds's story that he did it once and without knowledge. As baseball columnist Tom Boswell put it, "Granted, the presumption of Bonds's innocence now hangs by a thread. But Bonds is such an odd, extreme, gifted, and alienated character that he might do almost anything. Or not do anything. Just out of perversity." That is the most charitable commentary on Bonds I could find. More typically, pundits are brandishing torches and pitchforks. Former pitcher Jack McDowell, in an unintentionally hilarious assertion, suggested that he would have made the Hall of Fame if not for juiced players. (Yeah, Jack, I know how you feel. Me too.) McDowell believes that Bonds, Giambi, and anyone caught with an illegal substance should be banned for life, their names erased from the record books. He then derides anyone who thinks this is a "witch hunt." He's justified, in a way; an actual "witch hunt" usually involves a trifle less sanctimony.

Whether the anti-steroid furies are motivated by a desire to salve their egos, "protect the game," crush the players' union, or target Bonds, the fact remains: muscle enhancers cannot slam a 95 mph slider into McCovey Cove. Barry Bonds can—and Bush, Ashcroft, Selig, and all the others can kiss his asterisk. ◆

Michael Jordan Inc.

In a recent questionnaire, the youth of China were asked to name "the greatest man in world history." The survey produced a tie between Zhou Enlai and Michael Jordan. This is fitting company for Jordan who, like Zhou, never met an Asian labor camp he couldn't condone. A cheap shot? Maybe. But the unquestionably greatest basketball player of all time has never shirked his responsibilities as a soldier for mega-profits. Ralph Nader is fond of saying that "George W. Bush is a corporation in disguise as a human being." This never quite rang true to

me because Bush is much more like a bizarro-world King
Midas; everything he touches—from early oil ventures in the
appropriately named Arbusto Oil company to the U.S. economy—turns to shit. Jordan actually fits the bill. His basketball
resume needs no hype. He is a five-time Most Valuable Player,
and a six-time finals MVP. He is the all-time leader in points per
game and became the only person of forty years or older to
ever average twenty points per game. He has also been named
by ESPN and the *New York Times* as the Athlete of the Twentieth Century, in both cases besting Muhammad Ali.

While Ali was driven by a keen social conscience, Jordan
seems to get his motivation from a drive for profit. If Ali's most
iconic quote is the famed "I ain't got no quarrel with them Vietcong," then Jordan's was his response in 1990 to why he
wouldn't endorse Black North Carolina Democrat Harvey
Gantt in his Senate campaign against Republican Jesse Helms:
"Republicans buy shoes too." Michael Crowley of the *Boston
Phoenix* once wrote,

> If Ali's persona dramatically overshadows Jordan's, perhaps that's
> what we should expect. Maybe Michael Jordan reflects our times
> no less than Ali reflected his own. Just as Ali was a vessel for the
> social chaos and spiritual liberation of his day, so Jordan symbol-
> izes the political apathy and cultural shallowness of ours. Ali was a
> 1960s archetype in that he was a passionate and incendiary rebel.
> Michael Jordan is a 1990s archetype in that he is a value-neutral
> brand name.

In 2000, Forbes estimated "his Airness's" commercial value
to Corporate America at $43.7 billion. When he was rumored
to be returning to the NBA in March of 1995, the stocks of the
companies he endorsed increased in value a combined $3.84
billion. Jordan has shilled proudly for Nike, Coke, McDonalds,
Hanes, and Ball Park Franks. In the process, he has become
the first modern athlete, along with Magic Johnson, to make
the transition from being a corporate mouthpiece to being part

of the corporate world. Jordan's net worth is estimated at nine figures, he has made several efforts to buy an NBA team, and he runs his own division of Nike: Jumpman-23.

Yet Jordan's careful avoidance of social issues hasn't escaped criticism. Several well-known pro athletes—including Jim Brown, Hank Aaron, and the late Arthur Ashe—have knocked Jordan for standing on the sidelines. "He's more interested in his image for his shoe deals than he is in helping his own people," Brown said of Jordan in 1992. What has so frustrated older athlete-activists like Brown is the power Jordan could wield if he wanted to. When Nike's sweatshop labor practices in Southeast Asia received international exposure, a press conference from Jordan could have made a real difference. Instead Jordan said it wasn't his problem. Then, in 1997, he changed his tune, saying to the *Sporting News*, "I'm hearing a lot of different sides to the issue.... The best thing I can do is go to Asia and see it for myself. If there are issues...if it's an issue of slavery or sweatshops, [Nike executives] have to revise the situation." Yet even after acknowledging the specter of "slavery," Jordan never made the trip.

At this point, I think we need to revise our expectations of Jordan and athletes like him. Why should we expect him to have a social conscience in the first place? It is simply not in his interest to embarrass the Nike brass or puncture his own profits. Unfortunately, the kids in Southeast Asia don't have the luxury to wait for him to change his mind. If we want to stop sweatshops and child labor, we will have to look to someone else—perhaps even ourselves. Simply put, it's all right to want to Be Like Mike with our basketball shorts on. But we have to strive for better when we leave the locker room. ◆

Why Can't Kareem Coach?

NBA: Love It Live. That's the slick, traveling road show where smiling stars of yesteryear, from Moses Malone to World B. Free, comb back the grays and hype the league. But there is one man on the NBA Love It Live tour who has been shown very little love by the NBA: Kareem Abdul Jabbar. And it is eating him alive.

Kareem Abdul-Jabbar, the 7-foot-2 all-star center of the Los Angeles Lakers, is shown during an interview in New York City in 1975. (AP)

Kareem wants to be an NBA coach. Badly. This shouldn't be too difficult. In a typical off-season, one-third of NBA coaching positions are open or have just been filled. The job has about as much security as an American flag salesman in Tehran. Yet Kareem's phone does not ring. "I wish I knew why. I really do," he said in a radio interview. "I want to teach. I want to teach the game the way I was taught it, but I can't find the chance."

Kareem is an NBA legend, but his coaching resume is far broader than "icon for hire." Besides his three NCAA championships, six NBA titles, and record six MVP trophies, the man has proven his passion for teaching by working on the lowest rungs of the coaching food chain. In humid gyms throughout the Deep South, he coached the Oklahoma Storm of the United States Basketball League to a championship. In Whiteriver, Arizona, he coached a high school team on a Native American reservation. He was even an unpaid assistant for the Los Angeles Clippers. Kareem is also the author of several books, including the fabulous *Black Profiles in Courage*. And he is the all-time scoring champ, not just in the NBA but also on *Sports Celebrity Jeopardy*.

Now he wants to coach in the NBA, and according to Kareem, "I can't even get my calls returned. I just don't understand it." It's jarring to hear the resigned frustration in his voice. He doesn't sound like the legend of the Skyhook but a man in his mid-fifties who discovers that he's unwanted and expendable, an afterthought in a league built on his blood and sweat.

The question, of course, is why? Why is there no place for Kareem? Race always looms large when we speak of pro teams and coaches. There is a history of African-American former players, especially star players, being told that they lack, as Al Campanis said infamously, "the necessities" to coach or manage. But unlike pro football and Major League Baseball, the NBA has a solid record on this question. Roughly 50 percent of

NBA coaches are African-American. That's more than a tad higher than the NFL where the number sits at 17 percent (five out of thirty), or Division 1 college football where less than 1 percent of coaches are Black.

But if it's not racism, why can't Kareem find work? "Anonymous league sources" (don't you just automatically trust people who represent themselves as "anonymous league sources?) say it is because he is "difficult" and "surly." Kareem himself admits to being "enigmatic." But so what? Who would want to be stuck in an elevator with any of the stroke candidates that coach NBA teams? Forehead veins bulging, eyes bugging out of their heads; they're not exactly Care Bears. Larry Bird and Magic Johnson were hired as NBA head coaches, both with zero experience. And Bird is about as pleasant and personable as Donald Rumsfeld at an antiwar march. So the question remains, why not Kareem?

Kareem is being punished for what the NBA mafia considers the greatest sin of the modern athlete: a public career built on personal, political, and emotional honesty. In a cookie-cutter McWorld, where the words of Peyton Manning, Tiger Woods, and Tom Brady—among many others—all come from the same corporate handbook, Kareem has always been stubbornly human. Like Muhammad Ali, but without Ali's humor and love of the spotlight, he never feared standing apart from his identity as a basketball player, even if it meant standing alone.

When the Olympic Project for Human Rights asked Black athletes to boycott the 1968 Mexico City Olympics to protest poverty and racism, Kareem, then Lew Alcindor, stayed home. He later said his only athletic regret was not going and "pulling a Tommie Smith and John Carlos" by raising a defiant black-gloved fist on the medal stand. When his Islamic spiritual mentor's children were murdered in a brutal conflict with the Nation of Islam, Kareem, over the objections of team, agent, and league, was a pallbearer at the high-profile funeral. When confronted with racism, ignorance toward his faith, or invasions of his personal space, he lashed back. No PR firms. No canned clichés. No Charles Barkley smirk so we knew he was "just kidding." Kareem was and is the Anti-Sound Bite.

When young, the Anti-Sound Bite told painful truths to a media that didn't want to listen. Now he is a fifty-seven-year-old man who, honest to the end, refuses to hide that he is wounded and stung. "I don't know what I am going to do," he said recently, "I can be turned away only so many times before I have to think about another direction, another focus for the rest of my life." And now, as owners scramble for competent coaches, this man of immense pride, overwhelming talent, and proven commitment stands on the sidelines waiting, a pariah to an NBA that wants him seen but not heard. ◆

Don't Let Them Break You, Barry!

In the classic gangster film *Miller's Crossing*, mob counselor Tom Regan strides confidently into the women's "powder room" of a garish 1920s social club, sloshing his tall glass of bourbon from side to side. As the ladies screech and scamper toward the exit, Tom sidles up to a hard-edged woman named Verna, the moll secretly seeing Tom while two-timing his boss, the Kingpin known as Leo. Words are exchanged, voices are raised, and Verna tattoos Tom's chin with a stiff right cross. Momentarily stunned, Tom gathers himself and throws his drink with the speed and "accuracy" of a young Randy Johnson, shattering the mirror behind Verna's exquisitely coiffed head. As they breathe heavily with commingling desire and disgust, Verna puts herself together and coolly walks out of the

room, pausing only to sneer, "I bet you think you raised hell."
This should be the last word, the punctuation mark of their exchange. But Tom won't let it go. With a jagged, defiant scowl
ripping across his craggy face, he calls out, "Sister! When I've
raised hell you'll know it!"

The great Tom Regan has always reminded me of Barry
Bonds. Like Tom, Barry Bonds can be titanically arrogant,
with the capacity to verbally shred anyone in a room just to
show that he can. At one point in *Miller's Crossing*, Verna says
something to Tom that many a beat reporter has dreamed of
growling to Bonds: "I never met someone who made being a
sonuvabitch such a point of pride."

But also like Tom Regan, Barry Bonds's most enduring
characteristic is the defiant steel that runs up and down his
spine. He has always been, in my eyes, the Unbreakable Barry
Bonds. That's why it has been so shocking to see Barry Bonds
assume a new pose: that of a man broken.

After emerging from a ninety-minute session with San
Francisco Giants trainers, Bonds seemed to be in an imperme-
able fog of depression. Sitting next to his fifteen-year-old son,
Nikolai, Bonds spoke of retiring despite being within spitting
distance of surpassing Babe Ruth's and Henry Aaron's hallowed home run records.

"My son and I are just going to enjoy our lives," he said, in a
voice so soft reporters strained to hear. "You guys wanted to
hurt me bad enough, you finally got me." When asked to explain whom he was referring to, the seven-time MVP locked
eyes individually with every reporter in his sight-line and said
calmly, "You, you, you, you, you, you—the media, everybody.
You finally got there.... I'm tired of my kids crying. You wanted
me to jump off a bridge, I finally did. You finally brought me
and my family down.... So now go pick on a different person."

There is ample reason for Barry to be physically and emotionally exhausted. The *San Francisco Chronicle* has published an extensive series about an alleged ex-mistress detailing accusations of Bonds's steroid use and income tax evasion. She has now been subpoenaed by the BALCO grand jury, as prosecutors consider targeting Bonds for perjury. Bonds has certainly faced hardships before, but because of knees—which are now "cartilage on bone"—he doesn't even have the baseball diamond as sanctuary. He only has the self-image of a man over forty with a grueling rehab in his future, while his family life is clearly in crisis. Bonds has always thumbed his nose at many in media, saying in effect, "You can't touch me." But now both of his sanctuaries, family and baseball, are under siege, and the weight of that seems to be pushing even this most mighty of chips from his shoulder.

I am telling myself that Barry Bonds is just playing possum, that he is as indomitable as he has ever been. This is still the Barry Bonds that Congress feared to subpoena for their steroid photo-shoot. They knew Barry's voice would never crack with tears as he read a prepared statement. They knew Barry wouldn't break. They knew he would puncture their hypocrisy, asking them—as he's been asking reporters—when the hearings on cigarettes or chewing tobacco or alcohol might be scheduled. Congress said they wouldn't call Bonds because, in the words of committee chair Tom Davis, "then Barry would be the show." Just like Major League pitchers, Davis and his coterie of dime store Tricky Dicks were scared. (There is a lesson here for people on the left currently falling over themselves to show that they are as God-fearing, gay-bashing, and gun-loving as Republicans: If you are weak in the face of a right-wing assault, you only invite greater loss.)

No matter what the haters threw at him—slanders in the press, racist death threats, government investigations—Barry Bonds, it seemed, could withstand it all. This is the same

Bonds who reeled off a string of game-winning homeruns and RBIs the week of his father's death; the same Bonds who, unlike other suspected steroid users, never showed up to camp looking like he had spent the off-season on Atkins, coming back bigger every time; the same Bonds who, when asked if steroids were cheating, said, "Cheating is when the U.S. spends fifty cents to make a shirt in Korea and then sells it for $150.00 here."

This is the man who inspired Ben Nightengale, scribe for that radical publication *USA Today*, to write in February, "You don't want to hear what he says? Don't talk to him. You don't want to believe that he'd be treated differently if he were white and breaking Ruth's record? Look at his racist hate letters. You want a phony? Wrong guy.... He's not being disingenuous because that's what corporate America wants. He's not going to sit back and kiss the media's backside because we want him to. He's not going to pretend to be someone he's not."

This is not a man I want to see broken.

Some advice for Bonds: Look at history. This country tried to break another loud, polarizing Black athlete named Muhammad Ali. They stripped him of his title, and everyone from his closest friends to the Nation of Islam slunk away like the great man was radioactive and contagious. But instead of fading into obscurity, Ali embarked on a campus tour through which he spoke at four colleges a week for the whole year of 1968. Ali, unlike Bonds, had a mass antiwar movement as well as the Black freedom struggle to put the wind at his back. Bonds has no such support. But he does have the ear of the public. To fade away would be like putting chum in the water, intending to distract the encircling sharks but really only egging them on. Barry: Use the pulpit you have and draw strength from those—in the Bay Area particularly—who will have your back.

At the end of *Millers Crossing*, Tom Regan, also appearing

broken and vulnerable, comes out the apparent victor, but Tom Regan ends up alone. He seems to win, but really loses, left by himself with only his stubborn sense of pride. Maybe Barry thinks that's the best he can do: maintain his pride and walk away. But I know I speak for a lot of baseball fans, as well as fans of his indomitable will, when I say, Barry, please don't leave yet. Don't let them break you. Of course, you have to do what's best for your family and your own sanity, but I hope you return to the game and smash Babe Ruth's and Hank Aaron's home run records if only to ruin the day of every racist pen pal, congressional jock-sniffer, and hater who thinks strong wills are only meant to be broken. ◆

CHAPTER TEN

Stir of Echoes: A New Sporting Resistance?

There are very real signs that athletes and fans are starting to speak out for the first time in a generation. In 2004, baseball fans rebelled against the placing of movie ads on Major League bases, while a number of athletes challenged the limits on what they are supposed to think and say. "The Round Mound of Sound," Charles Barkley, spoke his mind about the war in Iraq and a number of other difficult truths. Carl Eller used his belated Hall of Fame induction to say something about Black America, much to the discomfort of NFL officialdom and to the delight of a mostly white and working-class Ohio crowd. Ricky Williams told the NFL where to get off and left fame and fortune to exert his right to be his own man. And three young athletes put themselves out there for criticism and scrutiny by taking courageous stands: Washington Wizards center Etan Thomas, Golden State Warriors Center Adonal Foyle, and Manhattanville College guard Toni Smith, who shocked the nation by turning her back on the flag during the national anthem. Will it all add up to a new sporting resistance? Only time will tell.

A Real Web Gem:
Fans Push Spiderman Off Base

Sometimes an everyday, innocuous indignity becomes the straw that breaks the camel's back. The American Revolution was sparked by a tax on tea. The Civil Rights movement ignited because Rosa Parks held down her seat on a Montgomery bus. Now Major League Baseball commissioner "Bud" Selig is learning the same lesson as King George and Bull Connor: You damn well better know how much straw the camel is willing to carry. When Commissioner Selig partnered with Columbia Pictures to put a six-by-six inch *Spider-Man 2* ad on the infield bases, the camels became bucking broncos. Fans across the country were incensed, and before you could say "Give me commercial free or give me death!" Selig and Columbia pulled the campaign. Both movie execs and Selig readily admitted that this "unexpected" fan backlash triggered their about-face.

"We saw some of the polls on the Internet that said that 81 percent of the fans didn't approve of it," said Geoffrey Ammer, president of worldwide marketing for Columbia. "Based on this reaction from the fans, we didn't want to do anything to take away from their enjoyment of the game and if that was the case with this element of the promotion, we could afford to do without it." Fans did far more than "not approve." In one ESPN.com poll, 79.4 percent of roughly 50,000 readers said they thought that baseball was "selling out" by allowing the *Spider-Man 2* advertisements on the field. Always the courageous leader, Big Bud told the Associated Press, "It isn't worth, frankly, having a debate about."

The question that comes to mind is, "Why this?" Why did a six-by-six inch blotch of spider web inflame the baseball masses? On the surface, it seems so trivial. But Spidey-fying the bases crossed a psychic line. Commercials assault our senses every minute of every day. From pop-up ads on computers to those jarring radio spots that seem to be written by the Marquis de Sade, we are all captives of corporate sponsorship. This is especially true in baseball. I have heard a lot of sports radio cement heads telling fans to "grow up," that this kind of commercialization is the future and they should "just deal with it." But the sports media elite, eating free press box sushi while the rest of us are paying $9.00 for a hot dog, could never understand what set our collective spidey senses tingling.

This is what we fans go through on a typical trip to the stadium: First we drive to a ballpark whose very name (or "naming rights") changes with every rise and fall of the tech markets. Then we park in a lot closer to the house we just left than the actual stadium—or ride on a subway packed tighter than a can of Pringles. This joyride is followed by an opportunity to pay through the nose for everything: bloated ticket prices, bloated food prices, and bloated beer prices for the privilege of building up our own bloat. Along the way, our bags are searched to make sure we aren't smuggling in a peanut butter sandwich. Finally, our journey ends with us sitting like contortionists in our nosebleed seats, as the jumbotron, the super jumbotron, and the super-mega jumbotron compete for our attention.

We suffer all this because the end goal, for the fan, is worth it: seeing a baseball diamond greener than the Irish hills. For every fan that played as a kid in a park strewn with broken bottles and the random syringe, a Major League Baseball diamond is the physical representation of how sweet it should have been. It's the inside of a cathedral. To us, putting ads on the bases is like gracing the altar of your church, mosque, or synagogue, with the words *"Hugh Jackman IS Van Helsing!"* Baseball has learned the hard way: know your boundaries, know your limits, and leave the field alone. Because it was ours long before it was ever yours. ◆

Charles Barkley:
The Round Mound of Sound

Charles Barkley, the basketball player, was always unique. He stands at barely 6 feet 5 inches, but became one of the all-time great rebounders, averaging just fewer than twelve boards a game for his career. He was mocked as "The Round Mound of Rebound" because he didn't have a ripple of muscle tone on his 260-pound pear-shaped frame, but he bent rims with his strength and once even threw the 350-pound Shaquille O'Neal to the floor. He was "too short, too fat, too slow" for the NBA, but is one of two players in NBA history, along with the legendary Wilt Chamberlain, to finish his career with 23,000 points, 12,000 rebounds, and 4,000 assists. He never won a championship but played huge in big games, scoring forty-four points and grabbing twenty-four rebounds in game seven of the 1993 conference finals against the Seattle Supersonics. He also averaged twenty-seven points in the NBA finals that year against Michael Jordan's Chicago Bulls.

Yet what really set Chuck apart from the pack was his utterly iconoclastic personality. In a league that produces corporate robots droning lines learned at the David Stern Finishing School, Barkley spoke his mind with the same reckless disregard that marked his playing style. Now, as a TNT studio analyst, he receives more attention than ever with his no-holds-barred approach to commentary. He makes us laugh with classic lines like the one he directed at hyper-religious A.C.

Green: "If god's so good, how come he didn't give you a jump shot?" But Barkley speaks to agitate as well as entertain. In the tradition of Muhammad Ali, Bill Russell, and Billie Jean King, Barkley uses his athletic prominence to spotlight issues not usually addressed by the "mainstream" political media—let alone the sports media—issues like racism and poverty. Early in his career, he caused a few jaws to drop by stating his desire to become the "first Black Republican governor of Alabama" after his playing days ended. But Barkley is neither Republican nor Democrat. He is a political being who lives to shock by stating his truth. Sometimes "Barkleyisms" are sharper and more provocative than anything uttered in the Beltway. And so, as a public service, I present the very best of Mista-Chuck.

Here is Charles on the Janet Jackson Super Bowl scandal:

> I wish people were more irate with the Bush administration for starting a war for profit than they are with Janet Jackson for showing her breast. But that's America…we don't know what's important and what's not important. It's much ado about nothing. It's not like she's going to traumatize anyone. Everyone is all offended now and bent out of shape. Give me a break. There are a lot of trashier things on television that what Janet Jackson did.

On basketball player Rasheed Wallace calling himself "exploited": "If you're a grunt for CNN, those people are exploited. The guy behind the camera I talk to, he's exploited. This guy is making $17 million, and he's exploited? That's the stupidest thing I've ever heard."

On the Enron scandal investigation: "Almost all those politicians took money from Enron, and there they are holding hearings. That's like O.J. Simpson getting in the Rae Carruth jury pool."

On racism: "Anytime something bad happens to a Black person because of racism, I feel it in my soul. I really do. You take the Abner Louima case. That let me know one thing: If some white guys wanted to stick a plunger up a Black guy's butt, and I'm the Black guy who happened to be around, I'd have a plunger up my butt."

On Saddam Hussein (circa 2002): "I think he's still alive.... Look at Osama bin Laden and Saddam Hussein—they used to both work for the United States and now they're enemies. That's part of the hypocrisy that goes on here."

On the flak celebrities get for their antiwar beliefs: "That's part of the hypocrisy that goes on when you're in the lime-light—if you say something, you're anti-American or unpatri-otic or too liberal. We're all free to say what we want to, but if you ever forget your place, we'll put you back in your place."

On politics: "Politics is too corrupt. You know how you can tell politics is corrupt? President Bush is going to raise $250 million for a job that pays $400,000. Now tell me there isn't something wrong there?"

On his priority in life: "My No. 1 priority is to help poor peo-ple. In this country, 90 percent of the money is controlled by 10 percent of the people, and that's not right."

Whether you agree or disagree, Charles Barkley recalls the words of Malcolm X in describing a young fighter named Cas-sius Clay: "Do not underestimate the quality of the mind he has in there. Although a clown can never imitate the wise man, the wise man can imitate a clown." ◆

Carl Eller Enters the Hall of Fame with Purpose

Most football fans wouldn't recognize Carl Eller if he walked the streets in his old Minnesota Vikings helmet tackling surly teenagers. Eller last played twenty-five years ago, before

ESPN, satellite cable, and the World Wide Web turned players into brand names, always available like potato chips in a 24-hour mini-mart.

Yet the anonymous Eller, the cornerstone of Minnesota's disco era "Purple People Eater" defense, entered the pro football Hall of Fame in Canton, Ohio, with the class of 2004, and he did it with style, substance, and a whole lot of soul. Eller was supposed to recede into the shadows, with the day belonging to two recently retired commercial icons: quarterback John Elway and running back Barry Sanders. Elway retired in storybook fashion after winning consecutive Super Bowls for the Denver Broncos. Sanders left the game an enigma, walking away from the hapless Detroit Lions at age thirty-one with his health intact and within spitting distance of the most hallowed rushing records in the game.

This was billed as their moment and they dressed for the part. Elway and Sanders stood erect and trim, beaming from their signature goldenrod Hall of Fame blazers. Next to these golden boys, Eller looked like he had wandered over from a nearby golf course in a too-tight yellow sports coat, lacking only the plaid pants. Yet when it was his turn to make a speech, Eller, the afterthought, shocked the Canton crowd by having something to say.

> What can I do with this honor? I want to use this platform to help young African-American males to participate fully in this society and to set a new direction in their lives…. I want that direction [to] be toward the great colleges and universities of our society, not to the prisons and the jail cells…. It breaks my heart, and it breaks all of our hearts…. This is not the future we fought for in the '50s, '60s, and '70s.

He then earned cheers from a predominantly white crowd of Elway and Sanders fans by saying: "Our country has turned its back on African-American males. Some have even given up hope. But I haven't given up on you."

Eller has earned the right to voice his frustrations about a nation that has more African-American men in prison than in college. Since retirement, he has been the executive director of Triumph Services, a chain of chemical dependency rehabilitation facilities located in Minneapolis/St. Paul. Eller is a certified chemical dependency counselor and was the National Football League consultant for alcohol and drug abuse issues. As a consultant to the NFL, Eller helped develop the league's first Employee Assistance Program.

To put it bluntly, he has spent many more years working on this issue than he ever did head-slapping offensive linemen. Yet criticism was still rained upon his salt-and-pepper Afro for stealing Elway and Sanders's thunder by being "political." *Denver Post* columnist Jim Armstrong wrote, "Memo to John Elway: Thanks for making the speech fun and not going all political on us. For a minute there, I thought Carl Eller was going to do a Michael Moore and call for Dubya's hide."

Some at ESPN radio wanted to nominate Eller for their "just shut up award" and even debated if Eller was "racist" for speaking about racism. (These must be the same folks who think Bush is a "peace president" and that John Kerry represented "electability.") Others called in to say that those who think Eller should just shut up, should in fact "just shut up." (Ahh, debate.)

But arguing whether or not Eller has the right to speak is a sad commentary on our times and, in addition, misses the point entirely. Eller took a ceremony about as exciting as a Shriners Award night and had the temerity to say something that wouldn't be immediately disposable. It's called having a backbone, principles, and being a human being instead of a brand. ◆

Ricky Williams: No More Running

Can someone be a sports hero for having the courage not to play? This is the question being posed by Ricky Williams, the NFL All-Pro running back who walked away from the Miami Dolphins last fall. Williams is twenty-seven years old, injury-free, and at the height of his football and earning powers. But such reasons wither in the light of the fact that the man simply has no interest in playing football.

"I just don't want to be in this business anymore," said Williams. "I was never strong enough to not play football, but I'm strong enough now. I've considered everything about this. Everyone has thrown every possible scenario at me about why I shouldn't do this, but they're in denial. I'm happy with my decision."

Williams has always marched to the beat of his own drum. When he came out of the University of Texas, he posed on the cover of *ESPN The Magazine* in a wedding dress. When he began to take anti-depressants, he went public with how they helped him and changed his life. When he failed his first NFL drug test for marijuana, he made no apologies. In August, he returned from an off-season traveling the world during which he experimented with releasing himself from all the trappings of wealth and fame

He talked with the homeless in Australia. He sat among the poor in Jamaica. He lived in a tent for seven dollars a day. "In my tent, I had about 30 books. And every morning, I'd wake up at about 5 a.m. And I'd take my flashlight and I'd read for a couple of hours." The bruising superstar said he came to realize, upon reflection, that he hates the macho crud and glorification of violence that engulfs the game of football. He doesn't like being told he can't smoke marijuana. And at the most basic level, one that transcends all analysis, he is miserable living the

NFL life.

He would have made $5 million this year, but he said, "It's blood money, as far as I'm concerned…. Playing in the National Football League, you're told, you know, where to be, when to be there, what to wear, how to be there," he said. "And being able to step away from that, I have an opportunity to look deeper into myself and look for what's real."

If Williams was looking to rile the right-wing establishment that runs the NFL like the five families in *The Godfather*, he couldn't have picked a juicier trifecta: an All-Pro retires because he hates violence, hates fame, and likes weed. Spousal abuse and steroids they can handle—and even excuse—but not this. So the collection of Montgomery Burnses who own NFL teams have "released the hounds" on Williams. The overwhelming majority of the talking yaks in the mainstream press and on sports radio are tearing Williams apart. He's been called everything from "a selfish ungrateful piece of garbage" to "a pathetic anti-American pot head" and a slew of other names reserved for those who don't play by the unwritten rules of big-time sports.

In the words of *Sporting News* columnist Paul Attner,

> Ricky's always been one of the most selfish, unpredictable, purposely bizarre, and more than slightly off-kilter athletes. He doesn't care that his behavior might affect anyone around him…. You know the type that fancy themselves as shining lights in a dull world. They try too hard to be unique. Instead of looking brave, they look foolish.

But Williams sheds such barbs as easily as he used to shed linebackers. "This is an opportunity to be a real role model. Everyone wants freedom. Human beings aren't supposed to be controlled and told what to do. They're supposed to be given direction and a path. Don't tell me what I can and can't do. Please."

Williams was not the kind of player to dazzle with pirouettes or blaze past free safeties with a sprinter's speed. He was a bull with burst that would run you over, step on your chest, and never break stride. He played with a violence completely in opposition to his personality. Now he's had enough and wants to walk away, not be carried on a cart, from this most violent of sports. "When would it have been OK for me to stop playing football?" He asked Mike Wallace on *60 Minutes.* "When my knees went out? When my shoulders went out? When I had too many concussions? When is it OK?"

Currently Williams is enrolled in a seventeen-month course at the California College of Ayurveda in Grass Valley, California, studying holistic medicine, giving not a thought to the millions he left on the table. He is putting his cars and Miami homes up for sale and is donating some of the money to a local school. He wants to teach in Latin America, to learn another language, to continue his studies. He wants to do everything but play football. Hardly aims that are "selfish" or "pathetic." Williams had thought it all through:

> Well, my whole thing in life is I just want freedom. And I thought that money would give me that freedom. I was wrong, of course. Because, especially when you're 21 and you're given as much money as I was given, it bound me more than it freed me. Because now, I have more things to worry about. I have more people asking for money. I had to buy a house and nice cars and do different things that people with money are supposed to do. It just seemed to create more problems.... The knowledge and the wisdom that I've gotten from this experience is priceless. So, the way I look at it, I'm still way, way, way up.... I'm finally free. I can't remember ever being this happy.

Ricky Williams is being pilloried for "running away." How wrong. Finally, the man has stopped running. ◆

The NBA's Etan Thomas: "I Am Totally Against This War"

Howard Cosell once said, "Rule Number One of the 'Jockocracy' is that pro athletes and politics should never mix." But in these times of war and resistance, a new wave of sports stars are demanding to be heard. In Major League Baseball, Blue Jays slugger Carlos Delgado has come out against the occupation of Iraq. At the Olympics, the Iraqi Soccer team publicly refused to be used as a symbol of a war they oppose. In the NBA, All-Star guard Steve Nash and forward Josh Howard have said that they were "for shooting jumpers not people." Now we can add NBA center/power forward Etan Thomas to the list of those athletic antiwar rebels who are rewriting the rules of the "Jockocracy."

Thomas came to the NBA's Washington Wizards from the Dallas Mavericks, having been chosen by Dallas in the first round of the 2000 draft after an All-American career at Syracuse. Since overcoming injuries in his rookie season, Thomas has been a force, leading the team in rebounds. But Thomas is as tenacious in front of a microphone as he is under the glass, and has been known to arrive, unannounced, at Washington, D.C. open-mike readings to share his incisive political verse. He has developed a reputation as a poet, and has written a book of poetry, called *More Than an Athlete*. Thomas sees poetry as "just another way to open people's minds up. I go to poetry slams in season, out of season. It is another way to get ideas across."

Unlike many pro athletes who would sooner try to dunk on Shaq than voice their political opinions, Thomas has spoken out publicly on issues ranging from the death penalty to affirmative action to, more recently, the war in Iraq. Fighting the death penalty is a passion for Etan because he sees it as the ultimate in political hypocrisy.

Etan Thomas, power forward/center for the Washington Wizards, has been an outspoken critic against both the death penalty and the U.S. war in Iraq. (Courtesy Washington Wizards)

I don't see how politicians can have the right to kill. And it blows my mind to see these Republicans talk on and on about pro-life and anti-abortion and then they are pro-death penalty. How can that principle not apply to both? That makes no sense to me. The death penalty is just wrong. When the ACLU contacted me about reading some of my poetry at a demonstration, I was more than willing to do it.

While speaking out has garnered respect for Thomas in some circles, in others he is told that he should be "seen and not heard." The mere idea makes this articulate, thoughtful man shake his head. "That is just so wrong to me. Seen and not heard? No way. I really believe that people who say that really do not see the athletes as real people who have opinions and ideas. They think that they are just athletes and that's all." He sees a racial message behind the idea that he should just "shut up and play." "Not to say that being an athlete isn't a great thing in itself, but the Black man has always been admired for his athletic ability, but when it comes to his mind, that's a whole other matter. I would like to be seen...in the tradition of athletes who used their position to be able to speak out on issues and make a difference."

Etan feels an imperative to speak anytime he sets foot on the street in Washington, D.C. and sees the incredible contrasts in the capital city. As he puts it,

There are two Washington, D.C.s. There is the capital and there are the people in the city who care very deeply about a host of issues and ideas. When I first moved here I was told that it was the crime capital of the country and I thought, "How can this be the capital and still have these problems?" And now when I am on U Street, because that is where a lot of the poetry readings are, it is like being in another world from Capital Hill. But I have met people on protests, I have met people on demonstrations and the people in this city really care about politics and issues. That's the kind of people I want to be around. That's the kind of place I want to be.

When Thomas began to speak out on the death penalty in

2003, he made it a point not to comment on Bush's war in Iraq. It was too hot-button, too controversial for the athlete. But last year, the crisis and resistance in the Middle East compelled Thomas to come forward. He spoke to *The Edge of Sports* first, only because, according to Thomas, a story the *Washington Times* was preparing—to profile his views—was "killed by higher ups" at the right-leaning paper.

"I am totally against this war," Thomas says adamantly. "But at the same time, I am completely for the troops. Republicans tried to paint the picture that if you were against the war, you were somehow unpatriotic, and that couldn't be further from the truth. What's truly unpatriotic is misleading an entire nation into war under false pretenses." Thomas shakes his head at Bush and Vice President Dick Cheney's criticism of John Kerry's call for a more "sensitive" war in the Middle East.

> [Bush and Cheney] missed the entire point. They should have been more sensitive to the 1,000+ American soldiers that lost their lives because of the ignorance of the White House. They should have been more sensitive to the fact that these were human lives they were ruining. I wonder what they would say to the mothers who will never see their sons again, or the children who will never see their fathers again. He has sent so many young children, who only signed up for the Army as a way to go to college, into a war that didn't need to happen. And people wonder why the casualties are so high. Eighteen-year-old babies are over there losing their lives everyday, and he has the audacity to say that "we are turning the corner."

Bush's arrogance has been a factor in Thomas's decision to speak out. He sees a quagmire developing because of Bush's oft-criticized "go it alone" style.

> He was so insistent about going against the UN and now we are bearing the burden alone. He said that he didn't need the help of any other country. Now, we need help and no other country wants to help us because of his unwillingness to allow the UN to do their job. The UN said that they didn't have enough evidence to invade

Iraq, but Bush insisted that they had these weapons of mass destruction, and come to find out, that was untrue. Now we are in way over our heads and progress is moving at a snail's pace.

Thomas also expresses frustration at the media's subservience to the war drive. Fox News, in particular, leaves him both astounded and annoyed.

> It amazes me that know-it-alls like Bill O'Reilly and Sean Hannity can actually defend [Bush]. O'Reilly said that he was simply given bad info, and he thought he was doing the right thing. Well, it's his job to know. That excuse—"I didn't know any better"—might work when you are seven years old, but not when you are the president of the United States.

Thomas knows he may feel some heat for speaking out against Bush's war but feels an obligation to do so.

> I have never had a problem standing up for what I believe in. I admire the athletes of the past, like Bill Russell, Muhammad Ali, Jim Brown, John Carlos and Tommie Smith, Kareem [Abdul-Jabbar]. Athletes that used their position as a platform to speak out on social issues and stand up for a cause. Basketball is not my life. To quote Bill Russell, "You're not going to reduce me to an entertainer. I'm a man who stands up for what I believe in and you're going to respect me for it." A quote I live by is, "I speak my mind because biting my tongue would make my pride bleed."

When athletes like Etan Thomas step forward and make their voices heard, they do more than rewrite the rules of Cosell's "Jockocracy." They reclaim the humanity of all athletes, who are generally presented as having muscles and tattoos but not minds. They also provide an outlet for the millions of people who oppose the priorities of this government yet, embattled and embittered, feel they stand alone. When 6-foot, 10-inch Etan Thomas stands up, you feel like you can straighten your back and walk tall by his side.

What follows is an excerpt of "The Penalty of Death" from *More Than an Athlete*.

> What makes you think the death by lethal injection is any less
>   sadistic than the gas chamber or public hangings
> The Firing Squad or the Electric Chair
> Being stoned to death or the Guillotine
> Or the Crucifix
> The answer is simply this
> Each method of capital punishment is equally sick and vicious
> What gives you the right to decide who deserves to die and who
>   doesn't
> If you play God too long, the real one might get upset
>   Only He knows
> He judges the ways of the wicked when that time comes so
> why are you trying to do God's job for Him
> You are not on that level
> A devil posing as an angel but I see through your disguise
> Your horns are protruding through your conservative lies

And from an untitled poem on the Iraq war:

> Out of the ashes of Iraq come soldiers dressed in fatigues of fire
> Wearing helmets secured in smoke
> They've choked off the lies spewed out of the mouth of a burning
>   bush
> The true warrior's existing wake
> Whose flames burned them at the stake
> Cremated their bodies
> And stuffed them in an urn wrapped in red, white, and blue...
>
> Rummaging through a forest set ablaze by one lethal match
> With witty catch phrases forever attached to the side of their
>   kingdom
> Operation Iraqi Freedom
> Links to Al Qaeda
> Eminent threats
> And weapons of mass destruction...
>
> They've been skillfully thrown into the lion's den
> Out of the frying pan and into the furnace

Their courage exceeds any measuring stick
But they can hear the footsteps of death creeping around the cor-
    ner
For they've been led into the eye of the storm
Transformed into peacekeepers
Lending a helping hand for the poorly planned post-war
    strategy... ◆

Adonal Foyle: Rebounder for Reforms, Master of the Lefty Layup

Adonal Foyle's singular life story is more fantastic than fiction.
He starts at center for the NBA's Golden State Warriors, but
that's the least interesting part. Foyle grew up on the Caribbean
island of Canouan—an area just 3.5 by 1.25 miles—and didn't
pick up a basketball until he was fifteen.

During the summer of 1990, two college professors from
America, Jay and Joan Mandle, were refereeing one of
Adonal's games and were blown away by his raw skills. After
speaking with him, they were equally impressed with his pol-
ished intellect. The Mandles asked Foyle to accompany them
back to the United States to compete for a basketball scholarship. Foyle agreed and, after playing two years of high school
ball in the States, was offered a free ride to all the traditional
college hoops powerhouses. Yet Foyle made a highly unortho-
dox decision: he decided to go to Colgate, a small liberal arts
college in upstate New York. This was an unheard of, counterintuitive move, akin to George W. Bush dumping Dick Cheney
in favor of Barbra Streisand. But, to Foyle, it made perfect
sense. His passions revolved around politics and social change
as much as sports. The Mandles also taught at Colgate, creat-

ing a warm environment and support system for Foyle. Their experiences in the Civil Rights and antiwar movements of the 1960s made the Mandles a perfect match for Foyle, and they now recognize him as their son, and Foyle refers to them as his parents.

Foyle tore up the overmatched Colgate basketball world, averaging 20.4 points, 12.7 rebounds, and 5.66 blocks a game in his three-year college career. His 492 career blocks are an NCAA record. In 1997, Adonal Foyle was selected in the first round of the 1997 NBA draft by the Golden State Warriors as the eighth overall pick.

In the summer of 2001, Adonal founded an organization called Democracy Matters, a nonpartisan student organization that fights for campaign finance reform. With an active presence on over thirty college campuses, Democracy Matters involves hundreds of students and faculty nationwide. Through teachins, letter writing and petition campaigns, educational seminars, and voter registration drives, Democracy Matters is trying to get big money out of politics from the bottom up (see www.democracymatters.org). When asked about why an NBA star would involve himself in such a project, Foyle says,

> My view is that democracy is harmed anywhere—including in the United States—when a small minority of people make the decisions for everyone else. In the United States, it is money that speaks loudest in political campaigns. In most cases, the person who spends the most money wins, and people who have average incomes and ordinary lives—that's most of us—are shut out of running for office. Because candidates must raise huge sums of money, they pay more attention to their big donors than to ordinary voters. And that means that important decisions about war and peace, the economy, the environment, civil rights are made by elected officials too often beholden to their funders rather than the people.

His sensitivity to issues of class starts with his very upbringing, which opened his eyes to poverty and oppression.

I grew up on a tiny island, Canouan, part of the country of St. Vincent and the Grenadines. On Canouan there were less than 1,000 people, no electricity, and my tiny house had no indoor toilet and a kitchen outside. I was raised by my grandmother and great-aunt, who "gardened"—growing peanuts and other ground crops. I grew up working in the garden and doing many other chores all day when I was not in school. Everyone is aware of politics in St. Vincent because the country is so small. People on Canouan and the other small Grenadine islands think that they get ignored and shortchanged by the main island where most of the politicians are from, so we are very aware of what is going on.

In college, when Foyle read about the Civil Rights movement for the first time, he learned what it meant to struggle for change.

The vision of justice for all and direct action to achieve it—especially by young people—is inspiring to me. In addition to that, my American parents—Joan and Jay Mandle—were part of the Civil Rights movement and the struggle to end the war in Vietnam. So our dinner table was always an education in itself—mostly about politics and social change.

But athletics and politics also came together for the young basketball player in the form of Muhammad Ali.

Ali's stand was a courageous one. Anyone who is a public person and speaks out—especially for an unpopular position that they believe in—is brave. I think he had every right to be public about what was on his mind. People think politics are only for elected officials—but that is one of the things that's wrong—everyone should have their voice heard.

Foyle believes that today's times are more challenging for activists. In an interview for the *Nation* magazine called "What Ever Happened to Jocks for Justice?" Foyle said,

The 1960s generation was against the war, people coming home in body bags, dogs gnawing at Black people's feet. Today issues are more complicated.... It is more complicated today because the issues are more complicated. To get people to think about money and politics is hard; to get them to see how it affects them every single day is hard even though it's true. People are so cynical and turned off of politics that they have given up. Through Democracy Matters I am trying to give people the hope that they can make a difference—that's what people in the 60s believed and it can be true again today. Civil rights activists didn't know they would win—they did it because it was right. Young people especially have to stand up for what they believe and trust that it will make a difference—because it will.

In the same *Nation* article, Foyle noted, "This mother of all democracies is one of the most corrupt systems, where a small minority make the decisions for everybody else."

He further explained,

Changing the way we fund campaigns would decisively change this dynamic. It would restore the equality of one-person one-vote in influencing elections and therefore our laws and social policy. If we had public funding of election campaigns as they do in Maine and Arizona, in New York City, Los Angeles and others, anyone with great ideas could run for office regardless of their wealth. Democracy Matters students are working to spread the word about the promise of public financing—as a workable way to fund campaigns that deepens democracy.

Finally, I asked Foyle what he says to people who believe that athletes have no business talking about politics, that they should just "shut up and play." He said,

We are role models as professional basketball players whether we want to be or not. I am using my influence to get young people and others interested in politics because I believe that a democracy can only work well if everyone is involved and participates. It isn't really much of a democracy when only a small proportion of people vote and most feel that their government isn't interested in them and doesn't represent them. I believe that everyone has the right and the responsibility to decide what kind of world we live in and ought to be involved in making these important decisions—including athletes. ◆

Toni Smith: Standing Tall

In 2003, Toni Smith was just another Division III athlete grinding through her senior year as captain of the women's basketball team at Manhattanville College. Yet her decision to protest the U.S. war against Iraq on the court—by turning her back on the American flag during the national anthem—sparked debate throughout the sports and political world. Today, Toni Smith is living in New York City, working for a young people's mentoring program called New York Youth at Risk (www.nyyouthatrisk.org).

Here Toni Smith speaks, looking back on the events of the last year and looking forward at the struggles to come.

Dave Zirin: It's been almost a year since you took your demonstration to the court. When did you first see the need to make a stand and why did you feel it was so important to take the actions that you did?

Toni Smith: I'm from a mixed racial and ethnic background. My mom is Jewish, and my dad is Black, white, and Cherokee. I was learning about the prison industrial complex and the wars against Native Americans. It made me very angry, but I never paid attention to how this history played out on the court. I never thought about the national anthem because I went to alternative schools. I never had to say the pledge. I never had to stand and salute anything before class. On the court I would just stand and let the time go by.... So last year, I was talking with my boyfriend. His family's very politically active also. They don't ever stand for the national anthem, and they're very clear on their position. We were talking about all the policies we dislike, and he said "Why do you stand for the anthem at your games?" And I said, "Well, I never really thought about it. I'm the captain of the team, and I have to be a team leader and a good role model." He said, "But that has nothing to do with who you are. This is not what you believe in. You just told me how much you dislike this flag and what it stands for." He's part Black and part Cherokee also, and he said to me, "This flag represents the slaughter of our ancestors," and I said, "You're absolutely right." We had a game a few days later, and as we stood up to sing the national anthem, I said no.

When was this?

This was probably the first week in December [2002]. It was at NYU. I thought, "No, this is not more important than my beliefs. This has nothing to do with who I am." I didn't tell anyone. I didn't really think of it as something that should be made public. It went unnoticed even by my teammates and family. Then one day the president of the school came up to me and said, "If anyone gives you any trouble, send them to me." I said "All right, but it's not an issue." And then he told me that there was this huge uproar, that there were several parents of the team who were furious and were threatening to go to the NCAA.

How did the uproar unfold?

A few of the parents went to the president of the school. The next thing that happened was one of my teammates called my dorm room and said, "You have to look on instant messenger. You have to see what our teammates are writing about you." There was this back-and-forth I.M. battle saying, "I can't believe Toni's doing this, what kind of a team captain is she?" All of this was done behind my back. No one asked me why, no one confronted me about it. The next day in the locker room I confronted the girl who began the I.M. discussion, and that turned into an explosion within the team.

Every news story said that you were protesting the war on Iraq in particular. Was that in fact the case?

Iraq was the icing on the cake. The war took me from angry at the general direction of the U.S. to "Are you kidding!?!" But it

Manhattanville College guard Toni Smith, second from left, turns her back on the American flag during the playing of the national anthem before a basketball game against Stevens Tech from New Jersey on Sunday, February 23, 2003. Smith is protesting both the impending war with Iraq and "injustices here at home." (AP Photo/Stuart Ramson)

wasn't just the war. It was everything before that. It was everything that the flag is built on, every thing that is continuing to happen and things that haven't even happened yet.

Why do you think your actions touched such a nerve?

The debate around the war, no question. We were playing a game at St. Joseph's. Their assistant coach had just been sent over to serve. They were angry. Nothing really came up about it at that game, but the next team we were scheduled to play was the Merchant Marine Academy. People at St. Joseph's called and warned them about me. In addition to that, a news reporter got a hold of it. The Merchant Marine Academy was the worst team in the league. They were something like zero and twenty-five. They don't have any fans, and let me tell you, this gym was packed. You can't even imagine what it was like. They had cadets lined up on the sidelines, each with their own flag that was about seven feet tall. Every single person in the stands was in uniform, with their own flag. They were shouting things at me—obscenities, curses, you name it. It was unbelievable. It was so bad that even the teammates who hated what I was doing had to put themselves in my place and defend my position. It came down to "You're not going to disrespect my team." That news reporter captured how angry everyone was at that game, and at the next game the [Associated Press] was there and the story took off.

Out of teammates, coaches, administration, school president—who was supportive and who wasn't?

Half of my teammates were completely against me. Completely against everything I was doing. There were four girls who were very against me and tried to make my life a living hell. The one who started the instant messenger drama sent a petition around the school, saying, "Sign this to demand that Toni Smith return all her financial aid, because she is disrespecting our school." What's the point in that? We were teammates in the middle of the season, one of the best seasons our school has ever had, and it just didn't make any sense. They talked to reporters when we were asked not to by the coach and by the president. When I finally decided to talk to the press it was because my teammates were speaking out without permission. It got to the point where either they're going to have lies out there or I speak up.

Did any teammates back you up?

Two of my teammates always stood next to me during the national anthem, one in front of me, one behind me, holding my hands—Melissa Solano and Dionne Walker. They were absolutely and completely supportive 100 percent, and would have taken a bullet for me. I couldn't hang out with anyone else on the team. Then there were four or so girls who were in between. It was, "I don't agree with your position but respect your right to do it, but I wish you weren't doing it because it's making life hell for the team." I can respect that. They tried to stay neutral because we were friends. And they were torn kind of between me and what their parents thought and the season was difficult for them.

What about your coach, Shawn Lincoln?

I have to give it to him. He took a lot of flack for not punishing me. I think it was very important for Manhattanville, promoting itself as a liberal arts college that promotes socially and ethically aware graduates, that he was so supportive. He made it a point not to include what his personal views were, and I still don't know what he thought, but he definitely supported my right to protest, whether he would rather I did it or not. I really commend him for that, because he didn't have to. Not just that, but he reprimanded those players who were deliberately going against his orders for the team [about talking to the press]. They were eventually held in check.

In the Merchant Marines story, you painted a picture of a team that was, despite its differences, able to pull together. Was that just a one-game thing?

There was tension throughout the season. It got to a point toward the end where we had to agree to disagree. It took a lot more energy for them to trash me and for me to hate them than to just play together. I think our team had so much potential to be a great team and that overpowered everything else that was going on. And I think everyone realized the potential that we had to have a really great season and to break records that our school, our team, has never broken, and I think that was more important. We ended up with the third best record in the history of Manhattanville. We all should take credit for that. For certain games I don't know how we pulled it off. I don't know how we just played together and did it, but we did. And we played very well as a team.

If someone were to come up to you and ask, "Protests were happening throughout the spring. Why demonstrate on the basketball court? Why take your stand there?" What would you say?

I would say that it wasn't really a stand. It was just, "I'm here to play basketball and I have to salute the flag? I don't want to." Manhattanville is a small Division III school. Our fans consisted of close friends, family, and a few girls. Not more than sixty people would be at the games. So it would not be the best place to get a message out.

What do you say to people who counter, "Sports is no place for political acts"?

I say that during World War II, when America decided that we needed to show our superiority to other countries, they implemented playing the national anthem before sporting events and when they did that they put politics in the middle of sports. The question is not why did I choose to turn my back on the flag. It's why do we have to do this at basketball games? If they don't want politics in sports then they need to take the national anthem out because that is inherently political.

We just passed the thirty-fifth anniversary of Tommie Smith and John Carlos's protest on the medal stand at the 1968 Olympics. When you were doing this, were you conscious that you were part of a tradition of sports and politics?

I was aware of Muhammad Ali, and I was aware of Tommie Smith and John Carlos. But I didn't connect myself to them. I saw one article that had my picture right next to theirs, and I was completely blown away. That was the first time I connected the two. I didn't feel in any way like it was on the same scale. I will say that like [Smith and Carlos] the point was not to put myself forward but to get people to talk about these issues. Last year people didn't want to acknowledge that we were going to war. They wanted to hide it. It can become really easy to not acknowledge the fact that we are killing people in other countries because it's not here. A big issue I had with September 11th was that was the first event since Pearl Harbor where there was an attack of such magnitude on this country. And you could see this all over the place, people going "never forget, never forget 9/11." 9/11 was terrible, but that level of destruction is every single day for other people in other countries. I think that it is unbelievably arrogant to say [in the aftermath of 9/11] "Now we can do whatever we want." It has sent the message that "We are better than you. We are superior human beings to everyone else in the world." It's really appalling.

Were you asked about speaking at any antiwar demonstrations?

After the season, I was asked once or twice to come and speak, and I declined. I felt like, if I was going to attend demonstrations, I was going to attend then as a regular person, not a person of importance. If it ever got to the point where I was speaking at a rally it would be because I had done the work, I had paid the dues, and I didn't feel like I deserved that.

Did you ever feel physically threatened during this whole process?

The guy who walked onto the court with the flag; I actually didn't feel threatened by him. I think we were all in too much shock—as to how he got onto the court and why he was interrupting our game to do this—to even be scared about it. It wasn't until afterwards, when my family and a few of my friends were really outraged. "How could this school let him get on the campus? What if he had a weapon? You're not safe." Then I got a bit concerned; but I still wasn't scared. I got one letter in the mail that was a death threat. It said, "I've seen you, I've been close enough to touch you, I'm a disabled veteran, I'll find you again, you won't be able to disrespect my country anymore, I'll make sure that it's an end for you." That scared me. I was a little bit frightened after that, and I was more cautious about where I went for a little while.

Did you feel like any of the coverage was skewed because of sexism?

I didn't think it at first. Someone brought it to my attention. They said, "You're threatening. You are saying things that no one is saying right now. You're protesting things that people are too afraid to protest, and you're a woman." And they said that even though Muhammad Ali and Tommie Smith and John Carlos protested and were reprimanded, they were men. That puts you in an entirely different category, and people don't know how to deal with it. That really got me thinking after that. I still don't know what conclusions I've come to because of it, but I definitely feel like it is a story of its own because people don't expect women to be bold and speak out. I think when women do then that puts you in another category, which is "You must be a lesbian, you must be mean, you're not a lady." It brings up hundreds of other stories. We've seen that happen with other female athletes; ones who don't pose for magazines, ones who come out and say they're lesbians. It completely discredits you as an athlete, as a person. People don't want to hear your story after that. Even in a lot of the letters I got, it went back to my looks. It all went back to my physical appearance. I got a lot of "You're a rich white girl who doesn't know anything." I want to know where they got that information. I'm definitely not rich, I'm not all white, and the white part of me is Jewish, so you're really off on that.

It's been a year. How has the stand you took changed your life?

I definitely have grown mentally. Part of that is due to the stand I took. Part of that is just the course that the world is taking and seeing it through my own eyes without the restraints of college, without the restraints of parents. I work for an organization where we deal with teenagers; I'm a lot more conscious of the development of teenagers and young people and their mindset.

What about the actual events in the world over the last year? Do you feel like the course of events in Iraq has validated the stand that you took?

It was always validated to me, and nothing anyone ever said invalidated or made me question what I did. The only thing I ever questioned was my safety and the safety of my family and friends. But the way I felt at the time was that there were many protests during the Vietnam War that outraged people. Then when circumstances came to light about how illegal the war was and how many were killed and died senselessly, people said, "Oh, now I get it." I think that's what's happening now. There are stories now that have been done about me—because it's the end of the year and people are recapping—and the tone is more supportive. There are a lot of people who were angry at the time, saying, "How dare you not support my son, he's going off to war." And now either their son has died or their son is still over there, and they realize that this war is bogus, and they don't have any health insurance or have to wait on line for food. Now they say, "Oh, I get it. Now I get what you were trying to say. And now my son is over there, my daughter's over there, and I can't help when I could have helped before." So I think a lot of that has come to light, as we knew it would—because they couldn't keep it hidden forever. If that validates it for other people, then I'm glad. They don't have to agree with me, but at least they can understand why.

Do you have any regrets?

None. I'm really big on not living with regrets. There are always things in your life you're not going to be happy with, choices you've made that you're not pleased with, but every choice you make, you make it for a reason, and you might not know what that reason is until later, and it might hurt you at the time, but eventually it pans out, and it shapes who you are as a person. Anything that I would have done differently would have altered who I am now.

Do you have any last comments?

Yes. I was one of those kids who went to overcrowded schools with no books and we had to recycle Xerox copies. That was a choice that I made, and that my mother made, and I've never regretted it. When I got to college, and I told my stories of high school—how we didn't have a gym, how we played in a junior high school across the street—they said "Oh my god! I can't believe you had to do this, I can't believe you didn't have this, you didn't have books!" And then we were assigned to write ten-page research papers, and none of them knew how to do it. I was in a higher writing class than any of my friends and they were complaining, "How can I write a three-page paper? What's an introduction? How do I end it?" They didn't know one thing from another. It is unfair that there is such unequal funding between school districts, but there is something to gain from every situation. Examine where you feel overlooked, uncounted, deemed unimportant, and use it to build yourself up. I would not trade the education I received for an education at a private school. It's all about what you take from life, not what you feel life is or is not giving you. The script is unwritten until we write our own stories. ◆

Afterword: We Are the Greatest

If the preceding pages have done nothing else, I hope they have shown that the two most common—and conflicting—views of sports don't help much when it comes to explaining the role of sports in today's United States. The idea that sports are just a pleasant distraction from the stresses of daily life, free from politics and broader implications, is as overly simplistic as insisting that pro sports are nothing more than reactionary refuse. To imagine that you can simply put your feet up, crack a beer, and watch the game—no harm, no foul—while a team mascot beats up on a man dressed like an Arab is absurd. But it is also ridiculous to claim that big-time athletics are nothing more than the motor driving a "values agenda" of war, oppression, and a "win or die" spirit of competition.

I understand why many people on the left find themselves looking at sports from the second perspective. If I had a dollar for everything that's wrong with sports, Bill Gates would be my butler. The sports industry fleeces fans every time we spend a dollar—from tickets to parking to concessions—and with the recent flurry of stadium deals, this multibillion-dollar business now has a hand in determining city budget priorities as well. That Washington, D.C. will spend $600 million on a new stadium while my wife teaches in a classroom without books is a monstrous demonstration of the "money game" that encircles sports like an anaconda.

This "money game" also grinds players into dust, treating them as little more than extensions of equipment. Athletes should, in theory, be the healthiest people in our society. Instead, too often, they become riddled with health problems and suffer crippling injuries, like paralyzed former wide receiver Darryl Stingley and brain-damaged boxer Greg Page, or die before their time, like Ken Caminiti and Lyle Alzado. There is also something twisted about the mind-warping attention lavished on peaking pro stars that turns off like a lamp when the glory days are done. The stories of drug addiction, deprivation, and bankruptcy from countless ex-athletes read like a Greek tragedy on permanent instant replay.

But only focusing on the militarism, sexism, racism, and exploitation that permeate pro sports produces a badly distorted sense of their significance—and of the people who love them. Sports are not popular because this is a right-wing country of "NASCAR Dads" and "Security Moms." Sports are popular because they are often fun, sometimes beautiful, and, at their best, represent an artistry that rivals anything in the National Gallery. To witness LeBron James threading no-look passes one play and hitting his head on the rim the next almost overwhelms the senses—like seeing some unholy progeny of Magic Johnson and Michael Jordan. The WNBA's Diana Taurasi, Barry Bonds, and Serena Williams dazzle us every time they play. Their strength, the grace and fluency of their movements, and the way they routinely seem to defy the laws of physics are all hypnotic. This is art, highly distorted, yes, but art all the same. And this is why fans, despite the abusive terms of their relationship with sports, keep coming back.

Pro sports can also provide fans with a window back to times when we were able to play team sports and experience the camaraderie involved in working together toward a realizable goal. Cooperation shadows competition throughout the play of team sports. The kind of satisfaction that comes from winning a game, or a championship, or simply interacting well together is not easily accessible in the workaday world. For many, rooting for a team is the closest they can come to being part of a team.

We have to be clear: arguing that sports are popular because of militarism and exploitation is kind of like arguing that TV violence is the direct result of viewer preference. If FOX had broadcast their World Series pre-game shows from the heart of an antiwar demonstration while the *SportsCenter* crew hid out in their gunner's nest, we might have a clearer view about the connection between people's love of sports and the drive toward war. But there are some choices we just don't get to make. We also have to realize that while these "games" often provide a place where the dominant ideas of our society are reinforced, they can also be sites where those ideas are challenged or downright rejected. The hidden history of Lester Rodney, Jackie Robinson, Muhammad Ali, Dave Meggyesy, Billie Jean King, John Carlos, and others is our history. The official sports hagiographers do everything they can to bury this legacy. We have to dig it up and spread it around. We want to be positioned to support and embrace athletes who risk their careers for principle. Our goal should be to engage and embrace not only the Etan Thomases, Toni Smiths, and Carlos Delgados, but also the fans that thrill to their exploits.

Some of my friends say that having "some kind of theory" or analysis drains the life out of sports. The opposite is in fact the case. By confronting the messages pumped out through our play, we can separate what we like from what we dislike, and begin to challenge sports—and our society—to change.

When warplanes fly overhead, we can ask how many pee-wee teams and physical education classes were cut to pay for each Blue Angel.

When Ted Cottrell, Norm Chow, or any of the other enormously talented NFL assistant coaches of color show up on screen, ask why they remain anonymous while Dennis Erickson (career record 40–54), late coach of the 49ers, got a top job.

When announcers and talking heads speak of an "athletic code of honor" and denounce Ricky Williams for saving his life, mind, and body by leaving the NFL, we can ask what happened to Ricky's right, as Bob Dylan put it, to "not be what you want me to be."

When cheap hits and taunts are decried and fined by league offices, we can ask why the X-Box and Playstation videogames that bear their "officially licensed" names contain more foul play than an Agatha Christie novel.

When college athletes are pilloried for taking under-the-table payoffs, we can ask whose blood, sweat, and tears paid for the brand, spanking-new enormo-domes that grace their campuses.

When the announcers on FOX become aghast as Southern belles during Reconstruction because a touchdown dancer gets raunchy, we can ask why a network that pays Bill O'Reilly millions and promotes shows like *Who's Your Daddy?* and *The Littlest Groom* should have the right to play purity police.

When our cities are soaked by sleazy stadium deals, we can stand up as sports fans and say, "Hey, we love baseball, but we're not going to give a billionaire a $350 million present for the privilege of watching it."

By speaking out for the political soul of the games we love, we begin to impose our own ideas on the world of sports—a counter morality to compete with the yawning hypocrisy of the pro leagues. These ideas allow us to embrace and cheer competition—when it is about appreciating the artistic talents of athletes and the strategic abilities of coaches and players alike. They allow us to recognize male and female athletes—and all women—as human beings with minds as well as bodies.

We also need to understand that sports do not exist in a vacuum. If we want more Muhammad Alis, more John Carloses, and more Billie Jean Kings, we need to build a broader movement for social justice outside the arena—so our "heroes" will also have people to look up to and places to turn for support.

Such a movement would break down the iron divide between the athlete and the spectator-fan. One of the most striking things about sports is that no matter how much we love to watch them, as a country we rarely play—too tired from the commute to the cubicle, too busy with bills and bunk. At the end of the day, play has been thoroughly outsourced from most of our lives. It doesn't have to be this way. Sports could be woven into the fabric of existence, more cooperative, more accessible, its competitive spirit removed from the cash pump and the destructive will to win at all costs. This would require a completely different world. But in such a world, there would be far less distance between the average person and the star athlete. Sports would become part of building integrated, whole people. Fun, yes, but also respectful, balanced, and available to all both to participate in and enjoy. In such a world, I might even be able to dunk—and that is a world worth fighting for. ◆

ALSO FROM HAYMARKET BOOKS

A People's History of Iraq: The Iraqi Communist Party, Workers' Movements, and the Left 1924–2004

Ilario Salucci   1 931859 14 0   April 2005
Iraqis have a long tradition of fighting against foreign and domestic tyranny. Here is their story.

The Case for Socialism

Alan Maass   1 931859 09 4   2004
"[Maass'] book charts a game plan for realistic radicals who haven't given up hope for making revolutionary changes in a society that finds itself in the grip of a remorseless political entropy."
—Jeffrey St. Clair, coeditor of CounterPunch

The Dispossessed: Chronicles of the Desterrados of Colombia

Alfredo Molano   1 931859 17 5   April 2005
Here in their own words are the stories of the Desterrados, or "dispossessed"—the thousands of Colombians displaced by years of war and state-backed terrorism, funded in part through U.S. aid to the Colombian government. With a preface by Aviva Chomsky.

Civil Rights in Peril: The Targeting of Arabs and Muslims

Elaine C. Hagopian, ed.   0 745322 64 6   2004
Civil Rights in Peril seeks to expose the impact of these new governmental powers on Muslims and Arabs, as well as other groups and individuals targeted as a part of the Bush administration's "war on terror," and to show how ordinary people can resist these attacks on our fundamental rights

The World Social Forum: Strategies of Resistance

José Corrêa Leite   1 931859 15 9   April 2005
The inside story of how the worldwide movement against corporate globalization has become such a force.

Women and Socialism

Sharon Smith   1 931859 11 6   May 2005
The fight for women's liberation is urgent—and must be linked to winning broader social change.

Your Money or Your Life (3rd edition)

Eric Toussaint   1 931859 18 3   June 2005
Globalization brings growth? Think again. Debt—engineered by the IMF and World Bank—sucks countries dry.